EthicsCentre.ca
Canadian Centre for Ethics & Corporate Policy

Ethics & Governance:
Developing & Maintaining An Ethical Corporate Culture

Fourth Edition

Leonard J. Brooks
Professor of Business Ethics & Accounting
Executive Director, The Clarkson Centre for Business Ethics & Board Effectiveness
Rotman School of Management, University of Toronto

David Selley
Past Chair, Canadian Centre for Ethics & Corporate Policy
Retired Partner, Ernst & Young LLP

Copyright © 2012
Canadian Centre for Ethics & Corporate Policy
Toronto, Canada
ISBN 978-0-9809641-1-0

Ethics & Governance: Developing & Maintaining An Ethical Corporate Culture

Contents

Useful Website Resources are located at http://www.ethicscentre.ca
      Glossary
      Resources and websites
      Case Summaries
      Recently published articles

Disclaimer

The views and opinions expressed in this publication are those of the authors and do not necessarily reflect the official policy or position of the Canadian Centre for Ethics & Corporate Policy.

Preface

The Canadian Centre for Ethics & Corporate Policy was incorporated as a not-for-profit organization in 1988, to champion the application of ethical values in the decision-making process of business and other organizations. Governed by volunteers and supported by organizations and individuals who share a commitment to ethical values, the Centre is dedicated to the promotion of an ethical orientation and culture in Canadian organizations.

Since its establishment, the Centre has carried out its mission through a variety of activities involving awareness building, learning, networking and referrals, collaborative relationships and the sponsoring of projects. One of its more ambitious projects was the 1995 publication of a book, *Ethics & Governance: Developing & Maintaining an Ethical Corporate Culture*. Published at a time when the subject of corporate ethics was in its infancy, the book has since been updated on several occasions to reflect changes and emerging trends in the business environment.

The publication of this 4th edition of the book represents a collaboration of two of the Centre's co-founders, Professor Leonard J. Brooks and David Selley, FCA.

Professor Brooks is a Professor of Business Ethics & Accounting and Executive Director of The Clarkson Centre for Business Ethics & Board Effectiveness at the Rotman School of Management, University of Toronto. With a long and distinguished career in the business ethics field, he is a recipient of the Ethics in Action Award for Ongoing Social Responsibility.

David Selley spent his career at Ernst & Young (and its predecessor Clarkson Gordon), Chartered Accountants, specializing in auditing standards and methodologies. Since his retirement in 1998, he has undertaken several professional activities in his specialty. He has also served on the board of Transparency International Canada. From these vantage points, David has been able to witness first-hand the ethical challenges that can be encountered by organizations and their leaders.

The book is dedicated to providing practical guidance on the core of governance reform – the development of a culture of integrity. It starts from the premise that an ethical corporate culture is essential for the ongoing success of a corporation and its executives, and proceeds to provide a detailed roadmap on how to develop and effectively maintain such a corporate culture. It includes checklists, tables and other helpful documents. In an effort to keep the guidance current, a companion website provides up-to-date hotlinks, websites and additional relevant readings.

Readers might query whether this latest revision of the book was necessary, considering that the previous edition was published a mere four years ago. We at the Centre firmly believe that the answer to that question lies in the global events experienced since 2008. In those few intervening years, circumstances under which corporations operate have changed dramatically, significantly increasing both the risks for those that do not behave ethically, as well as the impact of serious ethical lapses in business and other organizations on innocent third parties. (Some of these changes and increased risks are reviewed by the authors in Chapter 1.)

As the world continues to struggle with the fallout from the events of 2008, including the subprime lending crisis, the Directors of the Centre wish to contribute to the continuing conversation about the importance of ethics and good corporate governance to the well-being and prosperity of business organizations, governments and their citizens. It is their hope that the publication of this revised edition will offer practical guidance that can be easily implemented by business and other organizations striving to make ethical values the foundation of their decision-making processes.

Information about the Centre and membership can be obtained by accessing its web site at http://www.ethicscentre.ca or contacting the Centre at 416-368-7525.

Hélène Yaremko-Jarvis, B.C.L., LL.B.
Executive Director
Canadian Centre for Ethics & Corporate Policy

Understanding the Need for an Ethical Corporate Culture

Chapter 1
Introduction – Objectives, Developments, Evidence, Overview

There is no doubt there has been a worldwide reform of corporate governance over recent decades that seeks to restore credibility to corporate decision making, financial disclosure, and financial markets. This book is dedicated to providing practical guidance to the core of governance reform – the development of a *culture of integrity*.[1] An accompanying website is provided by the Canadian Centre for Ethics & Corporate Policy at http://www.ethicscentre.ca for the posting of updates, news, and commentary on governance and ethics matters. Checklists, tables, and other helpful documents referenced in this book are available in downloadable format from the website.

The primary focus of this book is ethical conduct within companies,[2] particularly publicly traded corporations. Nevertheless, the material in this book is also relevant to any organization with even minimal public accountability, an array of stakeholders, or simply looking for ideas on how to instill ethics as part of the decision-making process. This material will also be applicable to large public institutions such as hospitals; universities and other educational institutions; charitable organizations including NGOs; private companies of all sizes, from large wholly-owned subsidiaries of major corporations to small owner-managed businesses; and government bodies such as the RCMP. In particular, boards of directors of charitable organizations have strict fiduciary responsibilities, and history tells us that

---

1. *See for example*: Jim Goodfellow and Allan Willis, "CEO Challenge," *CAmagazine* 40:1 (2007): 35–42.
2. Use of the term "company(ies)" or "organization(s)" throughout this book encompasses all forms of organization including for-profit and not-for-profit corporations, partnerships, and co-operatives. More specific terms are used when the context requires it.

such organizations are by no means immune from ethical problems, including employee and management fraud.

It is vital to note that many successful organizations have benefited from instilling *a culture of integrity* long before the financial catastrophes of 2008 triggered the *Dodd-Frank Act* and similar legislation and guidelines created in Canada and other jurisdictions. They had been motivated to take a leading edge position on integrity or ethics by one or more of the following reasons:

- Good ethics are good business.
- Good ethics can support a competitive advantage.
- The enthusiastic support of some employees, customers, and other stakeholders depends on a culture of integrity.
- Employees at all levels, and company agents, need guidance about values or integrity expectations to make decisions that protect and further the company's strategic objectives.
- Company reputation and future profits depend significantly on demonstrating good corporate values.
- Sound risk management is based on ethical principles.
- They simply believed in doing what was right.

Governance reform has introduced the need for compliance with legislation such as the *Sarbanes-Oxley Act* (SOX) and the *Dodd-Frank Act*, and has forced CEOs and CFOs, as well as directors, to make sure that their company's internal controls are adequate to protect the company and ensure that financial reports are accurate. Consequently, good governance requirements and expectations now require an assessment of a company's culture of integrity to be part of the risk management and internal control review processes. Moreover, many Canadian companies and their auditors are subject to SOX and Securities & Exchange Commission (SEC) regulations, and Canadian securities regulators have formulated regulations that adopt certain, but not all, elements of this U.S. regulatory environment.

Developments since 2008

Since the third edition of *Ethics and Corporate Governance: Developing and Maintaining an Ethical Corporate Culture* was published in 2008, the circumstances under which corporations operate have changed significantly, and many of the changes increase the risks for corporations that do not behave ethically and therefore increase the need to set up a strong ethical corporate culture. Or, to put it another way, many changes have made it more likely that a corporation that transgresses will be found out, and their transgressions held up for all to see. This makes it even more imperative for corporations to instill an ethical corporate culture taking into account the interests of all significant stakeholders.

More specifically, these changes include:

- New legislation and regulation, and enhanced enforcement of older legislation, especially in the United States (i.e. The *Dodd-Frank Act* [2010] and the *Foreign Corrupt Practices Act* (FCPA) [1977]) and in the United Kingdom (i.e. the *Bribery Act* [2010]) and, to a lesser extent, in Canada (i.e. increased enforcement of anti-bribery legislation that had been on the books for years but was almost never enforced previously).

- An enormous increase in people's ability to access electronic media, especially in less developed regions of the world. This makes keeping things secret even more difficult than ever before.

- Mobile phone usage is now almost universal among young people in all except the very poorest nations, so there are hundreds of millions of people walking around with built-in cameras or video cameras, if not both. Nothing can be hidden for long.

- The explosive growth in social media such as YouTube, Facebook and Twitter means that any titillating event captured on a cell phone that could be embarrassing to a business is instantly transmitted to millions of people. Many corporations now find out about their problems at the same time as the rest of the world, or later. It is imperative to establish structures and processes that improve the chances that corporate officials will find out about problems first and be able to deal with them professionally.

- A financial collapse, the subprime lending scandal, caused a recession which made it more difficult for organizations and individuals to put ethics before their own financial well-being. Increasing unemployment, and the fear of unemployment, aggravates financial hardship and increases the incentives for individuals to improve their circumstances unethically, or even illegally.

- A spectacular increase in the income gap between the very rich and the merely rich, between the rich and the middle class; and between all of them and the poor has noticeably increased resentment among those who are losing out, relatively or absolutely. In 2011 this spawned "Occupy" movements that started on Wall Street but spread to other countries. A greater concern to the business world, however, is that employees who wish to act against their employers' interests now may find it easier to mentally justify their own actions. This is especially significant in companies where senior executives earn enormous salaries and reap other extravagant benefits.

- The growth in power and influence of China and the BRIC nations, whose ethical standards may differ from ours, highlight a clash of ethical cultures. More and more businesses are operating in those environments. Unless they are very careful, and very organized, they can easily lose control of own their ethical standards.
- Mass migration of workers to Western economies has brought different cultures right into Head Offices, requiring companies to ensure they are properly managing diverse cultural expectations to avoid embarrassment.
- Migration of jobs to less developed countries continues, straining relations with domestic employees and suppliers.

In addition, new expectations have been created as part of ethical reporting and performance standards published by the Global Reporting Initiative (GR3)[3] and the International Organization for Standardization (ISO 26000)[4], providing authoritative guidance throughout the world.

There is also the question of whether ethical performance by business has improved or worsened in this period. Has greed become more entrenched? Shenanigans on Wall Street and other financial centres have appalled observers, and there is little doubt that ethical conduct in that sector has deteriorated, or at the least corruption has been revealed, even among institutions that previously basked in an aura of respect. But is this true across the board for business and other organizations? Certainly there have been egregious examples of misconduct across the range of businesses and large public institutions, such as universities,[5] police and the military. At the same time, it seems clear that organizations are spending much more effort focusing on managing for ethical conduct, and that many have been successful. It is no longer unusual or surprising to hear corporate leaders emphasizing the importance of ethical conduct. And there are multiple examples[6] of ethical management of crises, such as the well-known Johnson & Johnson Tylenol recall case of 1982.

---

3. Global Reporting Initiative, GR3 Sustainability Reporting Guidelines, https://www. globalreporting.org/resourcelibrary/G3.1-Guidelines-Incl-Technical-Protocol.pdf.
4. International Organization for Standardization, ISO 26000 Guidance for social responsibility, http://www.iso.org/iso/home/standards/iso26000.htm
5. Such as the sexual abuse case involving a Penn State coach, *See*: p. 71
6. Such as the Maple Leaf Foods food contamination case in 2008–9. *See*: *CBC News*, "How Maple Leaf Foods is handling the Listeria outbreak," August 28, 2008, http://www.cbc.ca/news/ business/story/2008/08/27/f-crisisresponse.html (accessed June 11, 2012).

Compelling Evidence

Recently published studies have underscored how important an ethics program leading to the development and maintenance of an ethical corporate culture is to the ongoing success and reputation of a corporation and its executives. The following extracts and comments provide compelling evidence that an ethical corporate culture is relevant to success, and that corporations are responding.

KPMG's Ethics Survey, 2005–2006[7] compares corporations with and without an ethics program and finds that *an ethics program improves perceptions or behaviour significantly* as follows:

- 6–12% reduction in observed misconduct or violation of values and principles in the prior 12 months
- 9–16% improvement in prevention of misconduct
- 39–48% improvement in comfort in reporting misconduct to a supervisor
- 27–46% improvement in belief that appropriate action will follow reporting of misconduct
- 43–54% improvement in perception that CEO and other top executives set the right "tone at the top"
- 37–49% improvement in motivation to "do the right thing"

The *2009 National Business Ethics Survey* of the Ethics Resource Center[8] reports that a strong ethical culture reduces:

- pressure to compromise standards
- observed misconduct
- failure to report observed misconduct
- experienced retaliation for reporting

The PricewaterhouseCoopers' report on *Building a risk-aware culture for success*[9] states:

No matter how clearly you define your risk-appetite and controls, the

7. KPMG Forensic, *Integrity Survey 2005–2006* (KPMG LLP, 2005), http://www.us.kpmg.com/services/content.asp?l1id=10&l2id=30&cid=1972 and http://www.us.kpmg.com/news/index.asp?cid=2051.
8. Ethics Resource Center, *2009 National Business Ethics Survey*, http://www.ethics.org/resource/2009-national-business-ethics-survey.
9. PricewaterhouseCoopers, *Building a risk-aware culture for success*, http://www.pwc.com/gx/en/risk-regulation/risk-aware-culture.jhtml.

people who work for you won't consistently make the right decisions unless corporate culture reinforces "doing the right thing" naturally.

The *KPMG International Survey of Corporate Responsibility Reporting 2011*[10] states:

- Corporate responsibility (CR) reporting has become the *de facto* law for business.
- CR reporting enhances financial value.
- 95 percent of the 250 largest companies in the world (G250 companies) now report on their corporate responsibility (CR) activities, with two-thirds of the reporters based in the United States
- Almost 60 percent of China's largest companies already report corporate responsibility metrics.

Another example that focuses on the leadership role of the CEO, executives, and managers is research[11] that finds that to be perceived to be an ethical leader an individual must speak out about, and demonstrate, the ethical values the corporation or organization expects. If this is not done, employees will take the view that the only value that matters is making a profit. If the executives or leaders are silent on ethical matters, even if they are personally ethical, their reputation will be at considerable risk, as will be the corporation's.

There are still some executives and directors, as well as shareholders, who prefer to focus on making profits without making efforts to determine whether they are made ethically, or even legally. Such decision makers do not appreciate or care about the potential damage that may be caused in the long run by failing to consider the strategic significance of consistently making ethical decisions. With the increasing complexity and rising pace of operations in business, an even greater reliance will be placed on building relationships and managing risks ethically; which will require increasing attention on developing an additional point of reference for decision making – an ethical corporate culture to guide employees to behave ethically.

---

10. KPMG Forensic, *KPMG International Survey of Corporate Responsibility Reporting 2011*, http://www.kpmg.com/Global/en/IssuesAndInsights/ArticlesPublications/corporate-responsibility/Pages/2011-survey.aspx.
11. Linda Klebe Treviño, Laura Pincus Hartman, Michael Brown, "Moral Person and Moral Manager: How Executives Develop A Reputation for Ethical Leadership," *California Management Review* 42 (2000): 128–142.

Overview of the Book

Chapter 2 provides insights into what constitutes an ethical culture, and expands on why a culture of integrity is desirable. The following questions are specifically discussed:

- What constitutes an ethical culture, and why have one?
- What considerations or values define an ethical culture?
- Why is a corporate culture of integrity needed?

The chapter refers to Appendix B; which outlines the impact of regulation, notably SOX, SEC and Canadian regulations; and stock exchange guidance; on corporate governance and ethical requirements.

Chapter 3 follows, with practical insights into how to establish an effective ethical culture. Specific segments will cover:

- Creating a governance and leadership framework
- Motivating leaders
- Developing the core values and issues foundation

Chapter 4 offers insights for creating the guidance communications and framework, including the mission statement, code of conduct, and other decision aids; and for developing commitment to, and understanding of, the organization's ethical objectives by:

- Integration of core values into strategic objectives and operational goals
- Effective communication of values
- Building on input from all levels

Chapter 5 reviews how to launch a new ethical corporate culture successfully in order to develop understanding and commitment to its principles.

Chapter 6 is focussed on how organizations can work towards ongoing reinforcement of the organization's values and preferred practices, and on encouraging compliance with its policies. Techniques discussed include:

- Reinforcement of values
- Communication and feedback mechanisms
- Ombudsmen, hotlines, whistleblower programs, and inquiry services

Chapter 7 provides options for monitoring and reporting ethical performance, as well as Corporate Social Responsibility (CSR), which is a subject of growing interest for many organizations under pressure for transparency from external stakeholders. Issues examined include:

- What CSR means, and how it relates to ethical performance
- What frameworks for CSR measurement are being developed
- Where to look for comparators
- The audit of CSR reports

Chapter 8 presents several approaches to ethical decision making, which is a vital part of an ethical corporate culture since it protects the organization's values and reputation, and if proper techniques are applied correctly, leaves the executives and employees in a defensible position.

Chapter 9 deals with the important problems posed by conflicts of interest. These are omnipresent and very challenging, so companies need to consider carefully how they will deal with the inherent ethical risks presented.

Chapter 10 provides insights into the special ethical problems of financial institutions, including those that resulted in the Subprime Lending Crisis of 2008, which through the U.S. *Dodd-Frank Act* enacted July 21, 2010, produced another round of governance reform. It also offers some suggestions for avoiding these kinds of ethical problems going forward.

Chapter 11 comments on the ethical challenges presented by international operations including dealing with different cultures, practices, laws, enforcement differences, the potential impacts of dealing with emerging economies, and the issues related to guiding and controlling managers and agents from a distance.

Chapter 12 indicates how the issues discussed, and the suggestions made in this book can be applied to not-for-profit entities and small owner-managed enterprises. Not surprisingly, this book's full contents should be understood by the leaders of these organizations, and most of it is equally applicable to them, if not even more than to the world of big business.

Tables placed at the end of the book and at the end of some chapters have also been updated.

In addition to the commentary in each Chapter, readings, and a series of case commentaries are offered to outline, clarify, and illuminate issues causing or involved with important ethical problems facing corporations.

Finally, an accompanying website is available at http://www.ethics-centre.ca, where postings will be made, including updates, news, useful websites, and commentary on governance and ethics matters. Checklists and other helpful forms referenced in this book are downloadable from the website.

New in Fourth Edition of *Ethics & Governance*

In addition to normal updates, the fourth edition contains many enhancements of, and additions to, the issues covered and illustrative cases provided in the third edition, including the following:

Ch. 1   Commentary on developments since 2008
Compelling evidence for a culture of integrity
Summary of new items in the fourth edition

Ch. 2   New evidence of the pervasiveness of stakeholder interest in each organization's practice

Ch. 3   A new section on ethical leadership
A new emphasis on the role of the CEO

Ch. 4   New Illustrative case: J & J forced recall of liquid Tylenol for babies

Ch. 5   New emphasis on the role of the CEO

Ch. 6   New emphasis on the role of the CEO
New evidence regarding the effectiveness of whistleblowing
New Illustrative cases: Penn State, and the Roman Catholic Church

Ch. 7   Revised CSR and ethical performance scope and reporting sections
Revised Appendix A on CSR reports and ratings
New section on Ethics Risk Management
Updated Tables

Ch. 8   New Illustrative case: Moral Courage by the TD Bank CEO

Ch. 9   Revised conflicts of interest section

Ch. 10   New Chapter on ethical issues in the financial services industry and the subprime lending crisis and developments such as the

Dodd-Frank Act, and the recently identified concept of corporate psychopaths
New Illustrative cases: Credit Default Swaps, and the Goldman and Merrill abuse of clients

Ch. 11   Extensive revision of section on bribery
New Illustrative cases:
    On Worldwide Impact – Google vs. China
    On Bribery – SNC-Lavalin, Wal-Mart in Mexico, Lockheed, Daimler, and Niko Resources

Ch. 12   Expanded treatment of not-for-profit entities to cover small and large charities and NGOs
New Illustrative Case: Need to Operationalize Codes

The End of the Beginning

More executives and directors are beginning to understand that corporations are now accountable to shareholders *and to other stakeholders.* Leading companies have responded to this understanding, shifting expectations for all corporations. Governance reform, triggered by scandals, and introduced to restore corporate credibility and public confidence in capital markets, is now seen to depend on an ethical corporate culture that provides appropriate guidance for behaviour. Effective risk management, necessary to keep corporations on track, also depends upon this structure. Directors and senior executives must give adequate attention to the development and maintenance of an ethical corporate culture. Otherwise they must live with the personal vulnerability of inadequate due diligence, and/or failure to fully achieve strategic objectives.

Leonard J. Brooks
David Selley

August 2012

Understanding the Need for an Ethical Corporate Culture

Chapter 2
What is an ethical culture, and why have one?

Organizational Culture – Ethical Culture – Good Governance

The achievement of a corporation's strategic objectives cannot be left to chance. Directors and CEOs are now expected to ensure that employees are given adequate guidance and encouragement so that they further the company's strategic performance while minimizing risk. Since the early 1990s, the realization has grown that the organization's culture is critical to the desired guidance and encouragement process. Without a supportive ethical culture[1] – a *culture of integrity* – even well-intentioned directors and executives cannot expect accurate financial reporting and ethical operations that will generate and maintain the support of key stakeholder groups. Without support from an *ethical corporate culture*, the achievement of strategic business objectives cannot be attained on a sustained basis.

An organization's culture is the set of beliefs, norms and practices that are shared by the organization's members.[2] Employee actions flow from beliefs and norms that are conditioned to a significant extent by those of the organization as defined in mission statements, codes, and other reinforcing communications, as well as those that are informally observed from existing practices. However, employee beliefs are also determined with reference to their personal values as well as those they believe are held by their managers, and motivated or rewarded by their company. This chain of influence is portrayed in Figure 2.1. Further details concerning how a culture works are

---

1. Ethics have to do with deciding what is right and wrong, and an ethical corporate culture is one that encourages employees toward right, rather than wrong, behaviour.
2. Susan Key, "Organizational Ethical Culture: Real or Imagined?" *Journal of Business Ethics*, 20 (1999): 217-218.

Figure 2.1
Organizational Culture Influence Chain

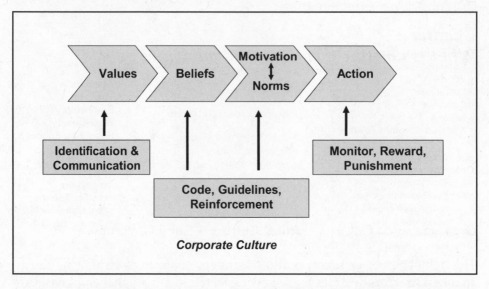

Adapted with permission from Figure 5.4 © 2012 L.J. Brooks & P. Dunn
Business & Professional Ethics for Directors, Executives & Accountants, South-Western, Cengage Learning

provided below, particularly in the chapters within Part 2, "Developing an Ethical Corporate Culture."

In 1982, in their classic book, *In Search of Excellence,* Peters and Waterman[3] identified how an organization's culture could contribute to success or failure by influencing the behaviour of the organization's members. Schein[4] followed in 1985, underscoring just how influential an organization's culture could be. Schein argued that culture is pervasive, and consists of a set of shared values or assumptions that motivate behaviour, provide the key to understanding organizations, define leadership, and can be taught or modified by leaders who wish to create change. He goes on to explore the elements of culture and how the change process works. A very brief summary of his book is found at http://www.tnellen.com/ted/tc/schein.html.

Figure 2.2 identifies the basic elements and reinforcers of an organizational culture, and shows the significant aspects of individual, team, and organizational performance that an effective culture can influence.

---

3. Thomas J. Peters and Robert H. Waterman. *In Search of Excellence: Lessons from America's Best-Run Companies* (New York: Harper & Row, 1984, ©1982).
4. Edgar H. Schein. *Organizational Culture and Leadership* (San Francisco: Jossey-Bass, 1985).

Figure 2.2
Organizational Culture, Individual/Team Outcomes, &
Organizational Effectiveness

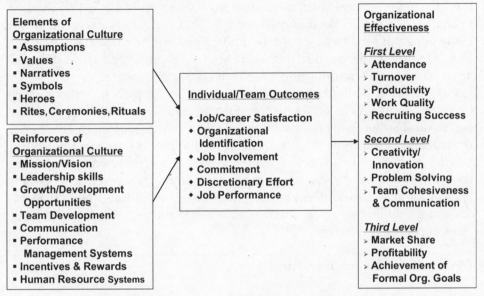

A Model of the Impact of Organizational Culture on Individual/Team Outcomes and Organizational Effectiveness, *The Business Case for Culture Change*, W. Reschke & R. Aldag, Center for Organizational Effectiveness, August 2000.

A properly thought out organizational culture provides a framework that motivates employee actions in accord with the organization's strategic goals. Values are a vital element of an organizational culture because they can define important behavioural principles, and therefore guide how employees will act with the organization's stakeholders. Given the potential gains and risks involved, it is surprising how few organizations have given adequate attention to their culture, and to the choice of values that are most supportive of their strategic objectives.

However, while values are important core touchstones for the establishment of patterns of motivation, norms and behaviour, an effective ethical system of governance requires more than just signposts pointing in the right direction. Experience and recent research have found that just identifying and articulating a set of corporate values, even with rules for their implementation, do not guarantee their use. In fact, codes of conduct are often skeptically referred to as "ethical art" to emphasize their limited usefulness as wall decoration unless accompanied by other support and reinforcement mechanisms. In this respect, ethical values and rules are perhaps even harder than health and safety objectives to get employees to observe; primarily because the positive value of an *ethics program* is not as intuitively evident to employees. They may believe that non-ethical behaviour is in their own self-interest and is profit maximizing for the corporation. To convince employees otherwise requires an all-out effort equivalent to that which would be mounted for a health and safety program or an environmental sensitivity program. Employees will not buy into an ethics program unless there is a strong, dedicated, well-resourced effort directed at developing and maintaining an ethical corporate culture.

Organizations embed and support their values in their narratives, publications, and speeches; when they choose their symbols and pick their heroes; and when they celebrate their successes. As indicated in Figure 2.2, organizations reinforce the importance of their values when they build them into the other aspects of their governance framework, including their mission or vision, their leadership skills and team development, their choices for growth and development, their communications, their performance management systems, their incentive and reward systems, and their human resource systems.

Can an Organization be Ethical?

The values chosen will determine whether employees are directed to behave in an ethical manner or not. For example, if employees believe that profit is all-important and to be maximized at any cost, there is a significant probability that they will be led to step over the line and act unethically. This is because they will very likely offend one or more of the interests of the corporation's stakeholders during an unbalanced pursuit of the interests of shareholders. Current thinking is that *in order to attain its strategic objectives on a sustained basis, a corporation needs the support of at least its key stakeholder groups,* so taking account of stakeholder interests is very important. While it is not possible to please all of the stakeholders all of the time, it is short-sighted not to build a corporation's strategy and culture on a multiplicity of stakeholder interests. Moreover, *the degree to which a corporate culture is based on ethical principles that respect the rights of a multiplicity of stakeholders will determine its degree of ethicality.* A self-assessment score sheet to assess the degree to which stakeholder interests or rights are respected is available on the accompanying website at http://www.ethicscentre.ca.

An *ethical corporate culture* provides a common frame of reference that can influence the behaviour of a corporation's employees. It instills principles of management and control that lead to desirable ethical outcomes. It is based upon and defines the values or principles for which an organization stands and thus its identity. Essentially it involves establishing a shared set

Figure 2.3
Key Stakeholder Support is Vital

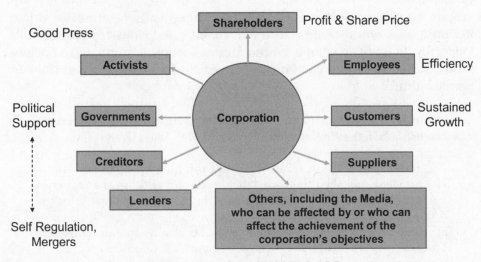

Adapted with permission from © 2012 L.J. Brooks & P. Dunn
Business & Professional Ethics for Directors, Executives & Accountants, South-Western, Cengage Learning

of organizational values that support and encourage ethical behaviour[5] and integrating these values into the day-to-day activities of management and employees.

How to define and establish a corporation's values is covered in the next chapter, but many corporations choose core values from such sources as:

- Reputation drivers[6] – trustworthiness, credibility, reliability, responsibility
- Hypernorms[7] – honesty, fairness, compassion, integrity, predictability, responsibility
- Ethical decision criteria[8] – net positive utility or consequences of

---

5. According to the *New Shorter Oxford Dictionary*, "ethics" refers to the moral principles by which any particular person is guided. "Ethical behaviour" is a term used herein to refer to activity or rules of conduct guided by moral conduct.
6. Charles J. Fombrun. *Reputation: Realizing Value from the Corporate Image* (Boston: Harvard Business School Press, 1996).
7. A hypernorm is a norm which is thought to be considered ethical in most cultures around the world. *See* T.L. Fort, "A Review of Donaldson and Dunfee's Ties That Bind: A Social Contracts Approach to Business Ethics," *Journal of Business Ethics* 28 (2000): 383–87.
8. These approaches to ethical decision making were outlined in the June 2004 Ethics Education Task Force Report of the Association to Advance Collegiate Schools of Business (AACSB), the worldwide accreditation body for business schools as recommendations for the education of business students, *See* http://www.aacsb.edu.

an action; observance of duties, rights and/or fairness; virtuosity expected

Some would argue that a corporation cannot really be ethical and that it would be a waste of time to try to make it so. However, authors like Harvard's Lynn Sharp Paine, whose seminal article is summarized below, argue that corporations can be very successful in instilling an ethical corporate culture.

> **Summary: Lynn Sharp Paine, "Managing for Organizational Integrity,"**
> *Harvard Business Review* **(March–April 1994): 106–117.**
>
> Paine set the stage in 1994 for current thinking on corporate ethics. Her article demolished the widely held idea that ethics was a matter of personal scruples and that the company bore no responsibility for the actions of individuals working within it or, as she puts it, "Ethics, after all, has nothing to do with management. ... typically, unethical business practice involves tacit, if not explicit, co-operation of others and reflects the values, attitudes, beliefs, language, and behavioural patterns that define an organization's operating culture. Ethics is as much an organizational as a personal issue."
>
> She also devastatingly dismissed a solely compliance-based approach as being adequate to allow an organization to qualify as ethical. Legal compliance is not enough, she argues. "The law does not generally seek to inspire human excellence or distinction. It is no guide for exemplary behaviour – or even good practice."
>
> She goes on to describe an ethical organization in more depth and provides examples from the public arena of ethical and unethical decisions by major corporations.

If there is one piece of reading that an aspiring ethics officer, or indeed any person with significant managerial responsibility should read, the Paine article is it.

Even those who argue that a corporation cannot really be ethical must recognize that a focussed devotion to maximizing profit alone is a focus on an imperfect measure. Profit does not take into account many aspects of a corporation's impact. Externalities, for example, represent important dimensions of corporate activity that are often not properly or quickly reflected in normal, historical, financial reports. Pollution created by a corporation is not reflected as a cost in its reports unless they clean it up or recompense an injured party. On the other hand, scholarships paid to employees' children are reflected as a cost in the corporation's accounts, but the benefits are not. In recognition of this lack of reflection in traditional reports, corporations are creating other forms of reporting to capture their impact, such as environmental impact reports or corporate social responsibility statements – and they are taking externalities into their strategic planning processes. The claim that all a company has to do is concentrate solely on its bottom line is both strategically short-sighted and misguided.

Why is a corporate culture of integrity needed?

It's Good Business: Corporations, as noted above, have entered an era in which stakeholders expect that their interests will be taken into account in return for their support. Unless a corporation enjoys the fully-committed support of its employees, costs will be higher than needed or opportunities will be lost through low effort. Unless a corporation enjoys the support of its customers, it will lose sales or margin, and in extreme cases may face consumer boycotts. This recent recognition of the impact of stakeholder expectations, and the related awakening of stakeholders' recognition of their power to influence corporate behaviour, have changed the regime faced by corporations from accountability to shareholders alone to accountability to stakeholders, including shareholders. Given this change, *it is just good business to be ethical and to take a multiplicity of stakeholder interests into account when determining strategy and implementing corporate goals and a supportive culture.* For an example, refer to the following case of the Holland America Line, which emphasizes the advantages that can accrue from good employee relations.

Illustrative Case: Positive Effects of an Ethical Culture

Holland America Line operates a fleet of cruise ships with worldwide itineraries. It has a first class reputation and its crews are admired by all its passengers.

Most of the crew, except for the senior officers, are from Indonesia or the Philippines. Crew members that come into contact with passengers are trained at a Holland America training facility in Indonesia (S/S Nieuw Jakarta). They learn the skills needed for their role, including English language skills. They do a tour of duty of up to one year and then get as much time off as they want with their family before applying to sign back on for another stint. During the tour of duty they work long hours for modest pay, but for more than they would earn at home, and they are learning skills that stand them in good stead for their entire working lives. They get to see the world and some establish permanent friendships with passengers.

Travellers on Holland America ships constantly praise the skill, friendliness, and cheerfulness of the crews, and Holland America thereby greatly benefits from repeat business.

Surely, Holland America's primary objective is not to be a beneficiary to Indonesians and Filipinos. Yet they obviously recognize that treating their crews fairly is good for business. Of course, there are still occasional complaints and injustices. The food provided to the crew looks pretty good when described by the Executive Chef, although one wonders why so many hustle off to McDonald's whenever they have the opportunity in port. However, the purpose of this case is not to illustrate perfection, but simply to show that concern for, and fair treatment of, employees, especially in a service industry, can be a major factor in business success.

Enhancing Trust and Reputation: An ethical corporate culture does not just provide strictures for employees to stay within; it can improve the level of trust in an organization. This is vital to the smooth functioning of employee groups, to the sharing of ideas, and to the willingness and pace of employee adaptation to change. Outsiders are also able and willing to rely more heavily on organizations engendering a high level of trust – a circumstance that works in favour of companies, particularly when they need tolerance in time of crisis.

As long ago as 1999 the *KPMG Business Ethics Survey* of senior executives in the public and private sectors concluded that chief executives see, "public demand for assurance of ethical practice in both the private and public sector as strong and increasing." In addition, respondents to the survey indicated that, "the most influential reason to invest resources in ethics initiatives was 'protection or enhancement of reputation.' "[9] As a result, corporations have increasingly recognized that they need to understand stakeholder expectations and that their actions and communications to stakeholders must demonstrate that they have this understanding. More and more large international corporations are devoting considerable resources to considering ethical issues and to disclosing how they are addressing these issues, as is evident in more recent studies that can be found on the Institute for Business Ethics website at http://www.ibe.org.uk/index.asp?upid=68&msid=12.

New Benchmarks for Profitable Behaviour: Fortunately this attention to stakeholder interests does not need to undermine long-term corporate prof-

---

9. Executive Briefing, *1999 KPMG Business Ethics Survey: Managing for Ethical Practice*, March 1999. *See summary*: http://cbe.bentley.edu/research/surveys/index#1999.

its. Many examples exist where ethical behaviour has led to competitive advantage and success, for example:

- In retailing – Walmart for their sustainability program and Loblaws for its green products
- In autos – GM and Nissan's plug-in electric cars, Toyota's hybrid green cars
- In community support – payment to Cornwall to permit the construction of the St. Lawrence Seaway

New Expectations for Corporate Citizenship and Corporate Social Responsibility: As the studies cited in Chapter 1 make clear, investors and other stakeholders now expect corporations to manage and report on their corporate social responsibility. Why else would:

> Ninety-five percent of the 250 largest companies in the world (G250 companies) now report on their corporate responsibility (CR) activities, two-thirds of the reporters are based in the US.[10]

Consequently, the linkage between an ethical corporate culture and *corporate citizenship* is well worth exploring. The view of both insider and outsider stakeholders is conditioned by the way the company's culture influences employees to deal with *corporate social responsibility (CSR)* issues and therefore influences *corporate social performance*. Directors, executives and managers should be aware that there are consulting services[11] in Canada, and worldwide, that measure and track CSR performance for investors and other activist stakeholders.

Awards are also given to companies with outstanding performance records.[12] Many companies are publishing their social goals and programs; and their performance on environmental impacts, community activities, and health and safety issues, on their websites and in special purpose reports. Corporations such as Shell, BP, and Nike provide ready examples. Significant worldwide efforts are also being made to develop and beta test

---

10. KPMG Forensics, *KPMG International Survey of Corporate Responsibility Reporting 2011*, http://www.kpmg.com/Global/en/IssuesAndInsights/ArticlesPublications/corporate-responsibility/Pages/2011-survey.aspx.
11. *See for example*: MSCI in the US and worldwide, EthicScan Canada Limited and Sustainalytics in Toronto, and Ethical Investment Research Services (EIRIS) in London.
12. Awards are given from such organizations as: PRNews/GeorgeTown University, http://www.prnewsonline.com/awards/csr/; CICA, http://www.cica.ca; and the Global Responsibility Initiative, http://www.globalreporting.org.

broad-disclosure frameworks[13] that go well beyond traditional financial reports to include environmental and social performance, and other disclosures of interest to stakeholders. The bottom line is that stakeholders who have a concern about an entity's business practices now, more than ever before, have the means to significantly impact a company's reputation and market share.

Evidence of the pervasiveness of stakeholder interest in an organization's practices is shown in "Appendix A: CSR and Sustainability Reports, Indexes, and Rankings" located at the end of the book and on the website http://www.ethicscentre.ca, which includes:

- Over 30 organizations with recent CSR reports on the Global Reporting Initiative (GRI) website (http://www.globalreporting.org)
- 10 companies accounting for 60 percent of the assets in two mutual funds that replicate the 60–company Jantzi Social Index®
- The top 15 North American and the top 10 Global companies based on overall Environmental, Social, and Governance (ESG) ratings by the FTSE
- 30 companies with highly regarded CSR reports and related website addresses

Stakeholder Expectations and Power Growth: Evidence of corporate social responsibility has further reinforced the desire of stakeholders to exert their power over corporations to make a difference. These influence attempts are sometimes direct, sometimes through the media, and sometimes through ethical investment funds. Managers of these funds screen corporate activities before investments are placed, and press for changes during the period of investment. The rate of return of these ethical funds can be in the top quartile of mutual funds on a continuing basis, so making such choices does not result in diminished returns. A review of socially responsible investing and investments is available at http://www.socialinvestment.ca/.

Speed and Depth of News Reporting – No Secrets: Not only have the expectations of stakeholders and their ability to exert their influence increased, but the speed of reporting unethical acts has increased dramatically. With satellite communication of news, actions on the other side of the world are known virtually instantly. Moreover, there is an extremely high likelihood that information hoped to be kept secret will leak out or be reported for revenge, or for the satisfaction of ethical principles, either internally within

---

13. *See for example*: AccountAbility, Triple Bottom Line Reporting, http://www.accountability.org and the Global Reporting Initiative (GRI), http://www.globalreporting.org.

a corporation or through an act of whistleblowing in public. Whistleblower protection laws are becoming more common that have reduced the risks for such reporting, and have even added some inducement to come forward.

Scandals Trigger Governance Reform: At the same time, shareholders and other stakeholders, including directors, have witnessed corporate scandals of a size and impact never imagined. The credibility of corporate governance, of their internal reporting and of the capital markets they draw on, has been thrown into crisis. The recovery of credibility lost due to the Enron, WorldCom, and Arthur Andersen scandals required the enactment of the governance reforming *Sarbanes-Oxley Act of 2002* (SOX), followed by regulations from the Canadian Securities Administrators. SOX and the U.S. Securities and Exchange Commission (SEC) regulations it spawned have been applied to all corporations wishing to solicit funds from the U.S. public and their subsidiaries, and has been emulated to varying degrees in other countries.

The Subprime Lending Crisis of 2008 provided another milestone where unbridled greed and unethical behavior in the real estate and financial sectors precipitated a worldwide economic crisis, and led to the creation of another U.S. statute with global reach when the *Dodd-Frank Wall Street Reform and Consumer Protection Act* became law on July 21, 2010. Much of the harm involved in this crisis was facilitated by unethical corporate cultures, as is outlined in Chapter 10.

Personal and Corporate Liability Soar: In the post-Enron, post-subprime lending crisis environment, personal and corporate legal liability for misdeeds has soared, and the preventative nature of a good governance system has been recognized by directors and shareholders. Leaving aside the good business aspect of a governance system that embodies an ethical corporate culture, the post-SOX, post Dodd-Frank governance framework laid out in SEC regulations, and extended in New York Stock Exchange guidelines, or Canadian Securities Administrators' Regulations and Toronto Stock Exchange (TSE/now TSX) guidelines, requires corporate directors more than ever to develop and monitor a sound governance structure that is based upon an ethical culture. The development of expectations for directors wishing to show due diligence in their oversight of corporate governance has been furthered by pronouncements on appropriate internal controls necessary to assure accurate accounting records and reports from the Canadian Institute of Chartered Accountants (CICA), the American Institute of Certified Public Accountants (AICPA), and the Public Company Accounting Oversight Board (PCAOB) which now sets auditing standards for SEC registrants. This governance and internal control framework is outlined in "Appendix B: Governance Framework Requirements," located at the end of the book. The impact of these laws, regulations, and pronouncements is such that while some may consider the resulting new governance framework to be too far-reaching, costly, and perhaps futile, legally it must nevertheless be implemented.

Prevention Requires Diligent Risk Management: Proper risk management provides one of the most important reasons for introducing an effective governance system based on an ethical corporate culture. Even though some argue the attempt to eliminate 100 percent of unethical acts is not possible, the majority of employees can be induced to behave ethically, and it is good risk management practice to encourage them to do so. Forensic specialists have long understood that employee behaviour can be described by the so-called 20/60/20 Rule. Although 10–20 percent of employees will never bend the rules, steal, or commit a fraud, 10–20 percent will do so regardless of what is put in place to stop them. The remaining majority of employees (60–80 percent) will bend the rules, steal, or commit a fraud if they think they can get away with it. This suggests that the directors of a corporation who do not try to provide sound ethical guidance and related internal controls could be vulnerable to illicit acts from 80–90 percent of their employees. On the other hand, directors who ensure the soundness of ethical guidance and related internal controls can take comfort that they have done everything reasonably possible to reduce vulnerability to illicit acts by all but a determined 10–20 percent of their employees.

Altruism: Finally, there are executives and employees who believe in, or are more comfortable, when "doing the right thing" or are proud to be associated with a corporation that demonstrates ethical values. Studies[14] have shown that MBAs from leading North American and European schools are reluctant to take interviews with corporations with questionable reputations or culture because these may cause them future embarrassment. Employees have been known to leave employers that suffer loss of ethical reputation. Recruiting and retaining the best and the brightest employees is increasingly difficult unless sufficient care is given to the development and maintenance of ethical reputation through the safeguards afforded by an ethical corporate culture.

Conclusions

Developing an ethical corporate culture involves going beyond an approach to ethics that focuses merely on concern for compliance with the

---

14. *See for example*: David B. Montgomery and Catherine A. Ramus, "Corporate Social Responsibility Reputation Effects on MBA Job Choice," GSB Research Paper #1805, May 2003.

law – the level usually regarded as the minimum for ethical performance. It means, as stated by Lynn Sharp Paine in, "Managing for Organizational Integrity," holding organizations to a more robust standard[15] that focusses on integrity as the force that drives the organization. It involves developing an *integrity strategy* that is characterized by a conception of ethics as a driving force of an enterprise. Ethical values shape the search for opportunities, the design of organizational systems, and the decision making processes used by individuals and groups. They provide a common frame of reference and serve as a unifying force across different functions, lines of business, and employee groups. *Organizational ethics* helps define what a company is and what it stands for.[16] An ethical corporate culture can, and should, also help a corporation ensure that its values and objectives are aligned with the interests of its key stakeholders. This can facilitate and enhance the organization's control systems and quality control processes to the benefit of directors, executives, shareholders, and other stakeholders.

Corporations are increasingly recognizing that sustained success in the marketplace and thus their long-term viability is very much dependent on their having continuing support from key stakeholders such as customers, employees, suppliers, and host communities. Good governance, dedicated to optimally achieving strategic objectives on a sustained basis, depends upon a culture of integrity to manage risks, maintain the support of key stakeholders, and maximize and sustain profits.

Moreover, the fact, as explained in Appendix B, that legislators and regulators are moving further into the business ethics field should not lead to complacency or a belief following the rules is enough to stay out of trouble. Far from it. Regulations tend to focus on form, sometimes at the expense of substance. Governance processes and internal control structures will work well only if those responsible for implementing them act in an ethical manner. When it comes to audit committees, for example, it appears that Enron had all the right structures in place. Indeed, some have said the audit committee's mandate was exemplary. However, the process failed because the people who were involved were not as diligent as they should have been. Diligence in matters ethical is a business imperative, whether there are rules or not.

---

15. Paine, Lynn Sharp, "Managing for Organizational Integrity," *Harvard Business Review* (March–April 1994): 111.
16. Ibid., 111.

Readings *located at the end of the book*

Jim Goodfellow and Allan Willis, "CEO Challenge," *CAmagazine* 40:1 (2007): 35–42.

Law Case Summary: *Caremark National Inc.*

Checklist – Creating & Implementing an Ethical Corporate Culture	
An Ethical Culture: Elements & Motivation	
✓	Do your organization's members share a common set of:
	• Beliefs
	• Values
	• Practices
	Is that common set of beliefs, values and practices supported by:
	• Specific identification & communications
	• Codes, guidelines & reinforcement
	• Monitoring, rewards & punishment
	Does your management team understand:
	• The elements of an ethical culture
	• The reinforcers of an ethical culture
	• Possible individual & team outcomes
	• Possible areas of improved effectiveness
	At what level does your company understand that ethical treatment is about how the interests of stakeholders are respected:
	• Board of Directors
	• Executives
	• Managers
	• Workers
	Does your ethical culture factor the need for stakeholder support into:
	• Strategic planning
	• Decision making

	Do your Board, executives, managers, and workers understand that an ethical culture:
	• Is good business
	• Enhances trust & reputation
	• Is subject of attention at an increasing number of companies
	• Is a new benchmark expectation for:
	○ Profit
	○ Corporate citizenship & corporate social responsibility
	○ Awards
	• Prevents surprises
	• Mitigates personal liability
	• Requires diligent risk management
	• Satisfies and encourages altruists

Developing an Ethical Corporate Culture

Chapter 3
Foundation – Effective Ethical Leadership, Core Values & Important Issues

Key Steps

As indicated in Chapter 2, an organization's culture is the set of beliefs, norms and practices that are shared by the organization's members.[1] This culture needs to be ethical – *a culture of integrity* – to ensure the continuing support of shareholder and other stakeholder groups that is necessary for a corporation to achieve its strategic objectives on a sustained basis. In the end, a properly thought out organizational culture – *an ethical culture* – provides a framework that motivates and guides appropriate employee decisions and actions in accord with the organization's strategic goals.

The major steps involved are illustrated in Figure 3.1, with *the first priority, and vital ingredient, being understanding the importance of effective ethical leadership*. Without a thorough understanding of what constitutes effective ethical leadership, a board of directors and CEO cannot pick the right people to lead in developing and managing a culture of integrity. Organizational values may not be developed properly, or communicated clearly, with genuine commitment. Developing strong support from followers will be unlikely, and monitoring and reinforcement processes will be ineffective. Understanding what ethical leadership means is clearly a precursor to developing and maintaining an ethical corporate culture.

Ethical Leadership: The Vital Role

Effective ethical leadership is becoming increasingly important to both cor-

---

1. Susan Key, "Organizational Ethical Culture: Real or Imagined?" *Journal of Business Ethics* 20 (1999): 217–218.

Figure 3.1
Creating & Implementing an Ethical Corporate Structure

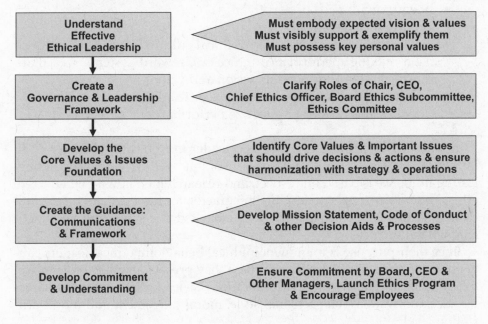

Understand Effective Ethical Leadership	**Must embody expected vision & values** **Must visibly support & exemplify them** **Must possess key personal values**
Create a Governance & Leadership Framework	**Clarify Roles of Chair, CEO, Chief Ethics Officer, Board Ethics Subcommittee, Ethics Committee**
Develop the Core Values & Issues Foundation	**Identify Core Values & Important Issues that should drive decisions & actions & ensure harmonization with strategy & operations**
Create the Guidance: Communications & Framework	**Develop Mission Statement, Code of Conduct & other Decision Aids & Processes**
Develop Commitment & Understanding	**Ensure Commitment by Board, CEO & Other Managers, Launch Ethics Program & Encourage Employees**

porations and to executives, managers and supervisors who wish to contribute successfully and to enhance their career. They need to understand what ethical leadership is, what it involves, and how to achieve it. It must also be understood that, although ethical leadership should come from all persons in leadership positions, an ethical corporate culture cannot be created or sustained without strong, visible ethical leadership from the CEO and the Board chair.

Ethical leaders have definite, important responsibilities that are discussed elsewhere in regard to the development and maintenance of a corporation's ethical culture. But there is an overarching role to be understood if their leadership is to be ethically effective. Essentially, *an ethical leader must embody the organization's vision and values, and influence others to follow their lead.*[2] Functionally, an ethical leader must:

2. R. Edward Freeman and Lisa Stewart, *Developing Ethical Leadership*, (Business Roundtable Institute for Corporate Ethics, 2006), 3, http://www.corporate-ethics.org. *See also* insert box.

- ensure that the vision and values of the organization are ethically sound
- identify with and support them
- communicate them
- ensure that the organization's ethical culture (code, training, decision making, performance indicators, reward systems, and monitoring system) supports its vision and values
- motivate other leaders and employees to adhere to them
- monitor and reward or penalize performance

In order to best achieve these goals, a leader must be able to successfully influence other executives and supervisors as well as employees. Long-lasting influence is based on respect, and research has shown that effective ethical leaders are respected for their character, for their care for others and their interests; for principled, fair and balanced decisions; and for practicing what they preach.[3]

Since their purpose is to influence ethical behaviour, ethical leaders cannot develop the necessary respect unless they present an ethical role model to be emulated. This requires consideration of a leader's personality characteristics, motivation, interpersonal style, moral judgement and moral utilization level.

Research has shown that the following personality characteristics can have a direct effect on effective ethical leadership:

- Agreeableness – Are they altruistic, trusting, kind and cooperative?
- Openness – Are they imaginative, curious, artistic, and insightful?
- Extraversion – Are they active, assertive, energetic, and outgoing?
- Conscientiousness – Are they dependable, responsible, dutiful, and determined?
- Neuroticism – Are they anxious, hostile, impulsive, or stressed? They should not be.[4]

These characteristics, which can be summarized as *integrity, trustworthiness, honesty, sincerity, and forthrightness or candor*,[5] identify ethical values or character traits an ethical leader should possess, to be considered non-

---

3. Michael E. Brown and Linda K. Treviño, "Ethical leadership: A review and future directions," *The Leadership Quarterly* 17 (2006): 595–616.
4. Ibid.
5. Linda Klebe Treviño, Laura Pincus Hartman, Michael Brown, "Moral Person and Moral Manager: How Executives Develop A Reputation for Ethical Leadership," *California Management Review* 42:4 (2000): 128–142.

hypocritical. They are key in building trust, with other leaders and employees, which is essential to their willingness to become followers and supporters of the organization's vision and values. Trust is vital in overcoming the natural cynicism that pervades organizations and reinforces the belief that a corporation's purpose is to make profit at any cost.

Organizational cynicism is also the reason why ethical leaders must visibly and audibly support their organization's ethical vision and values. If they stay silent, their silence will likely be interpreted to mean that they are supporters of the "profit at any cost" approach. If an ethical leader uses guile, deceit, or opportunism in their interpersonal relations, followers are likely to view any message about an ethical vision and values as nonsense. To be most effective, an ethical leader's use of power should not be egotistically focussed, but should recognize and incorporate the interests of employees and show concern for them.

Another aspect of ethical leadership that engenders trust is in the level of moral judgment[6] used. For example, if a leader wishes to convey an ethical message, it is more effective to appeal to followers based on ethical principles that are of value to everyone and positive social intersection rather than threats to their livelihood. Even if a leader thinks ethical thoughts, they must evidence this in their actions, such as by using fair practices, or their thoughts will not be correctly understood due to misperceived assumptions about how followers can best be developed and motivated, and to organizational cynicism.

It is helpful to recognize, as has been pointed out by Linda Treviño[7] and her colleagues, that a truly effective ethical leader must be a moral person as well as a moral manager. They proposed the following two dimensional schema to represent where executives rank on each dimension, and how each contributes to the reputation of the leader as an ethical leader.

In summary, if an ethical leader genuinely wants followers to learn appropriate behaviour and to avoid counterproductive or unethical behaviour, they must fully embody the vision and values intended, and must not only believe in them, but communicate that belief in actions and exhortations. Only then can they provide the right "tone at the top."

---

6. Lawrence Kohlberg's model of Moral Development identified six levels of what motivated moral reasoning, with the lowest level related to threats and the highest levels related to high moral principles. He, and others, have theorized and found that the higher the level of moral reasoning used, the more powerful the motivating potential. See L. Kohlberg, *Essays on Moral Development, Volumes 1 & 2*, (Harper & Row, 1981 & 1984).

7. Op. cit.

Figure 3.2
Dimensions of Ethical Leadership

EXECUTIVE REPUTATION & ETHICAL LEADERSHIP

MORAL PERSON

	Weak	Strong
Strong	Hypocritical	Ethical Leader
Weak	Unethical Leader	
	← Ethically Neutral Leader →	

MORAL MANAGER

Source: *"Moral Person and Moral Manager: How Executives Develop a Reputation for Ethical Leadership"*,
L.K. Treviño et al, California Management Review, Vol. 42, No. 4, Summer 2000.

Business Roundtable's View of Developing Ethical Leadership

According to Ed Freeman and Lisa Stewart,

Ethical leaders embody the purpose, vision, and values of the organization and of the constituents, within an understanding of ethical ideals. They connect the goals of the organization with those of the internal employees and external stakeholders.

Leaders see their constituents as not just followers, but rather as stakeholders striving to achieve that same common purpose, vision, and values. These follower and stakeholder constituents have their own individuality and autonomy which must be respected to maintain a moral community.

Leaders work to create an open, two-way conversation, thereby maintaining a charitable understanding of different views, values, and constituents' opinions. They are open to others' opinions and ideas because they know those ideas make the organization they are leading better.[8]

---

8. R. Edward Freeman and Lisa Stewart, *Developing Ethical Leadership*, (Business Roundtable Institute for Corporate Ethics, 2006), pp. 14, http://www.corporate-ethics.org.

Freeman and Stewart suggest that ethical leaders should have the following characteristics:

1. Articulate and embody the purpose and values of the organization.
2. Focus on organizational success rather than on personal ego.
3. Find the best people and develop them.
4. Create a living conversation about ethics, values and the creation of value for stakeholders.
5. Create mechanisms of dissent.
6. Take a charitable understanding of others' values.
7. Make tough calls while being imaginative.
8. Know the limits of the values[9] and ethical principles they live.
9. Frame actions in ethical terms.
10. Connect the basic value proposition to stakeholder support and societal legitimacy[10]

Creating an Ethical Governance and Leadership Framework

Strong leadership is absolutely necessary in the creation of an ethical corporate culture, as is strong support by senior leaders in the organization. For many organizations establishing an ethical culture is frontier territory compared to normal business functions, and the changes involved may challenge existing ways of thinking, of making decisions, and of getting things done. To overcome inertia or contrary momentum, to wrest turf away from those with a vested interest in the status quo, and to create an effective sustainable culture will require the identification and commitment of skilled and determined leaders supported by top management and resourced adequately. These lessons have been learned in the development of health and safety programs, environmental programs, and sustainability programs. Without the spark, guidance, and encouragement of strong leadership, developing an effective culture of integrity is not possible.

Leaders do not operate effectively unless their initiatives are in harmony with, and supported by, other aspects of a corporation's intended activities. In a modern corporation, all activities should be in support of a strategic plan that lays out strategic goals and related operational objectives. The organization's board of directors is expected to set and approve this strategic plan and its related objectives, and to monitor progress. The appointment of supportive executives and leaders who provide the right "tone at the top" is an essential element of the governance process, as is the oversight of

---

9. Values are rarely absolute, and their application needs to be tempered by judgment depending on circumstances.
10. Ibid, 3-7.

appropriate processes for the establishment, launch, and maintenance of an ethical culture, including the provision of needed resources.

Leaving a vacuum, instead of providing cogent guidance for employee behaviour, leaves the organization open to the risks of trial and error as employees make their inevitable mistakes. Because leaving employee actions to happenstance is not acceptable risk management practice in today's world, research[11] has been conducted into how to most effectively impact employee actions. It has become apparent that the best approach is to provide guidance on the values that underpin the organization's strategic objectives, coupled with the strong support of top management for those values. It turns out that values are a vital element of an organizational culture because they can define important behavioural principles, and therefore guide how employees will act with the organization's stakeholders. Consequently, ethical values need to be the focus of the first part of the establishment process.

Once the core values of the organization are established, the next step in the sequence is their integration into strategic and operational goals. Consistency between organizational goals and behaviour is essential to avoid confusion in the minds of employees, resulting in performance that conflicts with desired objectives.

After the strategic and operational parameters are in place, establishing a culture of integrity depends upon communicating organizational values and objectives effectively, and on making employees aware and willing to buy into, support and follow the recommended behaviour by making appropriate decisions.

Lastly, reinforcement mechanisms need to be put in place to ensure that employees renew their awareness, and their commitment, to the elements important to the organization's ethical culture.

Taken together, if executed effectively, these steps will design and establish a *corporate ethics program* that will reduce a corporation's risk of unethical and illegal actions by employees and agents, and respond to the interests of the company's stakeholders. It will also provide evidence of due diligence on the part of directors and executives who are expected to ensure and oversee appropriate governance structures and processes. In the future, reputations for ethical leadership will depend upon the active development, operation and advocacy of corporate ethics programs based upon the topics discussed in this chapter.

---

11. Gary R. Weaver, "Ethics Programs in Global Businesses: Culture's Role in Managing Ethics," *Journal of Business Ethics* 30: 1 (2001): 3–15, and Gary R. Weaver, Linda Klebe Treviño & Philip L. Cochran, "Corporate Ethics Programs as Control Systems: Influences of Executive Commitment and Environmental Factors," *The Academy of Management Journal* 42:1 (1999): 41–57.

Identifying and Motivating Leaders

Effective ethical leadership starts at the top. The CEO must endorse the goals, personnel involved, process, funding, and the results they produce, or the rest of the organization will only pay lip service to the concept. CEO support is so critical that ensuring proper "tone at the top" became an important governance requirement for boards of directors in the mid–1990s.[12] The support of the board chair is also important, particularly in the strategic sense, but is usually less obvious to employees than that of the CEO, CFO, and other senior officers.

It is important to note that it is not enough for a senior corporate leader to silently or passively support an ethical corporate culture if they want to be considered an ethical leader. Recent research has shown[13] that unless a leader is seen to be vocally or tangibly in support of the ethical corporate culture, employees will assume that the only meaningful guiding principle they should adhere to is to maximize profit, with little regard to how that profit is earned.

The task of championing the development of an ethical corporate culture can be delegated by the CEO to a well-regarded executive, provided that the CEO (and to a lesser extent, the board chair) practically and visibly retains leadership of the ethical culture initiative. The delegated champion may be assisted by an ethics officer or ombudsperson with expertise in managing an ethics program. The champion will report to, and keep the CEO informed, and will work with the CEO in arriving at a supportable ethics program that informs and fits with the organization's strategic goals and risk management preferences.

The champion will also need an ethics committee to assist in the development of the important elements of the ethical corporate culture, and to assist in the selling of the program to the rest of management and to other employees. Typically, the ethics committee assists in the identification of the values and the other elements of the ethics program, and then in the launch and early monitoring of the effectiveness of the launch and of the program itself. As well, the committee members act as facilitators or cheerleaders during the introduction of the program.

The CEO in turn will keep the board chair, the board, and its governance subcommittee informed. The governance committee should receive ongoing reports from the ethics officer and receive, vet, and approve, the

---

12. CICA Study, "Where were the Directors?" 1994.
13. Linda Klebe Treviño, Laura Pincus Hartman, Michael Brown, "Moral Person and Moral Manager: How Executives Develop A Reputation for Ethical Leadership," *California Management Review* 42:4 (2000): 128–142.

Figure 3.3
Establishing an Ethical Corporate Culture –
The Leadership Component

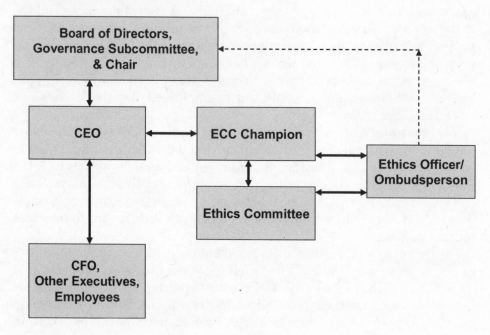

final report on the proposed ethical corporate culture prior to its launch. The champion for the development of the ethics program would probably lead the presentation and be charged with the responsibility for launching the program. Needless to say, the CEO, and possibly the chair of the board, should visibly sponsor and support the launch and the critical elements of the program, in order to assure management and employee buy in.

Developing the Core Values & Issues Component of an Ethical Culture

Central to the creation of an ethical corporate culture is the identification of the core values on which it is to be based. A comprehensive approach to this involves an analysis of stakeholder interests utilizing key frameworks for building reputation and developing core values, norms, and ethical decision criteria; as well as techniques for conducting ethics audits and ethics risk assessments. These are shown in Figure 3.4 and are discussed below.

Figure 3.4
Establishing an Ethical Corporate Culture –
The Core Values & Issues Component

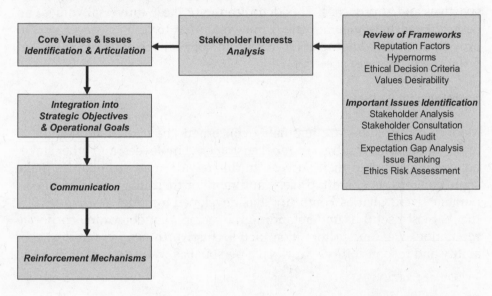

Identifying Core Values – The Basis for Cultural Guidance

Some corporations have a good sense of what they want to achieve, the image they want to project, and what is important to their success. Most companies, however, would benefit from an orderly examination of their goals, strategies, and processes to ensure that they fit well into an effective guidance mechanism. Such an examination would benefit from considering current thinking on the following points:

- The importance of stakeholders and their interests, and on the values most dear to them
- The key elements underlying reputation
- The making of ethical decisions
- The management of problems discovered in ethics audits and risk assessments.

Although it is not immediately apparent, much of this examination is focussed on identification of the key or "right" drivers of behaviour that are to be provided as guidance for employees, whose actions are responsible for success and for avoiding trouble. Interestingly, it will become clear that there is a set of common drivers – a combination of specific and universal values that earn respect – that coalesce from the different examination perspectives and approaches. The identification of these universal values can be facilitated by reviewing the frameworks that have been developed to provide an understanding of reputation and of a universal set of values that bring respect in most societies.

Reputational Values

Modern corporations are justifiably concerned about their reputation or image because it can attract or repel customers, employees, and other stakeholders important to their success. In this regard, many companies make significant efforts to craft, project, and monitor their image as a good corporate citizen. Charles Fombrun[14] has developed a model (see Figure 3.5) that is most useful in understanding the factors that determine corporate reputation. The four factors identified – trustworthiness, credibility, reliability and responsibility – work on a personal as well as a corporate level.

Figure 3.5
What makes a good reputation?

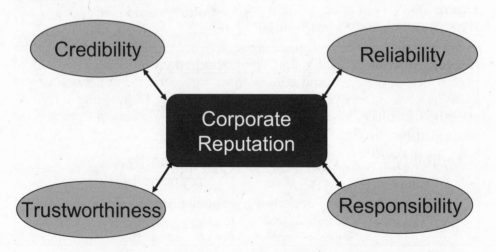

Charles J. Fombrun, *Reputation: Realizing Value from the Corporate Image* (Harvard Business School Press, 1996), 72.

---

14. Charles J. Fombrun. *Reputation: Realizing Value from the Corporate Image* (Harvard Business School Press, 1996).

For instance, they would be useful criteria for selecting a partner in life, or in a professional firm. *There may be additional criteria that are desirable or add value or value added, but the four identified by Fombrun can be regarded as a basic or core set of reputational values.*

Hypernorms – almost Universally Respected Values

Researchers have also been endeavouring to discover the values that are most universally respected by people from different cultures around the world, since these would provide excellent touchstones for the development of an ethical culture for enterprises doing business globally. The six most uniformly respected values, known as *hypernorms* – are *honesty, fairness, compassion, integrity, predictability, and responsibility.*[15]

Predictably, as reflected in Figure 3.6, strong hypernorms provide the basis for strong reputational factors and values. Consequently, the combined set of factors and values is worthy of adoption by any organization intent on establishing an ethical culture. Embedding the relationship between hypernorms and ethical reputation in the guidance underlying a company's ethical culture would be useful in establishing an understanding of the linkage in the minds of employees.

Figure 3.6
Hypernorms Support Reputational Factors

Reputation Factors	Hypernorms
Responsibility	Responsibility
Reliability	Predictability
Credibility	Honesty, integrity, responsibility
Trustworthiness	Fairness, compassion, integrity, responsibility

---

15. R.E. Berenbeim, The Conference Board, Director, Working Group on Global Business Ethics Principles, 1999.

AACSB Recommended Ethical Decision Making Approaches and Criteria

Hypernorm values and reputational factors are also present in the approaches and criteria recommended by the Association to Advance Collegiate Schools of Business (AACSB),[16] the worldwide accreditation body for business schools, to be taught to business students on ethical decision making, as shown in Figure 3.7. The AACSB's Ethics Education Committee recommends consideration of three approaches that have their roots in earlier philosophical thinking utilitarianism or its subset consequentialism, deontology, and virtue ethics. Leaving more detailed explanations until Chapter 8, these approaches examine the utility or consequences of a decision for the affected stakeholders, its impact on stakeholder rights, and how it corresponds to or demonstrates the virtues expected by stakeholders.

Figure 3.7
Ethical Decision-making Approaches and Criteria

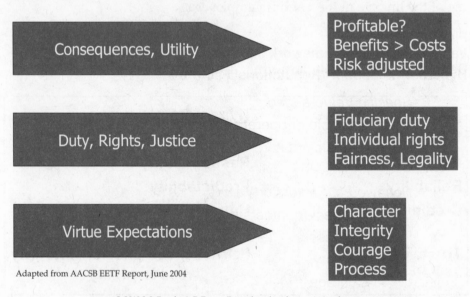

Adapted from AACSB EETF Report, June 2004

---

16. AACSB EETF Report, *Report of the Ethics Education Task Force: Ethics Education in Business Schools*, Association to Advance Collegiate Schools of Business, 2004, http://www.aacsb.edu.

Value Desirability Framework

In terms of the decision to choose a partner noted above, the three approaches of Reputational Factors, Hypernorms, and AACSB Ethical Decision Making, can be combined into a *Value Desirability Framework* that involves two dimensions – specific value-added and behavioural factors or values – as illustrated in Figure 3.8. To develop the full set of organizational values to underpin the ethical culture, the interests of each of the organization's stakeholder groups should be examined, asking what specific value-added factors and what behavioural factors or values are desired or expected.

Since one of the most common faults of corporate decision makers is to ignore some groups of stakeholders, including the media, which may later become very important to the achievement of the corporation's strategic objectives, it is advisable that all stakeholders and their interests be included in this review. It is important to bear in mind that stakeholders judged insignificant may, and often do, develop media-worthy issues, or ally themselves with stronger stakeholders, so that their interests become significant in the future.[17]

Figure 3.8
Value Desirability Framework Incorporating
Reputation Factors, Hypernorms, & Ethical Decision Criteria

Specific Value-added
  – Tangible or operational utility or consequences
  – Intrinsic or future-oriented considerations

Behavioural Factors or Values
  – Respect for others rights
  – Fairness
  – Integrity
  – Courage
  – Other value-related aspects of character.

---

17. For a more detailed discussion of this stakeholder impact dynamic, refer to Chapter 8.

Figure 3.9
Identifying Values for an Ethical Corporate Culture

Sources of Values	Tangible or Operational, Intrinsic & Behavioural Values

Stakeholder Interests	Shareholders
	    Tangible/Operational - Value Added, Net Profit,
	    Intangible - Competitive Advantage, Image, Reputation
	    Behavioural - Honesty (**H**), Integrity (**I**), Fairness (**F**), Credibility (**Cred**),
	          Reliability/Predictability (**R/P**), Responsibility (**R**)
	Consumer
	    Tangible/Operational - Value in use
	    Intrinsic Value - Innovativeness, Environmental Friendliness, ...
	    Behavioural - **H, I, F**, Compassion (**C**), **R/P, R**
	Employee - Fair Pay & Opportunity
	    - Ethical Reputation, ...
	    - **H, I, F, C, R/P, R**
	Environmentalists - Sustainability, **H, I, F, C, R/P, R**
	Community – Support, **H, I, F, C, R/P, R**
	Other – ....

Reputation Factors	**Trustworthiness, Cred**ibility, **R**eliability, **R**esponsibility
Hypernorms – key values in most cultures/societies	**H**onesty, **F**airness, **C**ompassion, **I**ntegrity, **P**redictability, **R**esponsibility

Ethical Decision Criteria
    See Chapter 8
	Net Positive Utility or Consequences from an action
	    Net profit, Net Cost-Benefit Analysis, Net Risk-Benefit Analysis
	Observance of Duties, Rights and/or Fairness
	Fulfillment of Virtues Expected

Figure 3.9 presents a set of values that result from an analysis of a typical company's stakeholders' interests. Shareholders, for example, are interested in profit or in some other form of value added such as competitive advantage, reputation, image, or control of assets or of processes that will produce future profits. In addition, they are interested in values and strategies that will support and sustain future activities, in addition to protecting their rights in terms of fair, complete, and transparent disclosure and distribution of profit earned. The interests of other stakeholders, such as consumers, employees, environmentalists, and community members, are also shown, as are the value elements included within the value-identification approaches – reputational factors, hypernorms, and ethical decision criteria. When reviewed as a whole, these stakeholder analyses fit well with the Value Desirability Framework, involving stakeholder-specific tangible and intangible value added, plus behavioural values.

In summary, in order to develop a set of core values to build into its ethics program, a corporation should analyse the interests of its stakeholders using a framework similar to the above, and referring to known reputation factors, hypernorms, ethical decision criteria, and a values desirability framework.

Identifying Important Ethical Issues for Cultural Guidance

During the stakeholder values analysis, the corporation should be alert to specific issues that are of concern, so that these can be adequately addressed in the ethical guidance given to employees. Often an issue, such as environmental sensitivity, can be covered by a general principle that flows from a specific set of values, but occasionally specific treatment is necessary to avoid confusion or to provide the best signal to all stakeholders that this is a matter of high priority or risk, and that its treatment, or specific aspects of that treatment are to be handled in a certain way.

In addition to a review of stakeholder interests and values, important issues can be identified from scans of industry and other company guidance documents such as mission statements, codes of conduct or ethics, and other policies. Electronic summaries of codes and code content are available on several websites that are referenced on the EthicsCentre website at http://www.ethicscentre.ca. Articles on the development of codes are also noted.

To make sure important issues are not overlooked, corporations can hire consultants to undertake environmental scans of the news media and provide up-to-date advice on issues of concern, or their own personnel can undertake these reviews. If the scans are done internally, corporations would be well-advised to seek expert advice on which issues are likely to emerge as significant risks, and how other companies are dealing with them.

Some companies convene *stakeholder consultation groups* in an effort to stay in touch with their constituents and their interests. These groups can also be useful in testing reactions to past events and proposed solutions. They create a bond that can be helpful in working through ongoing problems. Recognizing the importance of stakeholder consultation groups, the Canadian Standards Association (CSA) has developed a protocol for their formation and engagement.[18]

Some corporations engage in *ethics audits* as a means to identify and understand ethical issues affecting their strategies or activities, to ensure they are managed effectively from a risk perspective. An ethics audit involves reviewing all or part of an operation – its personnel, complaints by customers and suppliers; environmental and health and safety reports; quality standards and similar documents – in order to discover what the important issues are now and might be in the future. Sometimes audits are done by outside consultants, by squads of promising junior executives from other parts of the enterprise, or by the company's internal auditors. The audit re-

---

18. Canadian Standards Association, *A Guide to Public Involvement* (Z764), 1996.

port could be part of the ongoing ethics program, and be forwarded to the ethics officer, chief risk officer, CEO and relevant board subcommittee. The best known of these was the Dow Corning ethics audit[19] that unfortunately failed to raise the problems associated with the company's leaking silicone breast implants that were ultimately responsible for putting the company into bankruptcy. Even so, Dow Corning's CEO applauded its ethics audit process for its earlier successes. With proper guidance and understanding of audit and interview techniques, the ethics audit can be a very effective mechanism for ethics issues identification and assessment.

A logical output of the process of ethics issues identification and articulation is an understanding of which issues pose significant risks for the organization. Two further techniques can be used to identify and then rank the importance of the ethics risks involved. As part of the issues identification process, examiners can use *expectation gap analysis*, assessing the difference between what stakeholders expect and what the company is delivering, to identify *ethics risks*[20] and then classify their nature and significance.

Salience research by Mitchell, Agle and Wood[21] suggests that ethics issues can be classified into those dealing with:

- Legitimate claims from stakeholders – those protected by law or sanctioned by ethical norms
- Claims from powerful stakeholders – who have the power to influence the achievement of the corporation's objectives
- Urgent claims – often from victims or soon-to-be victims

Importantly, the urgent claims are usually the most significant, because of their ability to influence the media, who in turn influence the public and powerful politicians who have the power to regulate or influence corporate behaviour. The Mitchell, Agle and Wood Salience Model is reproduced in Figure 3.10. Care must be taken to remember the dynamic nature of the salience classification[22] when projecting developments in the future.

Figure 3.11 represents a three phase approach to the issue of ethics risk identification and ranking, and brings together several of the tasks suggested to date.

---

19. "Dow Corning Ethics Audit Case" in Leonard J. Brooks and Paul Dunn. *Business & Professional Ethics for Directors, Executives & Accountants*, 6e, (South-Western, Cengage, 2012), 340–342.
20. An ethics risk exists where stakeholder expectations are not met.
21. R.K. Mitchell, B.R., Agle, & D.J., Wood, "Toward a Theory of Stakeholder Identification and Salience: Defining the Principle of Who and What Really Counts," *Academy of Management Review* 22 (1997): 853–886.
22. T. Rowley, "Moving Beyond Dyadic Ties: A network Theory of Stakeholder Influences," *Academy of Management Review* 22 (1997): 887–910.

Figure 3.10
Stakeholder Interest/Claim Classification – Salience

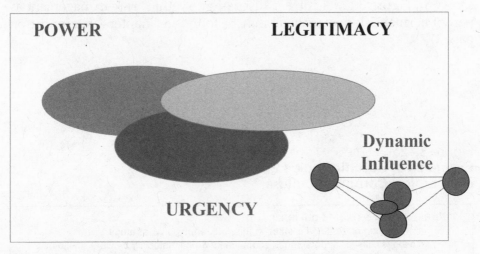

R.K Mitchell,., B.R., Agle, & D.J., Wood, "Toward a Theory of Stakeholder Identification and Salience: Defining the Principle of Who and What Really Counts," Academy of Management Review 22(1997): 853-886.
T. Rowley, "Moving Beyond Dyadic Ties: A network Theory of Stakeholder Influences", Academy of Management Review 22(1997): 887-910.

Figure 3.11
Ethics Risk & Opportunity Identification & Assessment

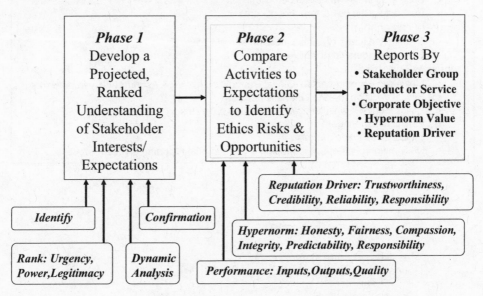

At the conclusion of the search for important ethical issues facing a corporation, a list of specific topics requiring treatment might emerge, such as shown in Figure 3.12. A further discussion of ethics risk management as part of normal risk management may be found in Chapter 7, beginning on page 177.

Figure 3.12
Examples of Specific Topics Requiring Treatment
in an Ethical Corporate Culture

Corporate values & related guidance
- Identification and rationale linked to mission, reputation & strategy
- Responsibility for endorsement, commitment & accountability by CEO & all others
- Responsibility for compliance, consultation & whistle-blowing
- Importance of character, integrity & courage

Stakeholder interests and expectations
- Fair treatment of customers & employees – pay, discrimination, complaints, etc.
- Respect for the environment for direct & indirect impacts, stewardship & sustainability
- Respect for the health of employees, customers & others influenced
- Conflicts of interest with shareholders
- Bribery and other unethical behaviour
- Respect for the law & for other cultures

Corporate citizenship
- Definition in terms of values, mission and activities
- External leadership objective

Processes endorsed
- Measurement of impacts – Global Reporting Initiative & AccountAbility frameworks
- Ethical decision making criteria & process
- Ethics inquiry & whistle-blower protection programs
- Ethical risk management
- Ethical crisis management
- Designation of an ethics champion & of an annual reporting & review process

	Checklist – Creating & Implementing an Ethical Corporate Culture	
	Leadership, Core Values & Important Issues	
✓	Understand the Importance of Effective Ethical Leadership	
	• Do leaders ensure that the vision and values of the organization are ethically sound?	
	• Do leaders embody the vision and values of the organization?	
	• Do leaders visibly support and exemplify the vision and values?	
	• Do leaders exhibit integrity, trustworthiness, honesty, sincerity, and forthrightness or candor?	
	• Do leaders communicate the vision and values?	
	• Do leaders ensure that the organization's ethical culture (code, training, decision making, performance indicators, reward systems, and monitoring system) supports its vision and values?	
	• Do leaders motivate other leaders and employees to adhere to the vision and values?	
	• Do leaders monitor and reward or penalize performance?	
	Create a Governance & Leadership Framework	
	Clarify roles of board, governance/ethics subcommittee, chair, & CEO	
	• Identify ethics champion, chief ethics officer & role of each	
	• Identify reporting relationships & expectations	
	• Identify responsibilities and performance expectations	
	Develop the Core Values & Issues Foundation	
	Develop Core Value set by considering:	
	• Reputational values – *trustworthiness, credibility, reliability, responsibility*	
	• Hypernorms – *honesty, fairness, compassion, integrity, predictability, and responsibility.*	
	• Ethical decision making criteria – stakeholder impact analysis	
	• Constructing a Values Desirability Framework	
	Identify important issues requiring cultural guidance by:	
	• Stakeholder Impact Analysis	
	• Environmental scanning	
	• Stakeholder consultation	
	• Ethics audit	
	• Expectations gap analysis	
	• Ranking issues – *urgent claims before powerful and legal claims*	
	• Ranking issues – ethics risk assessment	

Developing an Ethical Corporate Culture

Chapter 4
Guidance Communications –
Mission Statement, Code of Conduct, Decision Aids

In addition to the proper integration of the desired values into operational goals, implementing an ethical culture will require appropriate communication of values and initiation of reinforcement mechanisms.

Integration of Core Values into Strategic Objectives and Operational Goals

Strategic objectives should be set to optimize the corporation's potential to encourage the support of its key stakeholder groups because this support will determine the success of the organization in the future. The final set of objectives will certainly involve trade-offs between owners, management, customers, and other groups, so ignoring the interests and related core values of one or more of the stakeholder groups would be short-sighted. Consequently, whatever strategic objectives are adopted should be compared with, and adjusted to, reflect the set of core interests and values developed in the stakeholder analysis described above.

It may be more efficient to create a corporation's strategic objectives to reflect the findings of the stakeholder analysis in the first place. For example, the findings of the Values Desirability Analysis (*see* Figures 3.7 and 3.8) should identify the tangible and intrinsic interests, and the behavioural values desired by each stakeholder group. When combined with a vision of the future and an assessment of the resources of the organization, these findings should provide a guide to desired competitive advantages, values and behavioural principles. For example, if a substantial segment of customers want fuel-efficient cars because they value and want to protect the environment, or want to reduce costs, it would be highly risky to develop a vision and competitive advantage based upon high-powered, gas-guzzling vehicles, as some North American car manufacturers found in 2008.

Operational goals should flow from, and be compatible with, ethical strategic objectives, to avoid confusion and mistakes. If customers value honesty, integrity and transparency, it would be wise to craft strategic and operational objectives that signal their importance to the corporation's employees. In the case of General Motors' Saturn Division, this led to the establishment of "no haggle pricing" which found high appreciation from women who preferred to deal with credible dealers. On the other hand, Sears Automotive Repair operationalized their drive for profits by establishing a bonus scheme for service managers that, when coupled with an aggressive, insufficiently ethical culture, induced and allowed the managers to benefit from selling unneeded services to unsuspecting customers. With the immediate sharing of information via the internet, the damage to corporate reputation from unethical strategic objectives and operational goals can be swift and serious. Another example of this is Intel's decision not to recall a flawed math co-processor on their early Pentium 4 chip. Ethical core values need to be included in both strategic objectives and operational goals from the start.

Effective Communication of Values

A mission statement and a code of ethics or conduct are viewed by most companies as essential first steps in developing and communicating the values of an organization. On their own, however, they cannot result in the development of an ethical corporate culture.

A mission statement is a short, inspiring, visionary communication to employees and other stakeholders concerning the purpose, values, and objectives of an organization, and what is expected from employees in terms of promoting such values and objectives. The existence of a strong set of widely understood and generally accepted values has been cited as a reason why Johnson & Johnson was accorded iconic status in 1982 for quickly and effectively recalling poisoned Tylenol tablets. For reference, Johnson & Johnson's Mission Statement is reproduced as Figure 4.1.

A company that does not have a firm set of accepted values will be at a greater risk of unethical activities, and if a crisis occurs, may have to create these values on the fly. Such a company will find it very difficult to develop a solution that is well thought out and consistent with its longer-term objectives, and may end up making matters worse. Situations where absence of sound values has allowed poor practices in day-to-day operations or in crisis situations include:

Figure 4.1
Johnson & Johnson Credo

We believe our first responsibility is to the doctors, nurses, and patients, to mothers and all others who use our products and services. In meeting their needs everything we do must be of high quality. We must constantly strive to reduce our costs in order to maintain reasonable prices. Customers' orders must be serviced promptly and accurately. Our suppliers and distributors must have an opportunity to make a fair profit.

We are responsible to our employees, the men and women who work with us throughout the world. Everyone must be considered as an individual. We must respect their dignity and recognize their merit. They must have a sense of security in their jobs. Compensation must be fair and adequate and working conditions clean, orderly, and safe. Employees must feel free to make suggestions and complaints. There must be equal opportunity for employment, development and advancement for those qualified. We must provide competent management, and their actions must be just and ethical.

We are responsible to the communities in which we live and work and to the world community as well. We must be good citizens – support good works and charities and bear our fair share of taxes. We must encourage civic improvements and better health and education. We must maintain in good order the property we are privileged to use, protecting the environment and natural resources.

Our final responsibility is to our stockholders. Business must make a sound profit. We must experiment with new ideas. Research must be carried on, innovative programs developed and mistakes paid for. New equipment must be purchased, new facilities provided, and new products launched. Reserves must be created to provide for adverse times. When we operate according to these principles, the stockholders should realize a fair return.

- Surprisingly, in 2010, J & J was forced to withdraw infant liquid Tylenol cold products due to sloppy manufacturing practices. This caused a significant loss of revenue and profits, and was shockingly contrary to the iconic reputation-positive Tylenol recall mentioned above. *See* Insert box below.
- Firestone Tires on the Ford Explorer – Product recalls were initially denied to reduce legal liability, which signalled a lack of concern over customer safety to the public, and resulted in a loss of additional sales, as well as higher legal costs. Firestone was taken over by Bridgestone.
- Dow Corning Silicone Breast Implants – Dow Corning executives resisted product recalls and adequate restitution even though they knew silicone leakage was likely and that thousands of women were reporting similar illnesses. The entire company was ultimately put into receivership by the legal settlement.

Tylenol Recalls (2010): Losing an Iconic Reputation

Johnson & Johnson (J & J) enjoyed a halo effect for many decades after their iconic precautionary recall of Tylenol capsules in 1982. But that halo has now been lost due to the events that led to the company's forced recall of children's Tylenol and other children's medicines in 2009 and 2010.

On April 30, 2010, J & J's McNeil Consumer Healthcare, LLC (McNeil Division), "recalled some 50 children's versions of non-prescription drugs, including Tylenol, Motrin and Benadryl."[1] In total, 136 million bottles of liquid were involved.[2] This was the fourth recall in seven months. Earlier recalls included:

- November 2009 – 5 lots of Tylenol Arthritis Pain 100 count with the EZ-open cap due to reports of an unusual mouldy, musty, or mildew-like odour that led to some cases of nausea, stomach pain, vomiting and diarrhoea.
- December 2009 – November recall expanded to all lots of the product.
- January 2010 – an undisclosed number of containers of Tylenol, Motrin and over the counter drugs after consumers complained of feeling sick from an unusual odour.[3]

Prior to 2009, the FDA inspections had noted several problems with "laboratory controls, equipment cleaning processes, and a failure to investigate identified problems,"[4] but these were "generally fixed."[5] During 2009, the FDA identified several more problems. These incidents led the FDA to send a warning letter on January 15, 2010, to McNeil, but upper management at neither McNeil nor J & J responded to assure timely investigation and resolution of the issues raised.

On February 19, 2010, the FDA called senior officials from McNeill and its parent company J & J to a meeting to give them notice about the patterns of violation of cGMP[6] standards, recent recalls and warning letters, and failure to report information to the FDA in a timely manner. At the

---

1. Parija Kavilanz, "'Shocking' conditions at Tylenol plant," CNNMoney.com, May 14, 2010, (accessed May 14, 2010).
2. Joshua M. Sharfstein, Principal Deputy Commissioner, U.S. FDA, "Johnson and Johnson's Recall of Children's Tylenol and Other Children's Medicines" (Statement before the Committee of Oversight and Government Reform, U.S. House of Representatives, May, 21, 2010), http://www.fda.gov/NewsEvents/Testimony/ucm213640.htm, (accessed November 16, 2010).
3. Ibid.
4. Ibid.
5. Ibid.
6. cGMP refers to the Current Good Manufacturing Practice regulations enforced by the US Food and Drug Administration (FDA).

meeting, the FDA were told that structural changes, new management and a new consultant were to be put in place to deal with these problems. However, in April 2010, FDA investigators found additional similar violations at another plant.

On July 21, 2010, the FDA released a report on its investigations at another of J & J's plants that listed 12 types of violations, and indicated:

> "a pattern of ignoring rules for manufacturing and quality, failure to investigate problems that could affect the composition of products, carelessness in cleaning and maintaining equipment, and shoddy record-keeping"[7]

According to Associated Press, on the day the report was released, J & J's stock dropped 2.5% to $57.12. Estimates of the cost of recalls and the shutdown of the Fort Washington plant were $600 million in 2010. The Fort Washington plant manager had been fired and 300–400 workers had lost their jobs.[8]

Source: This case has been excerpted from a more comprehensive case entitled, "Tylenol Recalls (2010): It's Still About Reputation," drawn from L.J. Brooks and P. Dunn, *Business & Professional Ethics for Directors, Executives & Accountants*, 6e, (South-Western, Cengage Learning, 2012), 212–215.

A code of conduct or ethics is usually a much longer document than a mission statement. It covers the same purpose, values, and objectives found in the mission statement in greater depth, and usually goes on to propose principles and rules of conduct. It provides general and specific guidance, as well as rationale for expected behaviour.

A mission statement can be a focus-providing document of only one page, whereas a code of conduct is frequently published in a booklet form of twenty or more pages. A company's mission statement is usually featured on its public website, and a code of conduct is usually available via the company's Intranet. Both mission statements and codes of ethics or conduct can, and should, be used on an ongoing basis as a means of communicating an organization's values and objectives, and as a means of measuring and monitoring performance designed to achieve those objectives.

7. Associated Press, "New FDA report shows multiple lapses at J & J plant", CLEVELAND.COM, July 21, 2010, http://www.cleveland.com/business/index.ssf/2010/07/new_fda_report_shows_multiple.html , (accessed November 16, 2010).
8. Ibid.

The development and implementation of a process to articulate values, and to develop a mission statement and/or code, is often delegated to one department in an organization. It is essential, however, that managers at all levels of the organization, including top management, support the need to develop an ethical corporate culture, and that they are involved in the process. To be successful a mission statement or code should:

- Articulate the organization's strategically determined core reason for being and goals
- Reflect and articulate values, issues, and responsibilities to stakeholders that are important to success, to being the type of corporate citizen it wishes to be, and that ought to be shared throughout the organization
- Involve grassroots and front line buy-in throughout its development
- Take the outside world into account by determining where the organization can make a difference (mission) and by considering the real pressures under which the individual must make decisions (code)

Once the issues to be raised, and values to be signalled, are identified, an orientation method should be chosen for the mission statement or code of conduct. It is important to understand that this choice is an important contributor to the overall effectiveness of the code of conduct because the orientation of the code determines the degree of employee buy-in to the values it articulates. The choices of orientation noted by Treviño and her colleagues[9] are:

- An integrity, or values-based orientation
- A compliance-based orientation
- An orientation designed for the satisfaction of external stakeholders
- An orientation designed in order to protect top management from blame
- A combination of the above approaches

The Treviño research has shown that codes of conduct, and ethics programs, based upon integrity or shared values are more likely to be effective

---

9. Linda Klebe Treviño, Gary R. Weaver, David G. Gibson, and Barbara Ley Toffler, "Managing Ethics and Legal Compliance: What Works and What Hurts," *California Management Review* 41 (1999): 135–139.

than those based on compliance-oriented rules, protection for top management or satisfaction of external stakeholders. The most effective orientation, however, appears to be a combination approach in which shared values represent the dominant orientation, and compliance concerns are secondary. It is to be hoped that codes of conduct gravitate toward this values-dominated, combination approach.[10]

It should be noted that Lynn Sharp Paine believes that, "there is no one right integrity strategy. Factors such as management personality, company history, culture, lines of business, and industry regulations must be taken into account when shaping an appropriate set of values and designing an implementation program."[11] She describes the key features to developing a strategy-reinforcing integrity within an organization, by referring to efforts made by organizations that have achieved success in this area.

Ms. Paine goes on to say that, "success in creating a climate for responsible and ethically sound behaviour requires continuing effort and a considerable investment of time and resources. A glossy code of conduct, a high-ranking ethics officer, a training program, an annual ethics audit – these trappings of an ethics program do not necessarily add up to a responsible, law-abiding organization whose espoused values match its actions. A formal ethics program can serve as a catalyst and a support system, but organizational integrity depends on the integration of the company's values into its driving systems."[12]

Input from all Levels

When drafting the code, keep in mind the need to use plain language that can be understood by all readers. When the steering committee is comfortable with the draft, the chairman and CEO should read it to make sure they are willing to provide strong support.

---

10. Note that according to a 1999 Conference Board Report, the values orientation is only one of four identified, but it is the only one to be, "found in every region and is the dominant form in Europe." The four orientations that the Conference Board used are:
    - Instrumental – adherence is essential to success
    - Compliance – statement of do's and don'ts
    - Stakeholder Commitment – acknowledgment of company accountability to various constituencies
    - Values – declaration that certain ethics principles are essential to what it means to be an employee of the company

    US companies are said to, "rely most often on the instrumental justification," whereas, "Canadian, Japanese, and Latin American companies are more evenly divided among the four different categories." Ronald E. Berenbeim, *Global Corporate Ethics Practice: A Developing Consensus*, (New York: The Conference Board, Inc., 1999): 8.
11. Lynn Sharp Paine, "Managing for Organizational Integrity," *Harvard Business Review* (March–April 1994): 112.
12. Ibid., 112.

After the draft code is blessed by the chairman and CEO, it should be taken to representative groups of employees for their reactions, and suggestions for improvement, in its clarity, coverage, and sensitivity to local issues. These sessions can be useful for pre-training the corporation's trainers, and in gaining early understanding and commitment from informal leaders at all levels within the corporation. This can be particularly helpful when launching the code, and in its early interpretation.

It may be helpful for the steering group to start with input from stakeholders, particularly employees, prior to arriving at a first draft. The objective of this approach is to obtain employee input before major decisions are made, or even floated as ideas, rather than subsequently, as feedback. This is difficult to organize and achieve, but avoids the problem of negative feedback on a steering committee draft being inevitably seen by senior management as criticism of the document, that may lead them to inhibit the further flow of ideas from employees. Preliminary input may be obtained from small, facilitated groups of employees specifically selected to provide representation from various ranks, levels, departments, cultures, and genders.

Feedback Sessions and Gap Analysis

One helpful framework for feedback sessions involves sending out the draft code to be read in advance. When the session participants convene, the can be asked to debate the following questions:

- What did you expect to find in the code? What was missing?
- Was any aspect of the code unclear?
- Are there any barriers to the introduction and use of the code?
- What features do you think are the most important in the code?

The answers to these questions will facilitate a gap analysis that will permit the improvement of the code, its acceptance, and adherence to it. The final version of the code should be approved by the board of directors upon the favourable recommendation of the company's senior officers, all of whom must actively endorse it, and encourage its subsequent use.

Decision Aids

In addition to the organization's mission statement and code of conduct, other helpful aids are often produced to remind employees of what they should think about when considering a decision or action. IBM, for example, first produced a pocket-size guide, and later an online version, for ease of reference. Online guides with frequently asked questions (FAQs) are now expected. The intention is to ensure that the organization and its employees are in a defensible position legally and ethically, and to reduce the exposure of the corporation and its personnel to loss of reputation and competitive advantage.

Decision aids should include, in abbreviated form, the ethical values and major issues that employees should bear in mind. This might be arranged to cover decision-making approaches and issues, or a set of sniff tests and additional questions that cover the impacts on stakeholder interests. These are explored more fully in Chapter 8.

Organizational policy should hold employees responsible for using the decision aids provided, and if a potentially unethical decision is identified, the employee is responsible for consulting a manager with training in applying such analysis, or a designated person such as the company's chief ethics officer.[13]

Even if an organization does not have a quick reference decision aid, employees should have an understanding of ethical decision making, and know where and when to seek guidance. Ethical decision-making criteria need to be a formal part of an organization's ethical culture.

Checklist – Creating & Implementing an Ethical Corporate Culture	
Guidance Communications – **Mission Statement, Code of Conduct, Decision Aids**	
✓	Guidance communications should be based on core values & important issues that are integrated into :
	• Strategic goals
	• Operational goals
	Effective guidance communications should include:
	• Mission Statement
	○ Short, inspiring, focussed on key values

---

13. A chief ethics officer is charged with the overall responsibility for the ethics program for a company. Another title could be chief ethics & compliance officer. Additional details are available from the Ethics & Compliance Officer Association, http://www.theecoa.org.

	•	Code of Conduct
		○ Incorporate core values
		○ Cover important issues needing guidance
		○ Choose orientation – integrity or values-based vs. compliance-based, or combination approach
		○ Use input from all levels
		○ Use feedback sessions and gap analysis
	•	Decision Aids
		○ Online or not?
		○ Usage requirement
		○ Sniff tests
		○ Consultation required if problematic
		○ Key ethical decision criteria
		○ Reporting requirement

Developing an Ethical Corporate Culture

Chapter 5
Developing Commitment & Understanding – Launch

Training Program

An effective ethics-training program should cover all employees within an organization. It should be provided separately to agents and to providers of outsourced services. It should complement the launching of the mission statement or ethics code, and should be designed to help employees and agents:

- Understand the relevance of the mission statement or code and the values it puts forward to the organization's competitive advantage and strategy
- Understand the mission statement, ethical values, and principles of the organization
- Recognize, analyze, and resolve ethical issues in their own jobs
- Know what support resources are available to them if they have questions, or are faced with situations involving ethical dilemmas
- Provide feedback on current ethics issues, ethics performance and the training program

Ethics Workshops

Ethics workshops provide one way of training employees. The main advantage of holding workshops is that they enable employees to work together in small groups and to learn by doing.

Structure the workshops so that they involve employees from a single, small work group or from a small number of related work groups. This will allow the employees at the workshop to focus on issues relevant to their workplace. The workshop should be led by the person they report to, reinforcing management's commitment to, and responsibility for, ethics. If the manager is to participate directly as a presenter, it is important that they have had prior training and have demonstrated commitment to the mission and code, and to the values that underlie them. If this is not established in advance, it is better that the manager be part of the audience, rather than at the podium. Sometimes, it is beneficial to provide a facilitator to the group, but they should be a seasoned expert such as an ethics advisor or consultant, or an individual from the human resources department, the comptroller's department or the internal audit department.

Workshop Agenda

The workshop agenda should allow for open, informal, two-way communications, as well as a formal presentation. An appropriate way to achieve this is to have small group discussions of challenging issues or case studies, which are relevant to the particular group and its work. The discussions should be scheduled for a minimum of one to one and an half hours, with flexibility for more time if the discussion of issues is rewarding. If the group holding the workshop has regularly scheduled meetings, ethics workshops could be held as one of them. Whenever possible, the CEO should make a personal appearance during the launch. In very large organizations this may be impossible. In this case, he or she should send a message by video, and make a personal appearance at selected workshops, especially those for executive and senior management personnel.

A suggested workshop agenda is outlined below, with some supplementary tips added:

- Introduction (by the CEO in person or by video)
- Ethics program overview
- Mission statement review
- Video (include excerpts from code of ethics and a sponsoring presentation by senior management)
- Code of ethics content review
- Decision aids and frameworks for problems to be faced (*see* Chapter 8)
- Ethics resources
- Ethics inquiry/reporting process (available for guidance, support, and whistleblowing, including details of protection)
- Group discussion of issues raised in the code, in the workplace, or

in case studies from the group's workplace, showing how the code should be used as a reference tool

- Questionnaire (to provide anonymous feedback on ethics issues in the organization and workshop completeness in covering the details of the code, performance, and training program)
- Compliance sign-off (participants should be asked to sign a statement[1] agreeing to comply with the organization's ethics policy)

Workshop support

There are a number of generic support materials available in the marketplace for workshop leaders that can be accessed by the organization or the facilitator. A partial list of these is available from the Canadian Centre for Ethics & Corporate Policy.[2]

Workshop leaders would likely benefit from a training session which would review the materials available, prior to the choice of specific materials for specific workshop groups. In workshops for leaders, the following issues might be considered:

- The contents of the letter to employees from the workshop leader inviting them to attend the workshop. The letter should request employees to reread material presented to them during the launch of the mission statement or code, such as the letter from the CEO, the mission statement, and the code of ethics. Frequently, it would be prudent to provide copies of relevant material, particularly if it is several years old. The letter could also ask employees to identify, and think about, ethical issues which exist in their workplace.
- Agenda, video, overheads and handouts
- List of typical ethical issues likely to arise for discussion
- Reference to one or two articles, or extracts from a book. This will inform employees that business ethics is a widely considered and reputable academic and practical subject, and not just a whim of their particular management.
- Questionnaires and compliance sign-off cards
- Reinforcement – newsletters for after the session
- Assignment of responsibility, measurement of effectiveness, reports and reporting lines

---

1. Research suggests that physically signing such a statement engenders greater commitment to the underlying values than verbal or electronic endorsement. Subsequent annual sign-offs can be in electronic form.
2. Canadian Centre for Ethics & Corporate Policy website, http://www.ethicscentre.ca.

Follow-up

To reinforce management responsibility for ethics, the results of the training program should be reviewed by senior management as part of the normal management process. This should include review by a committee of the organization's Board of Directors. The facilitator would report on the questionnaire results, including new ideas for improving the training program, and ethics issues that need management attention.

Employees who miss sessions, or are called away from sessions for any length of time, should be reported and scheduled for replacement sessions, since these are vital to the future of both the organization and the individual. This is very important because if people see that it is acceptable to miss all or part of a session without consequences they may think management does not care about attendance. If a person is called away for an urgent business reason, it is even more important that the message get through that ethics is at least as important as business. Supervisors who frequently call people out of training sessions should be identified and corrected in their ways.

Employees should all receive a similar training session when they are hired, and be required follow the same initial physical sign-off procedure and subsequent annual sign-off process. The corporation's human resources department should be tasked with maintaining the file of sign-offs, and for advising the ethics officers and supervisors when someone has not complied with the annual sign-off procedure.

	Checklist – Creating & Implementing an Ethical Corporate Culture	
	Development of Commitment & Understanding – Launch	
✓	Training Program/Ethics Workshop	
	• Identify ongoing responsibility for development & presentation	
	• Organizational leaders speak in person or by video and endorse values & ethics program (CEO, other officers)	
	• Workshop leader/facilitator has training or experience	
	• Coverage should include:	
	○ Introduction	

		o	Ethics program overview
		o	Mission statement review
		o	Video (include excerpts from code of ethics and presentation by senior management)
		o	Code of ethics content review
		o	Decision aids and frameworks (see Chapter 8) for problems to be faced
		o	Ethics resources
		o	Ethics inquiry/reporting process (available for guidance, support, and whistleblowing including details of protection)
		o	Group discussion of issues raised in the code, in the workplace, or in case studies from the group's workplace showing how the code should be used as a reference tool
		o	Questionnaire (to provide anonymous feedback on ethics issues, completeness of coverage of the code, performance, and the training program)
		o	Compliance sign off agreeing to comply with the organization's ethics policy
	•	Workshop support should include:	
		o	Letter to employees from the workshop leader, inviting them to attend the workshop, and to suggest they anonymously submit ethical issues for possible discussion
		o	Agenda, video, overheads and handouts
		o	List of typical ethical issues likely to arise for discussion
		o	Articles or book extracts to frame key issues
		o	Questionnaires and compliance sign off cards
		o	Reinforcement – newsletters
		o	Assignment of responsibility, measurement of effectiveness, reports, and reporting lines
	•	Follow-up should include board & senior management review	

Maintaining an Ethical Corporate Culture

Chapter 6
Reinforcement & Compliance

Effective Reinforcement of Values

Once a mission statement or code of ethics has been developed, its adoption and the values inherent in it must be continually reinforced and supported by all of the organization's systems and functions. The board of directors should ensure that responsibility for this is defined and fully supported by the CEO, and that the effectiveness of reinforcement processes are reviewed periodically. Often the CEO will appoint an ethics officer and form an ethics committee composed of members from senior management to advise on employee training and compliance programs, and on communications regarding ethics.

Developing an ethical corporate culture depends upon CEO and management leadership and commitment to establish processes throughout the organization to assist all employees in understanding the values of the organization and incorporating these values in their day-to-day activities. Several aspects of organizational activity should be involved, including management communications, development and training programs, ethics workshops, job definition and reward systems, whistleblowing systems, and the role of ethics advisors and officers.

Management Communications Concerning Ethical Conduct

It is absolutely essential that all stakeholders see that the CEO and senior management are visibly involved and committed to developing an understanding of the mission statement and code of ethics. Ongoing management communications must emphasize support for the organization's mission statement and code of ethics, or employees will not use them. Such communications will reinforce the messages provided by management when launching the mission statement and during the ethics training programs. Ongoing management communications can take place in a number of ways:

- A visible contribution by the CEO at the beginning, possibly through the use of booklets, pocket cards, or other media such as videos, that are used to introduce the organization's ethics policy, mission, or code.
- Letters by the CEO to senior management, all employees, suppliers, contractors, customers, and shareholders that should provide a link to and introduce the mission or code, emphasize its importance, and relate it to the organization's values.
- A periodic ethics reminder letter can be sent from the CEO to employees, customers, suppliers, and agents on a quarterly or semi-annual basis. The letter may include discussion of the results of past training programs, future training plans, contemplated changes to the mission statement or code of ethics, current concerns or issues that need to be considered and relevant good or bad examples from company experience or the business world in general.
- The chief ethics officer[1] should present a report to the board or an appropriate subcommittee thereof, such as ethics, governance, or audit, on the status of the company's ethics program, any instances or patterns of conduct worthy of revised guidance or action, any trends noted in environmental scans[2] that will impact the company, and any suggested revisions to the ethics program.
- The annual report and annual meeting should include reports from the CEO and directors on how the ethics program is being managed, and how effectively that management is working.
- Speeches given by the CEO should include a reference to the code and ethical issues whenever appropriate.
- Employee newsletters and online blogs should include discussion of relevant ethical issues.
- Company forms and reports should be modified to reflect the mission statement and code of ethics.
- A company website could be established to house the code, updates, news events, and awards for good performance.

---

1. A chief ethics officer is responsible for the ethics program of a company. For further information, *see* the Ethics & Compliance Officer Association website at http://www.theecoa.org.
2. The term environmental scan is used here to refer to scans for issues likely to affect all stakeholders, not just environmentalists.

- Communications from senior management on specific issues, particularly on strategic and tactical plans, should contain appropriate references stressing compliance with the organization's code of ethics or conduct. For example, it is most helpful when senior management comment on the values that underpin the company's reputation, the importance of vigilance in the maintenance of those values, and on breaches and penalties imposed.

Communications from the CEO can also be very effective in introducing an ethics training program. As well, CEOs frequently meet with senior management in formal meetings, both large and small, and informally. The most effective reinforcement of all is for the CEO to behave ethically and to constantly refer to ethical values in all messages he or she delivers on all subjects. There is no important subject to which ethics is irrelevant.

Reinforcement through Management Capability Development

Discussion and consideration of ethical issues should be integrated, as much as possible, with normal systems and processes established by management. Management could, for example, use a portion of a regular meeting to discuss policy issues and specific matters that may need resolution. Management teams would also benefit from periodically meeting in order to do the following activities:

- Review the code of ethics and criteria, tools, and processes for identifying and resolving ethical issues.
- Discuss relevant ethical issues with a view to determining whether they were handled properly, whether feedback mechanisms were effective, and whether the code needs to be revised.
- Hear from, and provide feedback to, the corporation's ethics officer on the matters noted above for reporting to the board subcommittees.

Reinforcement through an Annual Ethics Training Program

Reinforcement of the original training program is needed to ensure success. One approach that might be taken is to develop a simplified and updated refresher workshop or online session that can be held annually. To be most effective, the refresher would differ from the original workshop in the following ways:

- Improved by incorporating suggestions provided by employees who participated in the original workshop.
- Enhanced relevance through introduction and discussion of cases; real if possible that would provide insight into current or projected problems. Cases can be disguised if necessary.
- Enhanced through the discussion of ethical decision-making aids and frameworks (*see* Chapter 8) as they are to be applied in cases and to issues expected to be encountered.
- Updated for changes to policies, issues, and resources.
- Updated to include the status of ethics issues, and concerns raised in questionnaires prepared for prior programs.
- Simplified by eliminating the video, and by reducing the amount of time taken to formally present the program.

As in the original training program, it will be important to have the CEO speak, at least on video, to have senior people attend, and to report the results of the workshops and of the questionnaires submitted by participants.

Reinforcement through Integration into General Training

There is growing recognition of the importance of integrating the mission statement or code of ethics into an organization's general training program. This approach emphasizes the important role that ethics plays in an organization. A discussion of ethics can easily be integrated with current examples into training programs in the following areas:

- Orientation
- Supervisory/management skills
- Risk management
- Safety
- Environmental protection and sustainability
- Legal issues and considerations
- Financial controls
- Internal audit

Mechanisms such as these are indicative of how pervasively an organization should look for ways to reinforce the values and other governance propositions to executives and other employees.

The board of directors itself should also be a focus for reinforcement sessions as their inability to govern according to reasonable ethical standards has been responsible for many recent financial scandals such as Enron, WorldCom, Adelphia, Tyco and Parmalat; bribery scandals such as those at SNC-Lavalin (see p. 166) and Wal-Mart (see p. 168); unethical practices at Goldman Sachs (see p. 142) and J.P. Morgan, and operating disasters such as the BP oil spill.

Some directors, executives, and managers still find it difficult to appreciate why a high level of reinforcement is needed for an effective ethics program. They should keep in mind, however, that an ethics program is absolutely critical to the company's reputation and stakeholder support, and therefore its future success.

Reinforcement through Feedback

Opportunities for employee feedback on ethical issues will increase employee involvement and interest in ethics. Employee feedback will also improve an organization's ability to become aware of ethical issues so that they can appropriately address them. Feedback can be facilitated in the following ways:

- Appointment of an ethics officer, or an ombudsperson
- Establishment of:
  - A subcommittee of the board of directors for general oversight
  - An ethics inquiry hotline
  - An ethics blog where questions can be addressed or answered
  - A protected whistleblowing program designed internally or outsourced to induce the greatest level of employee trust
  - Ethics committees in all relevant units
  - Employee assistance programs in all relevant units

These facilitations must be readily available and known to employees. Any responses must be treated as confidential. It is also important for management to establish processes to appropriately handle and respond to any feedback when it is received. Failure to do so will lead to employee cynicism about the process and will thus undermine its effectiveness. Some of the key elements of effective feedback processes can be summarized as follows:

- Allocate sufficient resources to the process to permit follow-up
- Document feedback received
- Identify criteria to help establish priorities
- Establish policies concerning confidentiality

- Involve management when policies are challenged on ethical grounds
- Establish a process to provide feedback to the individual who raised the matter, and when relevant, to all employees (such as by the ethics blog noted above)

Reinforcement through Recognition

The evaluation and promotion of individuals should be based in part on their adherence to the values of the organization. Management should also recognize and reward exemplary behaviour by individual employees or groups of employees. This will reinforce compliance with the mission statement or code of ethics. Recognition by management can take many forms. Employees can be recognized publicly in newsletters or privately in a letter from senior management.

Reinforcement through Job Descriptions and Reward Systems

Where possible, the systems of the corporation should bring the need for ethical behaviour to the forefront of employees' minds. Building the requirement for ethical action into job descriptions sends an early signal to everyone hired. Similarly, the inclusion of ethical activity as a dimension of assessable behaviour for annual merit increases will keep ethical behaviour in focus on a continuing basis. For example, the job description of the purchasing manager might specifically include the responsibility to ensure purchasing employees and agents are aware of, and follow the employer's values on matters such as not taking kickbacks, staying within stated limits for gifts or favours, objectively assessing supplier value, and being concerned about supplier sustainability and employee practices.

Illustrative Case: Kickbacks for Tires

X Ltd. was a medium-sized owner-managed company that distributed and repaired heavy construction tires. Sam, the owner, was a pillar of the community and as honest as the day is long. He was determined that his company would be run in a trustworthy and ethical manner. He had a written code of conduct that he required all employees to read. It was posted on notice boards throughout the premises. At that time, this was well ahead of common practice.

Furthermore, in the code was a specific prohibition on accepting or giving personal favours relating to the business of the company. Sam was scrupulous in this respect in all his own dealings.

Sam was absolutely mortified when he was told by his auditors that they suspected that his purchasing personnel were taking kickbacks for steering company business to particular suppliers. "It's right in the code," he said, "why did this happen?"

After an investigation by the auditors confirmed that kickbacks were in fact being taken, he asked what he could have done differently.

This case illustrates the necessity for putting the code into practice. Yes, there was a code; yes, kickbacks were prohibited. However, the code went no further than the notice board. Nowhere in the purchasing manager's job description was a responsibility for ensuring his department was conducting business on an ethical basis. The annual performance appraisals of the purchasing personnel never once touched on the issue of kickbacks.

The moral of this story is to operationalize your code. Build the ethical requirements right into job descriptions, communications, and performance appraisals.

Reinforcement through Whistleblower Programs & Inquiry Services

It is very easy to undermine an ethics program by failing to provide a mechanism for inquiry or consultation. The concepts included in a code of ethics or conduct are frequently complex and unfamiliar. Employees therefore often have questions about their applicability, and need someone to consult.

Unfortunately, employees may realize that something is wrong, but are afraid to ask about it or to bring the wrongdoing to the notice of company officials. In many cultures, it is not considered appropriate to tell or to snitch on someone. Consequences of doing so can involve hostility from fellow employees and retribution from the person reported on or managers who are caught up in the process who may have known about the problem, but took no action, or who are friends of the accused. In any of these cases the fall out for the person making the inquiry or report can be quite unpleasant, involving loss of merit, promotion, and often their jobs.

This negative reaction to doing what is right, and raising issues an ethical company would want to know about, is simply not in the interest of the individuals or the company (or particularly the board of directors) involved. Waiting until the company's culture changes to support ethical inquiries is not a sound prospect. Consequently, leading corporations are setting up ethics inquiry services where inquiries are encouraged and kept confidential. When unethical acts are reported, they are quickly and fairly investigated, and the reporter's name is kept confidential unless and until the matter has to go to court. Even then, the reporting individual is asked if he or she will permit his or her name to be used. Quarterly or annual reports of inquiries and follow-ups are made to very senior officers and to a subcommittee of the board of directors without revealing the names of the reporting individuals. These practices are essential to allay the often well-founded fears of the inquirers and reporters.

The findings of the Ethics Resource Center's 2011 National Business Ethics Survey: *Workplace Ethics in Transition*[3] reinforce these comments and provide interesting support for the development of ethical corporate cultures and reporting mechanisms. The U.S. survey reports that:

- The percentage of employees who witnessed misconduct at work fell to a new low of 45 percent. That compares to 49 percent in 2009 and is well down from the record high of 55 percent in 2007.
- Those who reported the bad behavior they saw reached a record high of 65 percent, up from 63 percent two years earlier and 12 percentage points higher than the record low of 53 percent in 2005.
- Retaliation against employee whistleblowers rose sharply. More than one in five employees (22 percent) who reported misconduct say they experienced some form of retaliation in return. That compares to 12 percent who experienced retaliation in 2007 and 15 percent in 2009.
- The percentage of employees who perceived pressure to compromise standards in order to do their jobs climbed five points to 13 percent, just shy of the all-time high of 14 percent in 2000.
- The share of companies with weak ethics cultures also climbed to near record levels at 42 percent, up from 35 percent two years ago.

These ethics inquiry systems and protected whistleblower programs are often under the jurisdiction of the organization's ethics officer, ombudsperson, human resources office, internal audit, or legal departments. Care should be taken not to send signals that would turn away employees from using the service. In this regard, locating the service within an internal audit department or legal department is not as attractive as locating it within a human resources department or as a stand-alone unit. A hotline to an undisclosed or third-party destination may also be suspect depending on the perception of its efficacy, trustworthiness and credibility. Over 50 per-

3. Executive Summary, p. 12, report is downloadable from http://www.ethics.org/nbes/ .

cent of the inquiries received by existing services are seeking information on personnel policies and practices, so basing the inquiry system in a human resource related or stand-alone unit that specializes in these matters is recommended.[4] While this may give rise to a conflict of interests in regard to poor human resource activities or policies, experience has shown this to be relatively rare compared to the volume of information-seeking calls.

Creating an Ongoing Monitoring or Review Mechanism

No significant ongoing process should be initiated without establishing a periodic process for monitoring performance, and ensuring consideration of changes that could bring continuous improvement. This should start with a review of the stated objectives for the ethical corporate culture, and the performance characteristics that were expected at the beginning of the review period. In the case of an ethical corporate culture this review should be undertaken at the direction and for the review of the ethics subcommittee of the board, by the chief ethics officer and the chief internal auditor, or those who occupy similar functions. Since monitoring and review is part of the maintenance process, it will be dealt with more fully in the next Chapter.

Employee and Management Compliance

Chapter 5 recommended having employees sign ethics compliance cards during the launch of the mission statement. This process is considered important because it focusses the attention of employees on the mission statement and code of ethics or conduct and requires them to confirm that they have read it, understood it, and that they will follow it. Periodic renewals of the sign-offs of compliance cards is also recommended because it will act as a reminder of the mission statement and related code and the organization's goals. Consideration should be given to extending the sign-off notification beyond an employee's own actions, so that when signing off, he or she would be confirming that they know of no other employee or corporate action that is unethical that has not been reported.

Senior management and the board of directors, as mentioned in Chapter 3, must lead and support the development and maintenance of an ethical corporate culture. Processes designed to evaluate CEO, management, and

---

4. For further information *see for example*, Leonard J. Brooks, "Whistleblowers – learn to love them!" *Canadian Business Review* (Summer 1993): 19–21.

board performance should take into account how effectively such leadership and support has been provided with regard to the items noted below:

- The ethics program generally
- Communications processes established
- Employee training programs, including lunch and learn sessions
- Reinforcement and compliance initiatives
- Handling of code violations and other ethical lapses
- Processes designed to obtain employee feedback and to follow-up on such feedback
- Processes designed to address violations and actions taken
- Processes designed to address new concerns and issues
- Integration of ethical performance goals into job descriptions and remuneration systems

The effectiveness of the CEO, chief ethics officer and his or her supporting ethics committee should also be evaluated with regard to reporting and actions taken.

Addressing Violations of the Code of Ethics

An appropriate process should be designed to address violations of the code of ethics. This process should consider:

- Who within the organization should address violations
- How employees involved with violations should be disciplined with regard to the investigation and hearing processes, and to the level of penalty to be assessed in the event that allegations are found to be true
- How violations will be communicated to all employees and other stakeholders

The seriousness of the violation, how senior the alleged perpetrator is, and the effect on the organization and its reputation may determine the process that is followed, and whether senior management or the board of directors become involved. However, since it is advisable for employees to believe that investigation and hearing processes are fair, timely, and credible, an organization should create and announce a standard process which is administered by the chief ethics officer.

Except in cases where the violation has legal implications, or there is a legitimate desire to protect the name of the violator, the nature of the violation and penalty should be made public, and compared to the company's guidance on the matter. As indicated in Chapter 2 in the discussion of the 20/60/20 Rule, since roughly 60 percent of employees will respond ethically if presented with proper guidance, knowledge of the nature of the violation and related penalty – from warning to termination – will reinforce ethical behaviour and add substantially to the culture of integrity the organization wants to maintain. Without such disclosure, rumours will abound about how the perpetrator got off, or how the company swept the matter under the rug. Sometimes insurance companies that are attempting to induce or enhance recoveries will press for nondisclosure, but the advantages cited should be weighed against the cultural benefit provided by disclosure. Legal action may be required if a law is violated.

Recent sexual abuse cases at Penn State and within the Roman Catholic Church, that are summarized below, offer evidence where organizations did not act effectively on unethical behaviour and lost significantly in terms of reputation, and the support of their stakeholders.

Reputation Cases involving sex abuse

Penn State Sex Abuse Scandal

This case, which exploded into public view in 2011, is primarily about allegations that several senior officers in the University and its sporting operations covered up or failed to pursue evidence that an assistant coach, Jerry Sandusky, had criminally abused underage boys on university premises over an extended period of time. Details became public knowledge first as a result of testimony given to a Grand Jury in 2011, then when Sandusky was convicted on 52 counts of abuse, and subsequently in July 2012 by the publication of a report by Louis Freeh, former director of the FBI, that devastatingly implicated coaches and senior University officials in a cover up. The affair brought down the University President, the Senior Vice-president for Finance and Business and, most spectacularly, coach Joe Paterno, probably the most famous football coach in recent US history. In late 2011, some good news came out of this scandal when the university's Board of Trustees wasted no time in firing them all, notwithstanding Paterno's immense reputation and the damage it would do to the university's football team, and later in 2012, when the University accepted Freeh's findings and vowed to implement them. The probable motivation for the cover up was to protect the reputation of the university and of its football team, which contributed tens of millions of dollars annually to university coffers. Surely none of those involved was anything but horrified by the sexual abuse of minors, yet they obviously thought that the greater good was to protect the reputation of their organization. The fact that such a twisted sense of morality could exist among otherwise very smart and upright people is a warning to all organizations that alertness to the perils of covering up problems should be built in to governance practices. The end result was penalties imposed by the National Collegiate Athletic Association that will cause catastrophic harm to Penn State's athletic program and finances for many years.

Wikipedia contains an excellent detailed account of the scandal, at http://en.wikipedia.org/wiki/Penn_State_sex_abuse_scandal. The site also contains a very extensive bibliography.

Roman Catholic Church Sex Abuse Scandals[5]

For many years, and in many countries, church leaders have consistently failed to report the activities of known pedophile priests and members of religious orders to legal authorities, which in some countries is itself a crime. In many cases, they simply transferred the offenders to different parishes or to other jobs within the church. In the United States, Ireland, Belgium and Germany, bishops and archbishops have admitted to cover ups. In an organization whose very foundation rests upon the need to confess to sins and seek redemption, the occurrence of such a twisted sense of priorities is astonishing – or perhaps it is not. Senior church officials could have believed that maintaining people's faith in their church was more important than protecting a few minors from molestation. But, when the truth was revealed, the damage was severe. This was especially the case in Ireland, where the damage was catastrophic to the church, which had enjoyed an overwhelmingly powerful loyalty from the Irish people for centuries. This vanished, almost in an instant.

This story illustrates that the protection of reputation must not countenance hiding seriously unethical or illegal acts. Furthermore, once the acts are in the public domain, it is critical for leaders in the organization to visibly take strong and immediate action to recover from the damage. In this case, unlike in Penn State, this did not happen. From The Vatican downwards, many church leaders remained in a state of denial or delayed taking firm action against the offenders in their midst, including those who actively participated in the cover ups.

Wikipedia, at http://en.wikipedia.org/wiki/Catholic_sex_abuse_cases, sets out comprehensive information about these cases around the world, as well as an extensive bibliography.

---

5. The Roman Catholic is not the only church that has suffered from cases of sexual misconduct.

Reinforcement and Compliance Summary

To reinforce employee understanding of the mission statement or code of ethics, strong support from the CEO is essential for all aspects of the corporation's reinforcement and compliance program. An ongoing management communications program is needed, which should include the CEO's remarks and provide evidence of the right tone at the top. Workshops to develop management capability are recommended. Refresher workshops should be part of the training program, at least annually, and ethical issues and treatments should be integrated into general training programs. Feedback opportunities should be provided, as well as a way of effectively responding to the feedback and resolving issues. Achieving compliance with the mission or code involves recognition of strong ethics performance and documenting of the intent to comply with the code. It also is reinforced by management reviews of each manager's contribution to the ethics management program. Lastly, ethics inquiries and violations must be effectively gathered, managed, and discipline appropriately applied. Procedures for measuring, monitoring, and reporting performance will support these essential activities.

For further information on compliance programs, refer to the following websites:

- Ethics & Compliance Officer Association: http://www.theecoa.org/
- Ethics Resource Center: http://www.ethics.org/resource/next-steps-designing-outcomes-based-ethics-and-compliance-program-evaluation

	Checklist – Maintaining an Ethical Corporate Culture
	Reinforcement & Compliance
✓	Reinforcement
	Effective Reinforcement of Values
	• Strong CEO commitment and visible support
	• Identify responsibility
	• Commitment of management leaders
	Management Communications Concerning Ethical Conduct
	• A visible contribution by the CEO at the beginning
	• Letters by the CEO to senior management, all employees, suppliers, contractors, customers and shareholders should link to and introduce the organization's code of ethics or conduct, stress its importance, and relate it to the organization's values
	• A periodic ethics reminder letter can be sent from the CEO to employees, customers, suppliers & agents on a quarterly or semi-annual basis
	• The chief ethics officer reports to the board, or to the ethics, governance, or audit subcommittees of the board, on the status of the company's ethics program, any instances or patterns of conduct worthy of revised guidance or action, any trends noted in environmental scans that will impact the company, and any suggested revisions to the ethics program
	• The annual report and annual meeting should include reports from the CEO & directors on how the ethics program is being managed and how effectively that management is working
	• Speeches given by the CEO should include a reference to the code and ethical issues, whenever appropriate
	• Employee newsletters and online blogs should include discussion of relevant ethical issues
	• Company forms and reports should be modified to reflect the mission statement or code of ethics
	• A company website could be established to house the code, updates, news events, and awards for good performance
	• Communications from senior management on specific issues, particularly on strategic and tactical plans, should contain references stressing compliance with the organization's code of ethics or conduct, as well as breaches and remedial actions imposed
	Reinforcement through Management Capability Development
	• Periodically review the code of ethics & criteria, tools, and processes that may be discussed for identifying and resolving ethical issues
	• Discuss relevant ethical issues with a view to determining whether they were handled properly, whether feedback mechanisms were effective, and whether the code needs to be revised
	• Hear from, and provide feedback to, the corporation's ethics officer on the matters noted above for reporting to the board subcommittees
	Reinforcement through an Annual Ethics Training Program
	• Enhanced and updated from past years, covering current problems

	Reinforcement through Integration into General Training	
	• Directors' and senior officer sessions	
	Reinforcement through Feedback	
	• Appointment of an ethics officer, or an ombudsperson	
	• Establishment of:	
	○ Subcommittee of the board of directors for general oversight	
	○ An ethics inquiry hotline	
	○ An ethics blog where questions can be addressed or answered	
	○ A protected whistleblowing program designed internally, or outsourced, to induce the greatest level of employee trust	
	○ Ethics committees in all relevant units	
	○ Subcommittee of the board of directors for general oversight	
	○ Employee assistance programs in all relevant units	
	○ A protected whistle-blowing program designed internally, or out-sourced, to induce the greatest level of employee trust	
	Effective Feedback Processes	
	• Sufficient resources to permit follow-up	
	• Documentation of feedback received	
	• Criteria to help establish priorities	
	• Policies concerning confidentiality	
	• Management involvement when policies are challenged on ethical grounds	
	• Feedback to the individual who raised the matter, and when relevant, to all employees	
	Reinforcement through Recognition	
	Reinforcement through Job Descriptions and Reward Systems	
	Reinforcement through Whistleblower Programs & Inquiry Services	
	• Whistleblower anonymity	
	• Whistleblower protection	
	• Rapid & fair investigation	
	• Confidentiality of findings	
	• Quarterly or annual reports of inquiries and follow-up made to very senior officers and to a subcommittee of the board of directors	
	Ongoing Monitoring or Review Mechanism	
	• Responsibility assigned	
	• Report to board subcommittee	
✓	Compliance	
	Employee and Management Compliance	
	• Sign off of compliance cards when hired	
	• Annual sign off	
	Evaluation of effectiveness of the Chief Ethics Officer and his or her supporting ethics committee with regard to reporting and actions taken with regard to the items noted below:	
	• The ethics program generally	

	•	Communications processes established
	•	Employee training programs, including lunch and learn sessions
	•	Reinforcement and compliance initiatives
	•	Handling of code violations and other ethical lapses
	•	Processes designed to obtain employee feedback and to follow-up on such feedback
	•	Processes designed to address violations and actions taken
	•	Processes designed to address new concerns and issues
	•	Integration of ethical performance goals into job descriptions and remuneration systems.
Addressing Violations of the Code of Ethics		
	•	Identification of responsibility for addressing violations
	•	Fairness & speed of hearing process
	•	Adequacy of penalties assessed
	•	Communication about violations to all employees and other stakeholders

Maintaining an Ethical Corporate Culture

Chapter 7
Monitoring & Reporting – Ethical, CSR, & Sustainability Performance – Ethics Risk Management

Monitoring and reporting corporate performance inevitably raises concerns about the nature, quality, and comprehensiveness of the performance and its disclosure, and whether the risks inherent in the corporation's actions have been identified, assessed and managed effectively. The first part of this chapter will examine the monitoring and reporting of ethical, CSR and sustainability activities, and the second part will comment on the monitoring and management of the ethics risks involved in company activities.

Part 1:
Monitoring & Reporting Ethical, CSR, & Sustainability Performance

Monitoring ethical performance effectively requires an evidence-based process that evaluates whether the organization's ethical performance objectives are being met in practice. In addition, an organization should consider how its corporate social responsibility (CSR) should be reported, whether the report will be designed to external general standards or company-defined standards, whether it should be verified or audited, and in what manner.

From a stakeholder perspective, ethical behaviour has to do with how the rights and interests of stakeholders are respected, and CSR reporting provides evidence of how this respect is demonstrated. Each corporation should decide which elements of CSR are to be reported internally, and which are to be reported to the public. The precise nature and degree of disclosure will determine the image of corporate citizenship that the corporation will take on.

Fortunately, a growing number of excellent guidelines, reports and protocols have appeared that should be consulted for assistance. Several are referred to below.

Thinking about CSR Scope and Management

Decisions about CSR should reflect a balance between a corporation's strategic objectives and the interests of its stakeholders, since both must be satisfied for long-run success. When thinking about the scope and depth of integration of stakeholder interests into a corporation's strategy, activities, monitoring and reporting, decision makers would be well advised to consult a recently published, comprehensive International Standard, *ISO 26000: Guidance on social responsibility*,[1] released on November 1, 2010, which has gained recognition as an important touchstone.

ISO 26000 covers the following:[2]

- Terms and definitions
- Understanding social responsibility
- Principles of social responsibility, including that an organization should:
    ○ Be accountable for its impacts on society, the economy and the environment.
    ○ Be transparent in its decisions and in activities that impact on society and the environment.
    ○ Behave ethically.
    ○ Respect, consider and respond to the interests of stakeholders.
    ○ Accept that respect for the rule of law is mandatory.
    ○ Respect international norms of behaviour, while adhering to the principle of respect for the rule of law.
    ○ Respect human rights and recognize both their importance and their universality.
- Recognizing social responsibility and engaging stakeholders
- Guidance on social responsibility core subjects, covering the following:
    ○ Organizational governance.

---

1. *ISO 26000* is available on the website of the International Standards Organization, http://www. iso.org.
2. Adapted from Table 1, *ISO 26000 Outline*, p. vii, and Clause 4.2–4.8.

- o Human rights.
- o Labour practices.
- o The environment.
- o Fair operating practices.
- o Consumer issues.
- o Community involvement and development.
- Guidance on integrating social responsibility throughout an organization
- Examples of voluntary initiatives and tools for social responsibility
- Bibliography

Schematically, *ISO 26000* is organized into the Clauses shown in ISO Figure 1,[3] reproduced below as Figure 7.1.

Figure 7.1
Schematic Overview of ISO 26000: Guidance on social responsibility

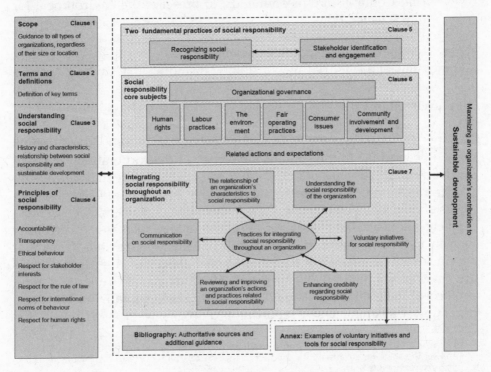

---

3.   Ibid, p. ix, reproduced with permission from the Standards Council of Canada.

It is noteworthy that the Tables included in *ISO 26000's Annex A* of voluntary initiatives and tools represent an outstanding overview of significant studies and/or pronouncements by most intergovernmental, multi-stakeholder, single stakeholder, and even sectoral organizations. Plans are underway already to revise *ISO 26000*, so constant scrutiny of the ISO website would be well-advised.

While *ISO 26000* provides useful guidance for the possible scope of CSR, many difficult strategy or policy choices have to be made by corporate boards. For example, if the corporation, as *ISO 26000* recommends, plans to develop a policy on environmental protection or sustainability, the board must decide whether to:

- Abide by the law in their home country or the foreign jurisdiction of operations, or the highest legal standard available
- Protect the environment to a level beyond simple compliance with the law and, if so, to what level
- Adopt a sustainability program that intends, and the UN's Brundtland Commission[4] recommends, to preserve the environment for future generations

The ensuing program design and reporting regime will clearly depend on those important choices.

Measurement of CSR

The specific measurements chosen for CSR should highlight key factors that will contribute to the strategic objectives of the corporation. This will involve defining strategic objectives and what they require in terms of support from domestic and foreign stakeholders. In addition, CSR measurements should be chosen to facilitate reports for customers, such as government purchasers, that may require CSR details, such as the percent of women and minorities on staff, or details of loans to minorities, for bids or assurance of CSR processes. Finally, as noted above, several organizations are developing guidance on aspects of standardized CSR reports or audit protocols,[5] and their efforts should be reviewed before finalizing a corporation's CSR measurement and reporting protocol.

4. The 1987 report, "Our Common Future," reviewed the prospect for environmental degradation and set the stage for sustainability conduct in the future. The report can be downloaded from http://www.un.org/esa/dsd/resources/res_publcorepubli.shtml.
5. *See for example*: the discussion of GRI, AA1000, and SA8000 that follows; the work of the Sustainability Standards Board at http://www.sasb.org/; or the work of the European Federation of Financial Analysts at http://effas.net/.

Measurements or indicators of CSR can take many forms. There are a number of organizations[6] that rate the CSR of many companies, and their list of criteria can be used as a guide in establishing an appropriate list of measures. For example, indicators of historical fact, based on voluntary surveys sent to senior corporate officers, are used by EthicScan Canada, first in their Corporate Ethics Monitor[7] and later in company profiles, including:

- Statements of guidance, their currency, efficacy, and reinforcement
- Employment record, including total staff, and number of women and minority group members in board or management positions
- Amounts of charitable donations in relation to other companies in the sector, and allowing comparison to profits as a means of assessing relative generosity
- Existence and nature of community relations programs
- Labour relations and health and safety
- Environmental management indicators
- Environmental performance indicators
- Ethical sourcing and trading policies

There are other measures that may be useful in revealing attitudes of managers and employees toward ethical issues. These may be useful in capturing information about actions that are about to happen, or about changes in attitude due to certain signals sent voluntarily or involuntarily by management, or read into circumstances by employees. Examples of such anticipatory measures are:

- Employee attitude surveys such as those undertaken by Walker Information[8]
- Customer or other stakeholder surveys
- Evaluation by paid shoppers or through solicited customer comments
- Other measures concentrate on the operational merit of the organization's support mechanisms for ethical behaviour. These could include quality assessments of:
  - Codes of conduct

---

6. *See for example*: in the US – KLD Research & Analytics, Inc., http://www.kld.com, in Canada – EthicScan Canada, http://www.ethicscan.ca, and Sustainalytics, http://www.sustainalytics.com/, and in the UK – Ethics Investment Research Service (EIRIS) at Email: ethics@eiris.win.uk.net.
7. The *Corporate Ethics Monitor* is published by EthicScan Canada: http://www.ethicscan.ca.
8. Walker Information's website is http://www.walkerinfo.com.

- Training programs
- Reinforcement mechanisms, including:
  - Newsletters, correspondence
  - Pay and reward systems
  - Promotions
  - Protection for whistleblowers
  - Follow-up on reported problems
  - Speed and fairness of investigations, hearings, and of penalties assigned

Measures are also available to indicate depth of involvement:

- The level of understanding that employees have of ethical issues[9]
- The principal motivator for an employee's ethical behaviour[10]
- Whether an employee is disposed to raise ethical concerns due to their perception of their ability to affect the outcome of such debates (locus of control tests)[11]
- The degree of inclusion of ethical concerns in, "the development of plans, setting of goals, search of opportunities, allocation of resources, gathering and communication of information, measurement of performance, and promotion and advancement of personnel"[12]

Table 1: Techniques for the Measurement of Ethical Processes & Performance, is offered at the end of this chapter to indicate measures that can be related to the attribute or process involved in maintaining an ethical corporate culture.

---

9. *See for instance*: the Defining Issues Test (DIT) as discussed in James R. Rest. *Development in Judging Moral Issues* (Minneapolis: University of Minnesota Press, 1979).
10. According to the subject's stage of moral reasoning per the schema developed by L. Kohlberg. *Essays in Moral Development, Volumes I and II: The Psychology of Moral Development* (San Francisco: Harper & Row, 1981 and 1984.)
11. "Locus of control is a self-regulatory aspect of character that captures individuals' tendency to feel that control of their lives rests in their own hands (internal locus of control) or in the hands of others (external locus of control). Those who are "internals" take responsibility for their actions, and are therefore more likely to act upon their ethical judgment. "Externals" are less likely to take responsibility for their actions and, therefore, are more susceptible to the pressures of the situation, feeling somewhat powerless." from Joanne Jones, Dawn W. Massey and Linda Thorne, "Auditors' Ethical Reasoning: Insights From Past Research And Implications For The Future," *Journal of Accounting Literature* (2003).
12. Lynn Sharp Paine, "Managing for Organizational Integrity," *Harvard Business Review* (March–April 1994): 112.

Monitoring CSR

The corporation that embarks on a CSR program needs to consider how it will measure, monitor, and report on performance, whether the report will be internal only or available to the public, and who will be charged with the responsibility for reviewing the report and pursuing program revisions on a continuous improvement basis. Internal reports can take on any form, but should be focussed on the program's performance objectives.

After the CSR measurements have been identified, the data gathered, and the report fashioned, the next step is monitoring how the corporation is doing. As with most measurement schemes, comparison can be helpful against:

- Strategic objective key success factors
- Similar organizations
- Best-practice alternatives for benchmarking
- Published standards such as those described above
- Industry statistics and averages
- Management targets
- Results obtained in earlier periods

Ethical performance could also be selectively monitored by reference to external studies. These may be found in books like *The 50 Best Ethical Stocks for Canadians*,[13] or in industry studies published in the *Corporate Ethics Monitor*[14] or by Sustainalytics. Alternatively, several annual studies are published such as the "100 Best Corporate Citizens" in *The Corporate Responsibility Magazine*.[15] This publication also features its Annual Business Ethics Awards that identifies companies judged to be outstanding performers.[16] For studies and rewards for Canadian companies, refer to the Corporate Knights website[17] and magazine, or the Chartered Accountants of Canada (CICA) and their Corporate Reporting Awards.[18] Even general business publications like *The Economist* periodically offers useful reports such as,

13. Deb Abbey and Michael C. Jantzi. *2001 Edition* (Toronto: McMillan Canada, 2000).
14. Industry studies published in *Corporate Ethics Monitor*, http://www.ethicscan.ca/education.html.
15. *The Corporate Responsibility Magazine*, http://thecro.com/.
16. Another awards program providing similar sources of best practice is organized by *Corporate Knights Magazine*. The Best 50 Corporate Citizens in Canada Annual Survey can be found at http://www.corporateknights.ca/reports/.
17. Corporate Knights website, http://www.corporateknights.com/reports/.
18. Chartered Accountants of Canada (CICA) and their Corporate Reporting Awards, http://www.cica.ca/about-cica/corporate-reporting-awards/index.aspx.

"Just Good Business,"[19] as well as sometimes skeptical opinions on CSR such as those in their 2005 special report.[20] Organizations also exist, such as the Social Investment Organization (SIO),[21] that provide CSR-derived information. It is possible to obtain a specific report on the CSR performance of a company from research organizations like Sustainalytics[22] or EthicScan Canada that provide them to the corporate and investment community. Hiring a consultant, such as a member of the Ethics Practitioners' Association of Canada (EPAC),[23] who specializes in ethical performance measurement, may be beneficial, especially if the consultant has experience with ethical processes in other organizations, that that can be used on a confidential basis for benchmarking purposes.

Reports will be most useful when reviewed and analyzed on a continuing basis, by senior management and the responsible board committee, with the objective of improving performance. The chief ethics officer and other individuals facilitating the review and analysis should be familiar with the ethical performance process, and should be committed to its improvement as well as to the improvement of performance itself. They should be formally charged with, and known throughout the organization to have, the responsibility for improving the process and for reporting to senior levels of management and/or a subset of the board of directors. These individuals may be part of, or report to, an ethics advisory committee with ongoing responsibility and authority to revise the company's ethics program, and/or to a subcommittee of the board of directors. An interesting example of this is reported in the article,[24] reproduced as a reading for this chapter, by Prakash Sethi, who was the Chair of the Mattel Independent Monitoring Council for Global Manufacturing Principles.

Chief ethics officers can remain up-to-date on measurement and review techniques through organizations such as the Ethics & Compliance Officers Association, http://www.theecoa.org/, or the EthicsCentre, http://www. ethicscentre.ca.

Public Reporting of CSR

Several organizations have created and published guidelines relating to as-

19. "Special Report: Corporate Social Responsibility: Just good business," *The Economist*, January 17, 2008, http://www.economist.com/node/10491077 (accessed June 3, 2012).
20. "Special report: Corporate social responsibility," *The Economist*, January 22, 2005.
21. Social Investment Organization (SIO), http://www.socialinvestment.ca/.
22. Sustainalytics company website, http://www.sustainalytics.com/.
23. Ethics Practitioners' Association of Canada (EPAC), http://www.epac-apec.ca/.
24. S. P. Sethi. "Codes of Conduct for Global Business: Prospects and Challenges of Implementation," *Principles of Stakeholder Management* (Toronto: The Clarkson Centre for Business Ethics, 1999): 9–20.

pects of CSR and sustainability reports, as well as to their audit. They are currently testing and refining their creations, and will be modifying them further. Consequently, it would be wise to maintain a watching brief on the following:

- Global Reporting Initiative (GRI) involves a comprehensive CSR/ sustainability reporting framework (G3), covering economic, environmental and social performance, that has been developed by a global group including noted stakeholder environmentalists, accountants and others, http://www.globalreporting.org. On June 1, 2012, the GRI website showed that its Sustainability Disclosure Database held a total of 10,034 sustainability reports, 9,346 GRI reports, and 3,889 organization profiles. Work has begun on the next version of the GRI guidelines (G4), which is expected to be circulated for comment in 2012.
- AccountAbility, a UK group, has developed the (AA1000) sustainability reporting principles that provide guidance on how to, "establish systematic accountability processes and how to assure how the underlying systems, processes and competencies live up to the AA1000 Assurance Standard," http://www.accountability.org.uk.
- Social Accountability International (SAI)[25] has developed, and provides training on, SA8000,® a voluntary, auditable standard for workplace conditions and human rights, based on, but transcending, International Labor Organization (ILO) and United Nations (UN) conventions and national laws. Formerly a department in SAI, the now-independent Social Accountability Accreditation Services (SAAS)[26] provides accreditation for organizations that act as independent workplace auditors, and that certify companies as SA8000®-compliant.

The G3 and AA1000 are useful frameworks for their respective purposes, and summaries of them are provided at the end of this chapter, in Table 2, Global Reporting Initiative's Sustainability Framework (G3) Guidelines, and Table 3, a summary of Accountability's AA1000 Assurance Standard.

Public reports are becoming more common. Reporting ethical performance can

- Heighten awareness of ethical issues within an organization

---

25. Social Accountability International (SAI), http://www.sa-intl.org/.
26. Social Accountability Accreditation Services (SAAS), http://www.saasaccreditation.org/.

- Provide encouragement for employees to adhere to ethical objectives
- Inform external stakeholders
- Enhance the image of a company

Internal reporting of ethical performance can take several forms. Newsletters can provide full or partial reports, scorecards, as well as recognition of exemplary behaviour by employees. Other internal reporting systems could include charts or progress reports on bulletin boards, partial or full reports as stand-alone documents, and verbal or video reports by senior management. Comparison of performance to benchmarks is becoming more common, with benchmarking services being offered by consultants or organizations such as GRI. Written reports can be prepared by internal staff, and can be certified by external agents like auditors, professors, or editors of ethics publications. Alternatively, reports can be prepared entirely by individuals independent of the corporation. Several organizations, including those certified through the SAAS[27] for SA8000®-compliance certification and EthicScan Canada in Toronto, train auditors to review social responsibility and ethics programs. Large public accounting firms offer related services including Ethics and Integrity (KPMG), Sustainability Assurance (PricewaterhouseCoopers), Climate Change and Sustainability (Ernst & Young) and Sustainability and Climate Change (Deloitte & Touche). Details are available on each organization's website.

Large corporations are releasing ethical performance reports to the public with greater frequency. Such reports may be a few paragraphs in the annual report and may, or may not, be specifically identified as ethical performance or corporate social responsibility or, more recently, as sustainability reports. For example, when Apple Inc., along with other computer and cell-phone manufacturers, was questioned about whether raw materials in its components were "conflict-free,"[28] submitted itself to an independent audit by the Fair Labor Association (FLA)[29] – the first technology company to do so. The audit resulted in the *Apple Supplier Responsibility: 2012 Progress Report*.[30] Another example of excellent CSR/accountability reporting is

---

27. Social Accountability Accreditation Services (SAAS), Accredited Certification Bodies, http://www.saasaccreditation.org/accredcertbodies.htm.
28. "Conflict minerals" are refined to become gold, tungsten and tantalum, but are mined under militia control in the Democratic Republic of Congo and neighbouring countries. *See for example*: Kristof, Nicholas D., "Death by gadget," *New York Times*, June 26, 2010, http://www.nytimes.com/2010/06/27/opinion/27kristof.html?_r=1 (accessed June 15, 2012).
29. Fair Labor Association (FLA), http://www.fairlabor.org/
30. *Apple Supplier Responsibility: 2012 Progress Report*, http://images.apple.com/supplierresponsibility/pdf/Apple_SR_2012_Progress_Report.pdf

that of PotashCorp (see below). Websites are available[31] that provide CSR disclosure examples, including those for specific CSR topics, which can be particularly useful for companies wishing to start down this road, or to improve their reporting if they have already started. "Appendix A: CSR and Sustainability Reports, Indexes, and Rankings," provides ready access to lists of companies, including:

- Over 30 organizations with recent CSR reports on the Global Reporting Initiative (GRI) website, http://www.globalreporting.org
- 10 companies accounting for 60 percent of the assets in two mutual funds that replicate the 60-company Jantzi Social Index®
- The top 15 North American and top 10 Global companies based on overall Environmental, Social, and Governance (ESG) rating by the FTSE
- 30 companies with highly regarded CSR reports and related website addresses

Reports from the following companies make very useful reading and can be accessed as indicated:

- PotashCorp – 2011 Online Annual Report, http://www.potashcorp. com/annual_reports/2011/gri/overview/
- Suncor – 2011 Report on Sustainability, http://sustainability.suncor. com/2011/en/responsible/1879.aspx
- Telus – 2011Corporate Social Responsibility Report, http://csr.telus. com/en/

Environmental performance reports, it should be noted, are mandatory disclosure in some parts of Europe.

Senior management may not support reporting, especially to external parties, if the results to be reported are unfavourable or if the possibility of legal action is significant. This is, however, an evolving area. Stakeholders are becoming increasingly interested in ethical performance, and leading companies are responding. Organizations are recognizing that it can be to their benefit to report even when the results are unfavourable. Even if unfavourable results are not initially reported (which may be considered unethical), the motivation of improvement remains as a reason for corrective action to be taken, because favourable results can then be reported in the future.

---

31. *See for example*: CSRwire website, http://www.csrwire.com/members

Audit or Verification of CSR Reports

One of the recent developments noted above, although there have been some examples of earlier attempts to audit or verify CSR claims, is the advent of so-called audits of CSR reports, particularly in Europe. European initiatives in environmental protection, and through the International Standards Association (ISO), have acted as a stimulus on corporate behaviour, requiring public disclosure of environmental performance. As a result, many individuals, and some large public accounting and other firms, have become involved in attesting to the reports issued. Reports by Bombardier, http://csr.bombardier.com/pdf/report/CSR2011_Report_en.pdf, and Ben & Jerry's, http://www.benjerry.com/company/sear/2010/sear10_16.0.cfm, for example, have been audited in whole or in part. Independent audits of labour practices in undeveloped and developing countries have become rather common for retailers, and their manufacturers, whose products come significantly from such sources, for example, Nike, Adidas and Umbro. Care should be taken when relying on certifications because auditing standards have not yet become generally accepted for this kind of reporting and may provide comment on adherence to reporting principles (i.e. from AA1000) rather on the specific quality of the disclosure. Increasingly, however, national and international accounting bodies such as IFAC,[32] and other organizations such as CEPAA and AccountAbility, are focussing on the need for appropriate auditing standards, including standards for the content of audit reports and certifications. As well, the next phase of ISO guidance may well push currently registered firms beyond documentation of systems to the reporting and audit levels.

It is possible for a corporation to have company personnel audit CSR reports. Internal audit staff may be used, as may managers from other divisions of a company. This managerial audit approach was used by Dow Corning, and was lionized in Harvard Business School cases, prior to the unfortunate breast implant scandal. It should be pointed out that the Chairman of the Conduct Committee of Dow Corning remained convinced of the worth of the company's ethics audit program, but acknowledged that audit improvements were warranted.[33]

---

32. International Federation of Accountants (IFAC), *Investor Demand for Environmental, Social, and Governance Disclosures: Implications for Professional Accountants in Business,* February 6, 2012, http://www.ifac.org/publications-resources/investor-demand-environmental-social-and-governance-disclosures (accessed June 3, 2012).
33. *See for example*: the quotation of the Chairman of the Conduct Committee of Dow Corning in the "Dow Corning Silicone Breast Implants Case," in L.J. Brooks & P. Dunn. *Business & Professional Ethics for Directors, Executives & Accountants,* 6e, (Mason, Ohio: South-Western, Cengage Learning, 2007): 340–342.

Questions provided in Table 4 at the end of the chapter can be used to guide auditors of an ethics program in which there is a written code.

Part 2:
Commentary on Monitoring and Managing Ethics Risks

Ethics Risk Management

Corporations should incorporate a review for ethics risks into their normal risk management program, as has been suggested earlier in this book, with many references to risk management and how a culture of integrity can prevent, control, or help mitigate serious problems an organization would otherwise face. However, although risk management has become commonly practiced, traditional Enterprise Risk Management (ERM), *does not focus on ethics risks, which are risks that stem from the failure to apply ethical values.* ERM needs to be enhanced to search specifically for ethics risks and the causes of those risks. The following discussion provides insights into a set of ethics risks, and the Enhanced Ethics Risk Management (ETHRM) processes needed to discover them.

Traditional Enterprise Risk Management does not Focus on Ethics Risks

The need to control risks to the achievement of their business objectives has been a priority for many farsighted companies for decades. In 2002, the *Sarbanes-Oxley Act* codified the expectation that corporations under its jurisdiction were required to maintain systems of internal control to facilitate risk management, and required, "managements to certify and auditors to attest to their effectiveness."[34] In 2004, the Committee of Sponsoring Organizations of the Treadway Commission (COSO) published *Enterprise Risk Management – Integrated Framework*, and it has become a *de facto* world standard, since many large companies have chosen to base their ERM programs on it. It has become known for its approach, that examines events and possible developments on the dimensions of the COSO framework pictured below, and discussed in the COSO documents.

Unfortunately traditional ERM is incomplete since:

---

34. *Enterprise Risk Management – Integrated Framework: Executive Summary*, COSO, 2004, Foreword, v.

Figure 7.2
COSO ERM Framework

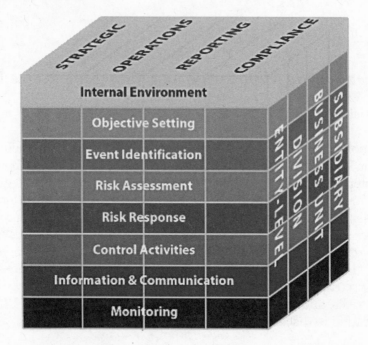

- It does not specifically examine for *ethics– or values–related risks* including:
  ○ Cultural support risks – that exist when the organization's culture fails to provide sufficient support and guidance to ensure a culture of integrity
  ○ Mindset risks – that exist when decision makers, employees, and agents are:
    - improperly motivated
    - use ethically unsound rationales for their decisions
  ○ Systemic ethics risks – that exist over and above specific outcome-oriented risks
- It is somewhat misdirected at identifying, assessing and remedying specific risk outcomes associated with events, rather than examining for ethics-related causality
- It is often undertaken as a perfunctory compliance exercise

In summary, while the traditional ERM approach can uncover some ethics-related risks, it does not examine thoroughly for all ethics risks, and the underlying ethics-related causes of other risks. Both shortcomings render prevention efforts ineffective, and unnecessarily consign companies to have to remedy costly problems.

Enhanced Ethics Risk Management (ETHRM)

Traditional ERM can be enhanced to address these shortcomings. The enhanced version will be referred to as Ethics Risk Management (ETHRM), and it will involve searching specifically for those situations in which the ethics or values being used are not likely to meet the expectations of the organization's stakeholders. The concern, which is articulated in Chapter 2, is that if the actions of the organization, its employees or its agents fall short of stakeholder expectations, then loss of reputation and stakeholder support is likely to follow, preventing the organization's full or efficient achievement of its strategic objectives. In summary, *ETHRM will search for, and assess, ethical or value shortfalls that could lead to ethics risks in general, and those specific ethics risks noted below.*

Figure 7.3
Enhanced Ethics Risk Management (ETHRM) Risk Coverage

Ethics Risks exist when the ethical expectations of stakeholders are not met:
- Resulting in loss of reputation and stakeholder support.
- Preventing full and/or efficient achievement of strategic objectives.

Specific Ethics Risks

- *Organizational culture risks* exist when the organization's culture fails to provide sufficient support and guidance to ensure a culture of integrity.
- *Mindset risks* exist when decision makers, employees, and agents are:
  - improperly motivated, or
  - use ethically unsound rationales for their decisions.
- *Systemic risks* exist over and above specific outcome-oriented risks.

Organizational Culture Risks

One of the most common types of ethics risks occur when *an organization's culture fails to provide sufficient support and guidance to ensure a culture of integrity*. In Chapter 2, the argument is made that an organization would be well-advised to develop a culture of integrity to provide guidance for employees and agents in their application of ethical policies. However, sometimes organizational cultures do not prove to be effective, and ethical problems arise. For example, risk that ethical malfeasance will take place will increase if:

- There is an ethics code, but no commitment to it
- There is no one responsible for the culture
- Organizational values encourage profit at any cost
- Reward systems encourage maximization of short-term profit (or some other measure such as revenue or new clients) by any means, regardless of the consequences

These are cultural red flags, which are indicators of cultural risks. They, and others like them, can be identified, and then assessed, if there is a review of the following important aspects of a culture of integrity:

- Values guidance: code, tone at the top, reinforcement
- Structural support: code, Chief Ethics Officer, ethics programs (training, monitoring, rewarding or punishing)
- Procedural observance:
  ○ Ethical decision making on daily matters, major decisions, and crises
  ○ Ethics inquiry service
  ○ Strong internal controls to protect against wrong-doers
- Failsafe mechanisms:
  ○ Whistleblower encouragement and protection programs reporting to the Board
  ○ Periodic ethics audit as discussed in Chapters 3 and 8
  ○ Periodic review of the organization's core values and their application – see Chapter 3

Mindset Risks

A second critically important area where failure to use ethical values can lead to serious ethics risks, but which traditional ERM does not search thor-

Figure 7.4
Fraud Triangle

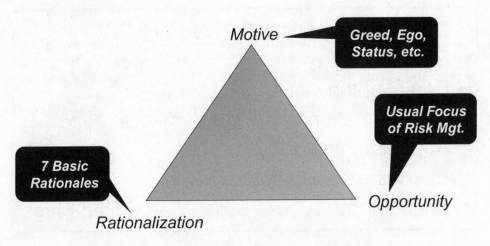

D.L. Crumbley et al, 2005, p. 3-131 – comments in white added

oughly, is *the set of risks caused when the mindsets of decision makers, employees, and/or agents are improperly motivated, or their decisions and actions are anchored in unethical rationales.*

Most investigative and forensic accountants subscribe to the logic that a fraudster:

- Has to have the opportunity to act improperly
- Has to be motived by an unbalanced self-interest based on greed, ego or status, and/or the need to pay for drugs or offset losses
- Has to use a faulty or unethical rationale for his/her decision

These dimensions have been organized into the *Fraud Triangle*, which is pictured above.

It has been known for a long time that decisions made on behalf of an organization can be affected by the self-interest or bias (greed, ego needs, status, discrimination) of the decision makers. These influences represent conflicts of interest that may produce decisions that are not in keeping with their organisation's long-term objectives, and may bias or undermine an organization's ethical treatment of its stakeholders.

In addition, a list of seven common unethical rationales (see below), has

Figure 7.5
Seven Common Rationalizations of Immoral Decisions

- Denial of responsibility
- Denial of injury
- Denial of the victim
- Condemnation of the condemners
- Appeal to higher loyalties
- Everyone else is doing it
- Entitlement

Red Flags

"Business Ethics and Moral Motivation: A Criminological Perspective"
Journal of Business Ethics, (2008), 83:595-614

been published by Joseph Heath, that provides a useful set of highly risky rationales to search for among decision makers, employees, and/or agents.

Some of these rationalizations are frequently encountered. How often have we heard that someone realized something was going wrong, but felt that it wasn't their responsibility to speak up or intervene? How often have we heard the remark that, although an action was questionable, the action was against a company that had a lot of money, and really wasn't injured significantly? How often have we heard that an action was ethically reasonable because there really wasn't a victim, because it was against the government or some other institution? Similarly, many people who act improperly often believe their action to be justified because the people who were arguing the action to be unethical or illegal had committed questionable acts themselves, and therefore lacked a moral right to criticise. Other wrongdoers justify their actions because they think they are doing good for others that outweighs the harm caused – such as justifying misleading investors in order to save a company from bankruptcy, so employees can continue to have jobs. Frequently, we hear the comments that cheating on your income tax or expense account is justified, because everyone is doing it; or that taking company resources is OK because you are entitled to them, since they don't pay you what you are worth, or that you built the company so it is yours anyway. Most of these rationales are kind to the interests of the decision maker and harmful to other stakeholders, and therefore very possibly unethical.

Mindset risks can be found by a review for abnormal instances of greed, ego satisfaction, status seeking, and/or personal indulgences, or for the use of any of the seven justifications for taking an immoral decision.[35] Employees and managers can be trained in ethical decision making, and made aware that they should be on the lookout for abnormal instances that bear reporting. Reports can be gathered annually by questionnaire or interview, from managers and heads of units, to ensure that they remain aware and vigilant on mindset issues. In addition, analysis of past problems, whistleblower reports, and brainstorming sessions can provide insights into problem procedures and trigger alteration of policies and training, or the remediation of problem individuals. Perhaps in time, psychological tests will be available to identify employee's propensities for improper motivators or rationalizations.

Systemic Ethics Risks

A systemic ethics risk is one that often originates outside an organization, and affects an entire system of activity, including more than one organization. For example, in the case of the subprime lending crisis, the undermining of the values underpinning the U.S. housing market led to the undermining of the financial markets around the world and the best work of all those involved in them. There was a systemic risk that undermined the housing finance system, and it went on to present a systemic risk to financial markets and their participants.

Normally, a traditional risk management system focusses on events or outcomes that can impede an organization's progress toward its strategic goals. While this type of assessment often does look at significant external influences to determine if there are currency exchange risks, or political risks, or new regulation risks for example, *it does not look for or assess the risk potential of the values or ethical principles underlying transactions or the raison d'être of an organization or a service being offered.* For example, the risk management practices in place before the subprime lending fiasco did not, in most instances, contemplate the unethical ramifications of offering unsustainable mortgages to uninformed people, buying unwarranted investment ratings on securitized mortgages to mislead investors, selling essentially uncollectible securitized mortgages to unsuspecting investors, undermining the

---

35. See further discussion in Chapter 9.

market price of previously sold securities against the interest of clients, and so on. Instead, the risk management practices in place were either ignored, overlooked, short-circuited, or assessed as normal business risks, but not as related to unethical values in their organization, or unethical values associated with a major dimension of the worldwide financial markets. In this case, when the unethical asset valuations and practices used proved to be unsustainable, the systemic ethics risk to the world's financial markets became evident, and a crash ensued. Only a few companies avoided the crash. Some did so because they understood that there were ethical weaknesses or risks to be avoided, as did the TD Bank, or they understood the precarious nature of the market caused by ethics risks. Further comment is provided in Chapter 10 on the Subprime Lending Crisis.

Ethics Values Review or Audit

Ethics risks in general, and systemic ethics risks, can best be identified by an ethics-values review, or audit of the values and practices underlying an organization's activities, and of the activities on which it relies. This review can be a demanding task.

After the values underpinning the company's activities are identified, a very reflective approach is required to project how these values are going to affect stakeholders in the short, medium and longer terms. A series of questions need to be asked, including:

- Do/will the values employed affect any stakeholders negatively?
- Are the values employed justifiable and sustainable?
- Are there alternative values that would be optimal and sustainable?

Needless to say, although it is a demanding task, the executives and investors caught on the downside of the subprime lending crisis would be glad to enjoy the benefits of such a values audit if given a second chance to avoid the losses they suffered.

Summary

The effective management of corporate ethical performance is facilitated by the measurement, monitoring, and reporting of performance. Attention to these aspects of an ethics program will go a long way toward developing and maintaining an ethical corporate culture, maintaining the support of stakeholders, and facilitating the achievement of corporate strategic objectives. Modifying normal risk management processes to specifically examine for ethics risks is essential to keeping the integrity of organizational cultures.

Readings *located at the end of the book*

S.P. Sethi. "Codes of Conduct for Global Business: Prospects and Challenges of Implementation," *Principles of Stakeholder Management* (Toronto: The Clarkson Centre for Business Ethics, 1999): 9–20.

Useful References

Richard M. Locke, Alvin J. Siteman, Professor of Entrepreneurship and Political Science, MIT, *The Promise and Perils of Globalization: The Case of Nike*, http://web.mit.edu/ipc/publications/pdf/02-007.pdf .

Nike's website: http://www.nikebiz.com/responsibility/cr_governance.html

Guideline for Corporate Social Responsibility (PLUS 9018), Canadian Standards Association (CSA), 2004.

Additional Readings and Useful References will noted on http://www.ethicscentre.ca

---

TABLE 1:
Techniques for the Measurement of Ethical Processes & Performance[13]

Attribute or Process / Measurement Techniques

Written objectives
    Existence – broad, specific by function
    Content – comprehensive set of values, clarity of coverage, relevance
    Date of most recent revision
Annual sign-off – yes/no, minimal or involving responsibility for reporting
Guidance given to directors, management, employees
    Process – training sessions, workshops, and employees
    Consultation with ombudsperson, others
    Comprehensiveness of coverage (e.g., new employees)
    Frequency, currency – board review, dissemination
Understanding of issues
    Rating developed by persons responsible for ethics program for each level of
        employee
    Some tests are available (e.g., defining issues test, stage of moral reasoning)
Inclusion of ethical concerns
    Evaluation by management in decision making
    In "the development of plans, setting of goals, search of opportunities, allocation
    of resources, gathering and communication of information, measurement of

performance, and promotion and advancement of personnel"[36]
> Frequency of coverage as agenda item

Commitment by all levels to the organization's ethical values
> Rating by ombudsperson
> Reports of ethical problems – fraud, customer and employee complaints
> Visible encouragement by top management

Achievement of ethical objectives
> Combination of – existence, stage of completion of plans, number of events, dollars spent, numbers experienced
> Monitoring and continuous improvement
> Identification of person(s) responsible
> Adequacy of resources allocated
> Periodic reports to senior management and Board
> Evident action based on feedback

Effectiveness of reporting
> Existence – internal, external
> Impact analysis on employees and external stakeholders
> Effectiveness analysis by researchers
> Favourable/unfavourable mentions in the media

TABLE 2:
Global Reporting Initiative's
Sustainability Framework (G3) Guidelines

Note: An expanded and updated version of this overview is available online as
GRI Sustainability Reporting Guidelines G3.1 – Reference Sheet
At https://www.globalreporting.org/resourcelibrary/G3.1-Quick-Reference-Sheet.pdf

---

Global Reporting Initiative
Sustainability Framework – G3 Guidelines
See http://www.globalreporting.org/ReportingFramework/G3Online/

Contents – *extracted 11.29.2009*

Defining Report Content
> Materiality, stakeholder inclusiveness, context completeness

Defining Report Quality
> Reliability, clarity, balance, comparability, accuracy, timeliness

Setting the Report Boundary
> Influence, significant influence, control

Profile Disclosures
> Strategy & analysis, org. profile, report parameters, governance

Management Approach, Goals, Policy, Performance Indicators, Org. Resp., Training, Monitoring, Follow-up, Contextual Info

- Economic Performance (EC): market presence, indirect impacts
- Environmental Performance (EN): materials; energy; water; biodiversity; emissions; effluents & waste; products & services; compliance; transport

Management Approach, Goals, Policy, etc. continued:

- Labor Practices & Decent Work (LA) – UN, ILO & Vienna Declarations; employment; labor/manage. relations; occupational health & safety; training & education; diversity & opportunity
- Human Rights (HR) – invest & procurement practices; non-discrimination; freedom of assoc.; child labor; forced & compulsory labor; security practices; indigenous rights
- Society (SO) – community; corruption; public policy; anti-competitive behavior
- Product Responsibility (PR) – customer health & safety; labeling; marketing communications; customer privacy; compliance

Indicator Search, Sector Supplements

---

36. Paine, Lynn Sharp, "Managing for Organizational Integrity," *Harvard Business Review* (March–April 1994).

TABLE 3:
AccountAbility's AA1000 Assurance Standard: Summary

Purpose, Sustainability Reporting and Assurance:

- The AA1000 Assurance Standard is a generally applicable standard for assessing, attesting to, and strengthening the credibility and quality of a reporting organizations' sustainability reporting, and its underlying processes, systems and competencies. It provides guidance on key elements of the assurance process, and is emerging as a standard guiding the audit of sustainability reporting.
- The AA1000 Assurance Standard is primarily intended for use by assurance providers, in guiding the manner in which their assurance assignments are designed and implemented.
- Assurance should provide confidence in the report's underlying information to the reporting organization's stakeholders, particularly the direct users of the report.

Assurance of sustainability reporting prepared in accordance with generally accepted standards:

- The AA1000 Assurance Standard supports assurance (whether made public or not) of reporting that adheres to specific standards and guidelines, and is customised by the reporting organisation. It is specifically designed to be consistent with, and to enhance, the Global Reporting Initiative Sustainability Reporting Guidelines, as well as other related standards.

Commitment by reporting organizations:

- Reporting organizations commit to (1) identify and understand their environment, (2) respond to their stakeholders' aspirations, and (3) provide an account to their stakeholders regarding the organization's decisions, actions and impacts.

Assurance principles:

- *Materiality*: the assurance provider must evaluate if the report contains all the important information about the reporting organization's sustainability performance, required by the organization's stakeholders, for making informed judgements, decisions and actions.
- *Completeness*: the assurance provider must evaluate the extent to which the reporting organization has not omitted any material aspects of its performance.
- *Responsiveness*: the assurance provider must evaluate whether the reporting organization has responded to stakeholders' concerns, policies, and relevant standards; and adequately communicated these responses in the report.

Evidence (supporting the reported figures and disclosures):

- The assurance provider must evaluate whether the reporting organization has provided adequate evidence to support the information contained in the report.

Assurance statement (i.e. auditor's opinion):

- The assurance statement should address the credibility of the report and the underlying systems, processes, and competencies that deliver the relevant

information and underpin the reporting organization's performance.
- Elements of the assurance statement (i.e. auditor's report):
  - Statement on use of AA1000
  - Description of work performed
  - Conclusion on the quality of the report and underlying organizational processes, systems, and competencies
  - Additional comments if necessary

Assurance provider standards (i.e. auditor's independence and competencies):

- The credibility of a report's assurance relies on the assurance provider's competencies, independence, and impartiality:
  - The assurance provider should be independent of the reporting organization and impartial with respect to the organisation's stakeholders. Any interests that detract from this independence and impartiality need to be transparently declared by the assurance provider.
  - The assurance provider must be impartial in its dealings with the reporting organization's stakeholders.
  - Assurance providers and the reporting organization must ensure that the individuals involved in any specific assurance process are demonstrably competent.
  - The organisations through which individuals provide assurance must be able to demonstrate adequate institutional competencies.

A full version of the AA1000 Assurance Standard, 2008, is available online at http://www.accountability.org/images/content/0/5/056/AA1000AS%202008.pdf

---

TABLE 4:
Ethics Audit Program Annual Audit Questions

Questions for each Business Unit

Responsibility:

- Is there a person at the business unit who is responsible for answering questions about, and administering the code? Who is this?
- Do the employees know of this person's responsibility with regard to the code?

Awareness and Commitment:

- Has the code been distributed to all employees and managers?
- Have all managers signed the representation letter confirming that, "during the past year, [they] and, to the best of their knowledge after due inquiry, [their] immediate subordinates who hold management responsibilities have complied with the code and also have taken appropriate actions to ensure compliance by other employees (who are [their] subordinates) and by contractors and consultants (whom [they] have engaged or are responsible for)?"
- Have all employees signed off during the past year, that they have observed the code and will continue to do so, and that they know of no unreported breaches of the code?
- Are all new employees signing off when they join the company?

- Do all suppliers, contractors, and consultants receive a written notification that it is understood that they will abide by the code, or specific provisions of it, such as those on gifts or inducements, conflicts of interest, health and safety, or environmental protection?

Training:

- Do new employees receive training on the code when they join the organization, before they sign the code sign-off?
- Have existing employees received training on the code during the past year? What is the nature of this training?
- Do suppliers, contractors and consultants receive a briefing on the code and their need to observe it?

Commitment and support provided by management:

- Has management above the business unit shown personal commitment and support for the code and the values on which it is based? How? (Speeches, memos, actions?)
- Has the management of the business unit shown personal commitment and support for the code and the values on which it is based? How? (Speeches, memos, actions?)
- Is the personal commitment and support for the code and underlying values of each manager built into job descriptions, monitored and included in performance reviews?
- Has there been reinforcing publicity in newsletters, or through publicity of good or bad examples of behaviour?

Operations:

- Do employees and managers have confidence in the business unit's systems for:
  - Answering ethics inquiries?
  - Bringing ethics concerns forward for investigation?
  - Investigation and sanction?

Survey 10 employees and 5 managers

- What are the annual usage statistics of each system?
- Were any significant ethical problems not handled appropriately?
- Were actions taken on a timely and appropriate basis?
- Do any items or issues require clarification to avoid further problems?
- Are there any suggestions for improvement of the code or the processes involved?
- Do timely periodic reports to division management exist, covering the activities of these systems?
- Are all items reported?
- Were you aware of unethical conduct that was not reported? If so, why do you think it was not reported?

Results

- Are there examples of company business decisions made that appear to contravene the code, or any other aspect of management's stated values?
- If so, were such matters openly communicated and explained? If they were not, cynicism about the Code will likely increase.

Questions to be asked of each Organizational Unit Overseeing a Business Unit Operation, Assessment and Continuous Improvement:

- Are there personnel assigned, if so, specify whom; and are systems in place to monitor and ensure:
  - ○ Compliance with the code in each business unit and at the division level?
  - ○ Effectiveness of the procedures for complying with the code, in such matters as training, sign-off, inquiry, investigation, and sanction?
  - ○ Assessment of operations and risks?
  - ○ Reinforcement and support?
- Are necessary actions taken in a timely and appropriate manner?
- Are timely reports prepared for and reviewed by division management?
- Are objectives related to the code built into the divisional and business unit yearly operating objective statements?
- Are appropriate actions taken and reinforced by division management?
- Is there appropriate reporting to head office to allow for remedial action and solutions to be shared across the company?
- Does head office react and respond to feed-forward or requests for clarification?
- Has management above the division level shown personal commitment and support for the code and the values on which it is based? How? (Speeches, memos, actions?)
- Do job descriptions and performance appraisal processes include reference to provisions of the Code?
- Are there any issues needing further clarification or suggestion?
- Are there any issues that should be reported to the board for information or action?

Checklist – Maintaining an Ethical Corporate Culture	
Monitoring & Reporting Ethical Performance	
✓	Measurement of CSR
	• Historical measures
	○ Existence of statements of guidance, their currency, and their reinforcement
	○ Employment record, including total staff, and number of women, and minority group members in board or management positions
	○ Amount of charitable donations
	○ Existence and nature of community relations programs
	○ Labour relations and health and safety
	○ Environmental management indicators
	○ Environmental performance indicators
	○ Ethical sourcing and trading policies

- Anticipatory measures
  - Employee attitude surveys such as those undertaken by Walker Information
  - Customer or other stakeholder surveys
  - Evaluation by paid shoppers or through solicited customer comments
- Quality assessments of
  - Codes of conduct
  - Training programs
  - Reinforcement mechanisms, including:
    - Newsletters, correspondence
    - Pay and reward systems
    - Promotion
    - Protection for whistle-blowers
    - Follow-up on reported problems
    - Speed
    - Fairness of investigation, hearing, and of penalty assigned
- Depth of involvement
  - The level of understanding that employees have of ethical issues
  - The principal motivator for an employee's ethical behaviour
  - Whether an employee is disposed to raise ethical concerns due to his or her perception of his or her ability to affect the outcome of such debates (locus of control tests)
  - The degree of inclusion of ethical concerns in, the development of plans, setting of goals, search of opportunities, allocation of resources, gathering and communication of information, measurement of performance, and promotion and advancement of personnel

Monitoring CSR
- Internal reports
- External reports
- Comparative assessment of results with:
  - Strategic objective key success factors
  - Similar organizations
  - Best-practice alternatives for benchmarking
  - Published standards such as those described in this chapter
  - Industry statistics and averages
  - Management by Objective targets
  - Results obtained in earlier periods
- Report to Board

	Public Reporting of CSR
	• Consider
	○ GRI (G3 or update G3.1)
	○ AccountAbility (AA1000)
	○ SA 8000
	• Audit or Verification of CSR Reports
	○ External Audit Firm
	○ External individual or committee
	Ethics Risk Management
	• Does the company review ethics- and values-related risks:
	○ During the normal risk management process?
	○ In general?
	○ Cultural support risks specifically?
	○ Mindset risks specifically?
	○ Systemic ethics risks specifically?
	○ In depth sufficient to discover ethics-related causalities?
	• Are ethics risks reported to senior management and the Board?
	See also Tables at end of Chapter

Special Topics

Chapter 8
Making Ethical Decisions

Several factors have stimulated interest in making ethical decisions that assist, rather than harm, an organization. Just as corporations have seen the logic in reducing the risk of unacceptable behaviour through the introduction of ethical guidance as part of their governance program, they are extending their guidance regime to provide ethical decision aids and frameworks. Leaving employees to their own values and interpretations of codes of conduct leaves corporations exposed to risks of:

- Unethical behaviour
- Damage to reputation
- Diminishment of profit
- Failure to keep the support of key stakeholders
- Failure to achieve the organization's strategic objectives

The discussion of ethical decision making that follows builds upon the discussion in Chapter 2 of corporate accountability to stakeholders, not just shareholders, and of reputation and its role in maintaining the support of key stakeholders. Not only do employees have to understand why and how their company expects them to behave, they need to know what questions to ask when attempting to identify the important aspects of the impact of their decisions that they need to take into account, and how to do so, before they make mistakes. The approach taken in making a decision, and the decision framework applied, can be essential in later justifying a decision, and avoiding a disaster.

Ethical Decision Aids and Frameworks

A code of conduct and some codes of ethics, can be used as an ethical decision aid or framework, and are often computerized and made available through the company intranet system. However, codes do not cover all possible eventualities explicitly. If they did, their authors could superhumanly foresee future business developments, and the codes would be so lengthy that few would read and remember their contents. That is why it is far more practical to develop a code of conduct that puts forth values or principles that can be interpreted to assist in future decisions as they arise, rather than just an exhaustive set of rules to be matched against problems. However, the code cannot be so broad as to leave employees nonplussed as to how to act. When the code is unclear or ambiguous for an employee making a specific decision, the employee needs to know where to turn for help, and needs to be aware that simply shrugging and taking the course of least resistance is not appropriate. Examples in the code, supporting auxiliary documents, and relevant training can clarify how to use the principles put forth, but keeping these clarifiers updated is a necessity.

In addition, as noted above, employees need guidance to ensure that they will ask all the questions required about a proposed action sufficient to ensure that their decision can be made based on a comprehensive set of information. Failing to ask one important question can leave the resulting decision ethically vulnerable.

Several approaches or frameworks exist for a company to ensure that its employees will recognize ethical problems and analyse them fully, or at least know whom to consult. For example, it would be wise for a company to have its employees consider their decisions and activities using a two-stage process – a quick "sniff" test stage, followed by a more thorough second stage consideration of impacts on stakeholders using a rigorous framework such as stakeholder impact analysis, if it is needed. These two approaches are discussed below.

Sniff Tests and Common Rules of Thumb

It is often appropriate for managers and other employees to be asked to check a proposed decision in a quick, preliminary manner, to see if an additional full-blown ethical analysis is required. These quick tests are often referred to as sniff tests. Commonly applied sniff tests include:

- Would I be comfortable if this action or decision were to appear on the front page of a national newspaper tomorrow morning?

- Will I be proud of this decision?
- Will my mother be proud of this decision?
- Is this action or decision in accord with the corporation's mission and code?
- Does this feel right to me?

If any of these quick tests are negative, employees are asked to seek out an ethics officer for consultation, or to perform a full-blown analysis of the proposed action. This analysis should be retained, and perhaps reviewed, by the ethics officer. A reading on "Sniff tests" is attached at the end of this book.[1]

Many executives have developed their own rules of thumb for deciding whether an action is ethical or not. For example, Carroll[2] identifies the following six rules as important, according to practicing managers:

Golden Rule:
- Do unto others as you would have them do unto you.

Disclosure Rule:
- If you are comfortable with an action or decision, after asking yourself whether you would mind if all your associates, friends, and family were aware of it, then you should act or decide.

The Intuition Ethic:
- Do what your "gut feeling" tells you to do.

The Categorical Imperative:
- You should not adopt principles of action unless they can, without inconsistency, be adopted by everyone else.

The Professional Ethic:
- Do only what can be explained before a committee of your professional peers.

The Utilitarian Principle:
- Do "the greatest good for the greatest number."

Unfortunately, although these rules of thumb are often very useful, they

---

1. Leonard J. Brooks, "Sniff Tests," *Corporate Ethics Monitor* 7:5 (1995): 65.
2. A.B. Carroll, "Principles of Business Ethics: Their Role in Decision making and Initial Consensus," *Management Decision* 28:8 (1990): 20–24, Figure 3.

Figure 8.1
Ethical Decision-making Approaches and Criteria

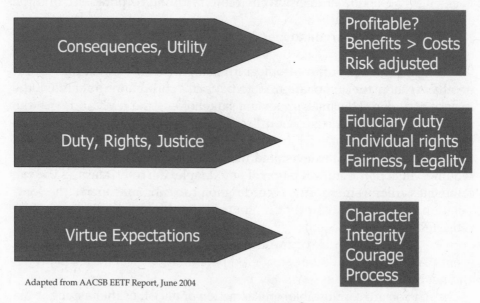

Consequences, Utility

Profitable?
Benefits > Costs
Risk adjusted

Duty, Rights, Justice

Fiduciary duty
Individual rights
Fairness, Legality

Virtue Expectations

Character
Integrity
Courage
Process

Adapted from AACSB EETF Report, June 2004

rarely, by themselves, represent a comprehensive examination of the decision, and therefore leave the individuals and corporation involved vulnerable to making an unethical decision. For this reason, the more comprehensive techniques of stakeholder impact analysis should be employed whenever a proposed decision is questionable, or likely to have significant consequences. Normally, this more sophisticated analysis would be performed by, or with the assistance of, an ethics officer, or by senior management.

Stakeholder Impact Analysis

Assessing the impact of a proposed action on the stakeholders to be affected by the decision, known as stakeholder impact analysis, can be undertaken in several ways, but these can be reduced to examining three fundamental aspects of the impact. Interestingly, in 2004 the AACSB, the worldwide accreditation body for schools of business, released an Ethics Education Task

Force Report[3] that calls for business school students to be educated in making ethical decisions using the three approaches identified in Figure 8.1. It is essential to note that an ethical decision may not result unless all three approaches are applied effectively.

· The first approach, or consequentialism stage, examines the consequences or usefulness of a proposed decision. Consequences must be considered for each stakeholder group – not just for shareholders. This is quite different than what many companies require. While a corporation's shareholders may be considered the most important stakeholders, the realization that the achievement of strategic goals requires the support of other key stakeholders necessitates the consideration of their interests and the impacts upon them. In other words, the consideration of shareholders' interests is a legal requirement, but the consideration of key stakeholder interests is a strategic or business requirement. This consideration can take the form of the computation of projected net profit or contribution for shareholders, and the projected costs and benefits for other stakeholders. Such projections can even be adjusted for risk or the probability of the occurrence of related events. A decision would be considered potentially ethical if the net profits and net benefits (benefits-costs) are positive.

The next stage of analysis involves the examination of the impact of the proposed decision on the duties, rights, or fair treatment of all stakeholders.[4] Relevant questions could be:

- Are all fiduciary duties owed by company personnel to other stakeholders properly discharged?
- Are property, legal, and other rights (for example, health, safety, life, fair treatment and freedom of speech) respected?

A decision would be considered potentially ethical if all stakeholder duties and rights were discharged and/or respected.

The final, or virtue expectations stage of analysis, considers whether the behaviour of a company's personnel and agents that is inherent in the proposed decision matches stakeholder expectations. Has the company, or its personnel and agents demonstrated the virtues expected of them? Have they demonstrated the honesty, integrity, forthrightness, courage, compassion, and other aspects of character that their stakeholders expected in their company's decisions, activities, or processes? For example, although a line

---

3.   AACSB EETF Report, *Report of the Ethics Education Task Force: Ethics Education in Business Schools, Association to Advance Collegiate Schools of Business*, 2004, http://www.aacsb.edu/publications/researchreports/archives.asp
4.   Referred to as "deontology," as it has to do with the study of obligations.

of car tires has not been declared unsafe by regulators, has the manufacturer informed customers about abnormally high incidences of blow-outs or instituted a recall? Or, has a company mistreated animals in its testing processes? A decision to act (or a decision not to act) would be considered potentially ethical if the virtues expected were delivered.

Only after all three stages of analysis have been completed do we know if each stage has yielded a positive or ethical verdict. It may be that a proposed decision is profitable, but not fair to all stakeholders. Or a proposed action could be profitable, but not live up to the expectations of customers or employees – who are disenchanted and buy elsewhere, or change employers, or work with lowered enthusiasm or effectiveness thus lowering profits in the longer term. Accordingly, *a corporation cannot be confident that a proposed action is ethical unless, and until, all three analytical approaches are completed* and the results found to be positive. Fortunately, if the results of one of the tests are negative, the proposed decision can be revised on an iterative basis until the negative aspect is removed,[5] if possible.

It is unlikely that a stakeholder will be favourably disposed to a decision that leaves him or her worse off, so looking for an option that leaves everyone better off is best, and if that is not available, one that leaves no one worse off would be desirable. Unfortunately, it is not always possible to find such a solution, which means that some stakeholders may have to be worse off. In this case, the question to be asked is whether, taking all stakeholder impacts into account, the overall impact of the proposed decision will be a net benefit or a net cost.

If the overall net impact of the proposed decision is positive, there is still a question of whether the decision is fair to all stakeholder groups. If not, some stakeholders will be worse off, and the question is whether the overall gain warrants disadvantaging some. Again, the extent of this disadvantaging or unfairness will have to be assessed to see if the trade-off is warranted.

One way to assess the degree of unfairness is to examine what impact the proposed decision will have on the rights of the decision maker, the corporation, and the other stakeholders. The rights attributable to stakeholders depend partly upon several factors, including the culture of the individuals affected, and the law of the country involved. However, there are some rights that are held to be universal, particularly in North America, and worldwide by North American stakeholders. They include the right to the following:

---

5. For a wider discussion of stakeholder impact analysis *see* Leonard J. Brooks & Paul Dunn. *Business & Professional Ethics for Directors, Executives & Accountants*, 6e (South Western, Cengage Learning, 2012), Ch. 4.

- Life
- Health and safety
- Exercise of conscience
- Dignity and privacy
- Freedom of speech (albeit constrained in some situations by the obligation not to disclose confidential information)
- Freedom of association
- Fairness
- The keeping of agreements, including oral agreements

It should be noted that some of these rights are not strictly or absolutely observed in many trading partner countries around the world. In these cases, the degree of variance from North American practice should be known to the board so that the board can consciously make the decision to deviate from North American standards fully considering the benefits of doing so and the potential risks involved to reputation and future profits.

The Modified Tucker Framework

Stakeholder impact analysis can be distilled into decision frameworks, or into a set of questions that employees are encouraged to use when they are called upon to make decisions. One of the simplest of these is the framework that Graham Tucker suggested in the article in the readings section.[6] Tucker's framework, modified to incorporate a question on expected virtues, suggests that proposed actions be challenged by asking the questions posed in Figure 8.2.

A proposed action or decision that passes all challenges positively is ethical. Sometimes the challenges will reveal a negative aspect that can be improved to be neutral or positive in impact through redesign of the decision. Often the proposed decision involves trade-offs between two or more stakeholders, and therefore will rely upon the judgment of the decision maker and outside experts to arrive at the most ethical resolution.

There are some limitations to the Tucker framework that should be noted. It focusses on profit, which potentially is very short run in perspective. Moreover, profit doesn't take into account any externalities, such as pollution, that are not usually captured in traditional financial statements, at least in the short run, but are nevertheless the result of a corporation's actions and represent impacts on stakeholders. If the proposed decision

6. Graham Tucker. "Ethical analysis for environmental problem solving," *Agenda for Action Conference Proceedings* (Canadian Centre for Ethics & Corporate Policy, 1990), 53–57.

Figure 8.2
Modified Tucker Framework for Stakeholder Impact Analysis

Questions To Challenge Actions or Decisions

1. Is it profitable?
2. Is it legal?
3. Is it fair?
4. Is it right?
5. Does it demonstrate the virtues expected?
6. Optional question: Is it sustainable (environmentally/over time)?

Modify using moral imagination and optimize

---

under review involves a longer-term problem, or externalities, the assessment ought to be upgraded to include a cost-benefit analysis with an appropriately longer time horizon, or even more sophisticated techniques.

Another enhancement that should be considered is the assessment and ranking of the severity of impact of the proposed decision on each stakeholder group. All impacts are not equal in severity of impact and therefore cannot be considered to be of equal consequence from an ethical perspective. For example, an employee's health and safety is not, in North America, considered to be of equal consequence to the earning of a profit for shareholders. Trading off an employee's health or safety for more profit would not be considered ethical. Similarly, disadvantaging vulnerable stakeholder groups, such as children, is frowned upon, as is advantaging a stakeholder group with lots of resources in order to disadvantage a group with very few resources. In assessing trade-offs such as these, it is often wise to consider how the public, the media, and the corporation's primary stakeholder groups will view the impacts.

In addition to the article by Tucker, a more complete treatment of ethical decision making, including additional approaches and examples can be found in Chapter 4 of *Business & Professional Ethics for Directors, Executives & Accountants.*[7]

---

7.   Op. Cit.

Common Ethical Decision-making Pitfalls

There are several pitfalls that unaware decision makers fall into repeatedly. These include:

Focusing on Short-term Profit and Shareholder-only Impacts

Often, the most significant impacts of a proposed action are those that surface in the future, and those that befall non-shareholder stakeholders. Frequently, only after non-shareholders react, do shareholders bear the cost for misdeeds. The remedy for this myopia is to ensure an adequate time horizon for the analysis, and to take into account all externalities on a cost-benefit basis even though the impact measured is felt initially by a non-shareholder group.

Focusing only on Legalities

Many managers are only concerned with whether or not an action is legal. They argue, "If it's legal, it's ethical." Unfortunately, many find their corporation unnecessarily subject to consumer boycotts, employee slowdowns or inefficiency, increasing government regulation to cover loopholes, and fines. Some managers don't care because they are only intending to stay at the corporation for a short while. The fact is that laws and regulations often lag behind public expectations. One reason for this is that corporations lobby against rule changes. For example, auto companies lobbied against the adoption of 21 miles per hour rear crash tests for over five years, until the Ford Pinto lawsuits were settled. Caution is called for – just because a proposed action is legal, that does not make it ethical.

Limits to Fairness

Sometimes decision makers only want to be fair to groups they like. Unfortunately for them, they do not have the ability to control public opinion, and may end up paying for their oversight. Many executives have been put off by activist organizations, such as Greenpeace, but have learned that environmental issues are ignored at their peril. A full review of fairness to all stakeholders is vital to ensuring an ethical decision.

Limits to Rights Canvassed

Bias influences decisions in many ways. Decision makers should canvass the impact on all rights for all stakeholder groups – not just their favourites.

Decision makers should be encouraged to take their own values into account when making a decision. Courts in North America no longer react favourably to the defense that, "I was ordered to do it by my boss." Employees are expected to use their own judgment, and many jurisdictions[8] have set up protective whistleblowing and "right to refuse" statutes to encourage employees to do so. Often, managers that force unfortunate actions on subordinates are really not acting in the best interests of shareholders.

Conflicts of Interest

Bias based on prejudice is not the only reason for faulty assessments of proposed actions. Judgment can be clouded by conflicting interests – the decision maker's personal interest versus the corporation's best interest, or the interests of groups the decision maker is partial to versus the corporation's best interest, can both account for erroneous assessments and decisions.

Failure to Identify all Stakeholder Groups, Rank their Interests, and Understand their Interconnectedness

The need to identify all stakeholder groups and interests before assessing the impacts on each is self-evident. However, this is a step that is repeatedly taken for granted, with the result that important issues go unnoticed. A useful approach to assist with this problem is to speculate on the downside of a proposed action, try to assess how the media will react, and how that reaction can lead to interest by other influential or legally powerful stakeholders. This often leads to the identification of, and focus on, the most vulnerable stakeholder groups, who have the most urgent claims, and whose plight the media naturally tend to favour.

The media and public opinion will almost always side with employees rather than shareholders. For example, there was media and public outrage after the Enron bankruptcy when it was revealed that employees were exhorted to buy even more Enron stock when senior executives were selling theirs. Many lost their life savings. There was little evidence of similar outrage at the losses suffered by shareholders who were not employees.

---

8. *See for example*: the New York State *Whistleblower Protection Law* that has been copied in many states, and the "right to refuse" statutes in Ontario labour, water, and pollution laws.

Frequently decision makers fail to anticipate that what they do to one group will trigger action by another. For example, despoiling the environment in a far-off country can be picked up by domestic customers and capital markets on other continents due to TV shows with satellite feeds like CNN, or on Internet websites. Categorizing the interests or claims of stakeholders as urgent, powerful or influential, and legal or legitimate can be helpful in appreciating those interests likely to become most important to the achievement of the corporation's strategic objectives, and facilitate the decision-making process.

Failure to Appreciate How Important Expected Virtues are to Stakeholders

Many executives are so focussed on making a profit, and/or are uncomfortable or unfamiliar with the idea that they should be concerned about virtues, that they fail to realize how important virtues are to customers, employees, and other stakeholders who are looking for people, relationships and corporations that they can trust. Nowadays the media are increasingly interested in stories showing executives who really didn't grasp or grapple with what was expected in this respect.

Failure to Exercise Moral Courage

Frequently executives and managers will correctly identify and analyse an ethical problem, but they fail to have the courage to behave ethically because the temptation to act unethically is too great to resist, or because everyone is behaving unethically, and they would look foolish to do otherwise. Ed Clark, the CEO of TD Bank, unlike almost all other executives prior to the subprime lending crisis, exercised moral courage in not investing in derivative securities backed by mortgage loans. His story appears below.

Moral Courage: Toronto-Dominion Bank CEO Refuses to Invest in High-Risk Asset-Backed Commercial Paper[9]

Although Canadian banks did not suffer as much as other financial institutions around the world, they have not been immune from the economic consequences of the subprime mortgage meltdown. In Canada,

---

9. This case is an edited version of a case by the same name in L.J. Brooks and Paul Dunn. *Business & Professional Ethics for Directors, Executives and Accountants*, 6e, (South-Western Cengage Learning, 2012).

the earliest crisis concerned the liquidity of asset-backed commercial paper (ABCP) that was affected by the precipitous decline of U.S. housing prices and the related mortgage-backed securities on which those prices were based.

ABCP are short-term debt obligations, generally issued by a specially formed entity or trust, and secured by a bundle of assets such as mortgages and other types of consumer loans. The repayment and maturity of these ABCPs is dependent on the cash flow of the underlying assets. The ABCPs were issued to investors by trusts that were sponsored or managed by either banks or nonbank financial institutions. The nonbank-sponsored portion of the Canadian market was approximately $35 billion.

In July 2007, as the U.S. subprime mortgage market began to deteriorate, the Canadian issuers began to fear that they, too, could face a liquidity crisis that would prevent the recovery of capital, or refinancing of borrowings, when they came due. As such, in August, a number of nonbank ABCP sponsors agreed to a sixty-day standstill period, called the Montreal Accord, during which the holders (those who had invested in the ABCP) promised not to roll over or redeem their paper at maturity, and the issuers agreed not to make any collateral calls. A committee, chaired by Toronto lawyer Purdy Crawford, then began to work out a deal whereby the short-term ABCP could be converted into long-term floating-rate debt that would have a much greater likelihood of recovery or refinance, because the underlying assets would eventually recover their value.

The agreement required the support of the five major banks in Canada. They were each to pay $500 million in order to shore up the country's debt market. However, Canada's third largest bank, the Toronto-Dominion Bank (TD), balked at the suggestion on the basis that, three years earlier, the bank intentionally had moved to eliminate its exposure in the nonbank ABCP market.

In May 2005, Edmund Clark, CEO of the TD, announced that the bank would exit the structured loans products market, including interest rate derivatives and collateralized debt obligations such as ABCPs. He had been briefed by experts who traded these securities on the nature of credit and equity products and concluded the risk was too great. "The whole thing didn't make sense to me. You're going to get all your money back, or you're going to get none of your money back. I said 'wow!' if this ever went against us, we could take some serious losses here." The TD generates 80 percent of its profit from consumer lending and money management. "I'm an old school banker. I don't think you should do something you don't understand, hoping there's somebody at the bottom of the organization who does."[10]

---

10. Pasternak, Sean, "Toronto-Dominion Avoids Subprime as Banks Costs Rise," *Bloomberg.com*, May 26, 2008, http://www.bloomberg.com/apps/news?pid=newsarchive&sid=aeAsOI6GUU1Y.

Meanwhile, all of the other major Canadian banks were investing in the ABCP market. They collectively controlled two-thirds of the ABCP market.[11] The yields were high and everyone was on the bandwagon. It took great courage for Clark to go against the tide. As David Baskin of Baskin Financial Services said, "He's absolutely to be commended for not getting caught up in the subprime frenzy."[12] And Clark was right. When the ABCP market collapsed, the other banks reported large write-downs on their securities, estimated to be in excess of $2 billion.[13]

As the commercial credit market began to collapse, the Montreal Accord was being extended. TD was under a lot of pressure to help participate in the repair of the credit market, but Clark's attitude was, "that it would not be in the best interest of TD shareholders to assume incremental risk for activities in which we were not involved."[14] TD was not part of the problem, so he thought it should not be part of the solution. Finally, the federal government, through the Bank of Canada, weighed in saying that it wanted the problem solved, and that it was in both the public interest and the interest of the financial marketplace that all the banks participate in restructuring the commercial paper segment of the market. Since TD was part of the financial community, although it had not created the problem, it had a moral and financial obligation to help.

TD could have held out, but as one analyst said, "It's like protesting going to your mother-in-law's house for Christmas. Despite your protest, you know you're going because it's been determined that it's in your best interest to do so. In my view, the Bank of Canada will win the' argument."[15] On March 13, 2008, the five major Canadian banks, including TD, said that they would provide $950 million to support the newly restructured credit market, in which $32 billion of short-term commercial paper would be swapped for long-term notes.[16]

It takes courage to oppose a trend, or to blow the whistle. Ed Clark set a worthy example that signaled his view of appropriate behavior for everyone in his bank.

11. *CBC News*, "Credit Crunch Could be 'Quite Ugly' for Months: TD CEO," September 11, 2007, http://www.cbc.ca/money/story/2007/09/11/credit.html?ref=rss.
12. Pasternak, op. cit.
13. "TD Bank will Consider Montreal Accord Proposals on ABCP but Won't Take Risks, December 17, 2007.
14. Mordant, Nicole, "TD Bank Throws Wrench into Canada ABCP Repair," *Reuters*, December 17, 2007.
15. Critchley, Barry, "TD May Join ABCP Bailout," *Financial Post*, December 19, 2007.
16. Alexander, Doug and Pasternak, Sean, "Canada Commercial Paper Group Gets Credit Protection, *Bloomberg.com*, March 17, 2008, http://www.bloomberg.com/apps/news?pid=newsarchive&sid=aO.ysqLVjxUc.

Competitors are Stakeholders Too

Much is written about the need for companies to act ethically towards their investors, employees, customers, suppliers, regulators and the environment. Less is written about the need to act ethically towards one's competitors. This may be because cutthroat no-holds-barred competition is still regarded as necessary by some business leaders for success in the capitalist system.

Many companies believe that competition must be fair, and some incorporate specific policies into their operating practices to prohibit unacceptable practices. Others do not. However, getting caught competing in a manner deemed unethical can result in bad publicity and lawsuits that can be very costly. It can also damage personal reputations. Two examples in the airline industry are illustrated in the cases that follow.

Laissez-faire capitalism, based as it is on the presumption that competition is a good thing, inevitably generates the risk that it will be overdone. In most developed economies there are laws and regulations aimed at eliminating abuse, but there are many more areas that most stakeholders would regard as unethical, and could generate lawsuits.

Examples of unethical competition include:

- Direct theft of confidential data from competitors, such as customer lists and pricing information.
- Pressuring personnel formerly employed by competitors to reveal confidential information. Worse still, luring personnel from competitors for this purpose.
- Spreading unflattering or false information about competitors, either directly through advertising, or indirectly by word of mouth to key stakeholders.
- Using predatory pricing that creates losses until smaller competitors are driven out of business, at which time more monopolistic prices can be put in place.
- Conspiracies to deprive competitors of access to preferred suppliers.
- Dissemination of information stating that products are of superior quality to those of competitors when it is known that they are not.

Illustrative Case: Two Airlines Caught Out

Two interesting and somewhat similar cases of unethical conduct have occurred in recent years in the airline industry.

In 1991, British Airways (BA) was caught stealing data from its major transatlantic competitor, Virgin Atlantic (Virgin).[17] They also sent employees to steal people out of Virgin's check-in lines by offering them cheaper (unadvertised) fares. They were found out when a BA employee spilled the beans, resulting in dreadful publicity and a major lawsuit that was settled for a substantial sum. The Chairman of BA, Lord King, subsequently resigned. Although ostensibly his leaving was not for this reason, the press and the public were understandably skeptical. The important thing about this case is that nobody in the company, or in the media, ever attempted to justify this conduct as acceptable business conduct. The situation could presumably have been avoided if those in BA who instigated, or who knew about, these activities had called a halt either on ethical grounds or on the grounds that it was too risky and would be damaging if found out. Competition between BA and Virgin was exceptionally intense at that time. Virgin was an upstart enterprise run by an entrepreneur who had a very high (and favourable) public image. BA was a traditionally-run corporation with an excellent, but rather staid reputation, and it had previously had little or no real competition over the Atlantic from other British companies. Their reaction may have been understandable, but not excusable, and internal structures should have been sufficient to prevent these events from occurring.

More than a decade later, in 2004, it became known that a senior West-Jet official had pressured a former Air Canada employee, who still had password access to detailed Air Canada database information, to provide that access to obtain flight scheduling information that would benefit WestJet's business. The individual was concerned about the propriety of this and asked for, and received, a signed indemnification from West-Jet from any damages that might ensue. An employee eventually spilled the beans. A law suit ensued, which WestJet settled, and Clive Beddoe, the Chairman of WestJet suffered damage to his personal reputation because it is alleged that he knew what was going on. Again, nobody has suggested that WestJet's conduct was appropriate business practice, but it is interesting that Beddoe, in defending his personal reputation, stressed that he had always run his business in an ethical manner.[18] He

---

17. BBC News online, "BA Dirty Tricks Cost £3m" http://news.bbc.co.uk/onthisday/hi/dates/stories/january/11/newsid_2520000/2520189.stm

18. On a 2004 conference call he is reported to have said, "I built this company based on integrity and honesty…" Brent Jang and Paul Waldie, "What Clive Beddoe knew," *Globe and Mail*, October 3, 2006.

has since apologized to Air Canada. This case raises the same issues as the earlier BA case, with the added element that corporate ethics has progressed significantly since then, and the primary focus of Beddoe's response to being found out was to look to ethical metaphors to save his own, and his company's reputation. Of course, the other thing that the situation illustrates is that WestJet personnel were unfamiliar with the history of this kind of conduct in their industry. And as in the BA case, competition was intense, WestJet was viewed as an "upstart," and Air Canada's pricing policies had themselves been the subject of criticism in the past. In the end, though, this kind of conduct was universally deemed unacceptable and unethical.

Leaving out one of the Key Stakeholder Impact Analysis Approaches: Consequentialism, Rights and Duties, and Virtue Expectations

As pointed out above, a comprehensive ethical decision cannot be made if one of these three approaches is overlooked. Repeatedly however, decision makers short-circuit their assessments, and suffer the consequences.

Failure to exercise Moral Imagination

One of the most important steps in ethical decision making involves taking the time to assess whether there is a better or more ethical choice that can be made. This is called exercising moral imagination. Frequently, an outstanding improvement can be made. For example, Ford sold the Pinto in North America with a gas tank that ruptured on impact from the rear at 21 miles per hour or higher. In the UK, Ford sold a similar car named the Bobcat in which the gas tank placement was raised to avoid the rupturing problem, and thereby save many lives as well as Ford's reputation and profits.

The Shell Brent Spar oil storage vessel disposal fiasco presents another example. The original decommission solution of sinking the huge storage tank in the deepest part of the North Sea was furiously opposed and stymied by Greenpeace, causing significant harm to the reputations and fortunes of Shell Oil. Ultimately, the 137 metre deep vessel was happily used to support a pier to dock ships in a fiord. Had this solution been identified earlier, through the exercise of moral imagination, all of the upset could have been avoided.

Steps for an Ethical Decision

To summarize the comments made on ethical decision making, the following steps should be taken when challenging a proposed action:

1. Identify all stakeholder groups and interests.
2. Rank the stakeholders and their interests, weighting the most important more heavily than other issues in the analysis. As discussed above, urgent claims like threats to life and health are generally considered more important than financial interests, and should be considered so by decision makers. Organizations should specify a ranking for key interests such as employee concerns, environmental concerns, and financial concerns.
3. Assess the impact of the proposed action on each stakeholder group's interests with regard to the consequences, rights and duties impact, and virtues expected:
   - Use a comprehensive framework of questions covering the following areas:
     o Consequences
        - Will the action generate a net profit or benefit?
     o Duty, rights, and justice
        - Is the action legal?
        - Is the action fair?
        - Does the action offend the rights of any stakeholders?
     o Virtue expectations
        - Does the action demonstrate the aspects of character that are expected, including integrity and courage?
   - Avoid the problems set out above, including:
     o Focussing on only short-term profit and shareholder impacts
     o Focussing only on legalities
     o Being fair only to groups management approve of
     o Ignoring the impact on the rights of the decision maker
     o Failing to identify and rank all stakeholder groups' interests
     o Leaving out one of the main elements such as virtues expected
     o Failing to exercise moral imagination
4. Iterate. Take the time to exercise moral imagination to optimize the decision.

Ethical Decision Making Aids

Some corporate executives have decided to provide their employees with ethical decision-making aids in an easily-carried form such as a pocket card or digital app. IBM and Bell Canada, for example, started with such a card. IBM now provides a website on the IBM Intranet to guide its employees. Both are good ideas.

An Illustration of Ethical Decision Making – Dealing with Disappointed Apple iPhone Customers

On September 5, 2007, Steve Jobs, the CEO of Apple Inc., announced that the spectacularly successful iPhone would be reduced in price by $200 from $599, its introductory price of roughly two months earlier.[19] Needless to say, he received hundreds of emails from irate customers. Two days later he offered early customers who had paid full price a $100 credit good at Apple's retail and online stores. Was this decision to mitigate the $200 price decrease, and the manner of doing so, appropriate from an ethical perspective?

If Apple management had used a *sniff test* prior to the decision, they might have come to the conclusion that their mothers wouldn't have been proud of or comfortable with it. Similarly, they might have discovered that the price reduction may have offended the Apple Code of Conduct for treatment of customers.

If Apple had considered the *stakeholder impacts* that the decision involved, they would have realized that, while past consumers would be most affected, the reputation of Apple would also be tarnished, and that could affect future consumers who they were trying to attract. In addition, Apple employees – many of whom had been attracted by the strong Apple reputation for providing innovative solution of high quality – would question the company's motives, which could weaken their loyalty and commitment.

If Apple had applied *traditional ethical tests*, they would have found the following:

- Consequentialism
  From a profit perspective, Apple was expecting to more than offset the $200 per unit drop in margin with a gain in volume of sales. For the iPhone alone, this may have been correct, but Apple has many products that are bought by other customers who could be affected negatively and who would see the decision as an opportunistic price decrease from an extraordinarily high starting price. Gouging behaviour could be suspected, which would undermine Apple's

---

19. David Ho, "Apple CEO apologizes to customers," *The Toronto Star*, September 7, 2007, B4.

wholesome value proposition, and non-iPhone sales would suffer as a result. Overall, management might not be certain of making a combined net profit on sales of iPhones and other products.

- Duty, Rights and Justice issues
  Apple executives have a duty to make profits, as long as doing so doesn't violate any laws. In this case, early customers of the iPhone might have a legally enforceable right to sue for unfair practices, but individual actions would be far less likely than a class action lawsuit. While no lawsuit was filed, the prospect of further bad press that tarnishes Apple's image is of considerable concern, due to the ripple effects noted above. The impact of the unfairness of the price reduction could be magnified significantly by bad press.[20] It is unlikely, although the early purchasers had the notoriety of having the newest technology available, that Apple management would have thought the $200 price reduction was fair if they had been personally affected.

- Virtues Expected
  In the minds of Apple's customers and employees, Jobs had the image of a far-sighted technical genius who had been driven to provide great value for his stakeholders, and this image has been transferred to Apple itself. For many stakeholders, the $200 price decrease doesn't match up to the expectations they came to expect of Jobs or Apple.

Apple might also have used the questions developed in the modified *Tucker Framework* to test the proposed $200 price decrease. If so, the answers could have been as follows:

1. Is it profitable? – outcome is not clear, as discussed above
2. Is it legal? – probably, unless a consumer protection act is offended
3. Is it fair? – not accordingly to some customers and employees
4. Is it right? – no, according to some executives, employees, and potential customers
5. Does it demonstrate the expected virtues? – no, as discussed above
6. Optional question: Is it sustainable (environmentally or over time)? The environmental impact issue is not involved in this decision, but

---

20. *See summary article*: Jim Dalrymple, "Lessons learned from the iPhone Price Cuts", Macworld, Sept. 11, 2007, http://www.pcworld.com/article/137046/lessons_learned_from_the_iphone_price_cuts.html

the medium and longer-term impacts are likely to be negative and may be significant. It would be unwise to repeat such a decision, or to ignore the possible future negative impacts to reputation.

On balance, Apple should consider the $200 price decrease to be unfair and unwise, without some mitigation for early purchasers of the iPhone. Is the credit of $100 adequate, and its restricted use appropriate? Another analysis could be run, and a sound solution arrived at in an iterative fashion, applying moral imagination where possible. In this case it is probable that judgement will have to be applied. Time will tell. In any event, Jobs could have avoided the initial negative press and damage to his and Apple's reputation, if Apple had used ethical decision-making tools to analyse the decision before putting it into action.

It should be noted that, while price discounts of the type described in this case are not uncommon, and are not generally regarded as serious ethical problems, they have an ethical aspect that can be assessed using the ethical decision-making approaches discussed in this chapter. They certainly represent risks which could weaken the reputation of executives and the company involved.

Readings *located at the end of the book*

Leonard J. Brooks, "Sniff Tests," *Corporate Ethics Monitor* 7:5 (1995): 65.

Graham Tucker, "Ethical analysis for environmental problem solving," *Agenda for Action Conference Proceedings*, the Canadian Centre for Ethics & Corporate Policy, 1990, 53–57.

	Checklist – Special Topics	
	Making Ethical Decisions	
✓	Ethical Decision Aids & Frameworks	
	• Are frameworks in use	
	○ Voluntary?	
	○ Mandatory?	
	• Training Session	
	• Refresher session(s)	
	• Sniff tests	
	• Stakeholder Impact Analysis used to assess:	
	○ Identification of all stakeholders' interests	
	○ Ranking of all stakeholders' interests	
	○ Potential consequences of decisions or actions	
	○ Duty, right, and justice impacts	
	○ Demonstration of expected virtues	
	○ Overall Net Benefit	
	○ Sustainability	
	○ Moral Imagination	
	○ Iteration	
	• Avoid Commons Pitfalls	
	○ Focusing on short-term profit and shareholder-only impacts	
	○ Focusing only on legalities	
	○ Fairness, but not for all stakeholders	
	○ Respect for rights, but not for all stakeholders	
	○ Conflicts of interest	
	○ Failure to identify all stakeholder groups, rank their interests, and understand their interconnectedness	
	○ Leaving out one of the Key Stakeholder Impact Analysis Approaches:	
	• Consequentialism	
	• Rights and Duties	
	• Virtue Expectations	
	○ Failure to appreciate how important expected virtues are to stakeholders	
	○ Failure to exercise Moral Imagination	
	• Decision Aids	
	○ Do they exist?	
	○ Are they online?	
	○ Are they mandatory?	
	• Documentation & Reporting Guidance	
	• Required Consultation if initial assessment indicates problems	
	• Identification of knowledgeable counsellor (chief ethics officer)	

Special Topics

Chapter 9
Conflicts of Interest

From a practical perspective, some of the most troublesome ethical problems faced by business people are those involving conflicts of interest. These are almost impossible to avoid, so the emphasis should be on increasing awareness of the dilemmas involved, and on how to minimize their impact. There are two types of conflict of interest described below: individual and corporate.

Individual Conflicts of Interest

An individual conflict of interest is a situation in which a person may be motivated to action or inaction by an interest other than the interest that is appropriate in the circumstances. For example, purchasing agents should make decisions for the benefit of their employer, and they should not allow a supplier to charge more than a fairly-bargained price for goods or services. Sometimes suppliers try to obtain a higher price by offering purchasing agents an incentive that appeals to their self-interest. If the purchasing agent accepts and acts on the offer, they are placing their interest and the supplier's interest ahead of their employer's interest. This is contrary to the expectation of the employer of a fair day's work, and loyalty, for a fair day's pay.

Conflicts of interest may be categorized as shown in Figure 9.1. An *apparent* conflict of interests exists when it is readily evident to an observer that a decision maker or major influencer is likely to be motivated to arrange an outcome that is not in the interest of her/his employer. Most often, however, conflicts of interest are *not apparent*, but some may be anticipated based on past history or analysis.

Figure 9.1
Types of Conflict of Interest & Risk of Potential Impact

Nature of Conflict of Interest	Risk of Potential Impact On				
	Conflicted Person		Their Organization		Others
INDIVIDUAL					
Visibility	Reputation	Economic	Reputation	Economic	
Apparent or Not-apparent	-------------------- Depends on extent of management ----------------------- but public perceptions of apparent concerns must be countered or the impact will probably be worse than necessary.				
Extent of Management					
Unmanaged	Very High	Very High	Very High	Very High	Very High
Managed	Low	Low	Low	Low	Very Low
Avoided	None	Low but opportunities could be lost	None	Low but opportunities could be lost	Very Low, opportunities could be lost
CORPORATE	All stakeholders (Goldman Sachs systemically unethical)				

Whether a conflict of interest is apparent or not, there may be controls, safeguards, or offsetting influences in place that would prevent harmful outcomes from occurring. On occasion, these offsetting influences occur naturally, but increasingly organizations are putting controls in place to *manage* the conflict to minimize the harmful risks identified. Sometimes it is possible to *avoid* conflict of interest risks entirely by completely ruling out or banning some transactions, relationships, or attempts to improperly influence a decision. Most of the time, however, a complete ban is not possible, or even desirable, from an economic opportunity point of view.

A conflict of interests can create harm for the decision maker, their organization, and other stakeholders because of the potential effects on reputation, economic opportunity and performance. A decision maker who has a conflict of interest with their employer, whether it is apparent or not, can suffer a severe loss of reputation because concern over that person's bad judgement could lead to lack of trust of the individual or their actions. A decision maker's transgressions can also cause loss of reputation to his/her employer, because it could be presumed that the employer lacks sufficient awareness to prevent or manage the problem, and does not have codes, training and monitoring in place to mitigate such ethical risks. This may give rise to a lack of trust in the employer's activities, its leadership, and its ability to serve its stakeholders well.

The case[1] of Mississauga's long-serving mayor, Hazel McCallion, is illustrative of this. She pressed landowners to sell property close to city hall to construct a hotel and conference centre. Mayor McCallion's son was a principal in the development company (which she claimed not to know) and stood to gain significantly from the transaction. Her actions were investigated thoroughly and she was reprimanded. Her sanction would probably have been far more serious, and have included breach of trust charges, if she had not been so effective for years as a mayor, and not close to 90 years of age. Even so, a glittering reputation and career has been tainted.

In a corporate setting, the legal ramifications could have been far more serious for both the employee and employer. Trust could have been seriously undermined, and future relationships as well as economic opportunities, including future partnerships, could have been cut off. Conrad Black's conflict of interest situation is illustrative. He was convicted[2] of self-dealing by arranging, as a senior officer, and without proper approval of his Board, for part of the sale price of one of his company's newspapers to be paid to himself (and other executives), and has served jail time for it. His chain of companies, Ravelston, Hollinger, and Hollinger Inc., has been seriously devalued during the aftermath of the discovery. Therefore, other shareholders and stakeholders have been negatively impacted.

Other examples of reputational and economic impacts flowing from conflicts of interest would include the cases of rogue traders at Barings Bank or Société Générale; insider trading at Galleon Group, aided by tipsters like recently convicted Rajat Gupta; abusing clients as Goldman Sachs did during the subprime lending crisis, by selling them likely-to-fail securitized investments, and then trading against their interests; or the misuse of corporate resources at Tyco, Adelphia or HealthSouth.

The risks associated with unmanaged conflicts of interest, whether apparent or not, are now so severe that corporations are actively looking for conflicts, and putting in place codes of conduct, inquiry and guidance services, and active monitoring systems in order to identify and mitigate the risks involved. The objective is to ensure that conflicted employees are adequately counselled and supervised so that no harm results. In cases where the public is likely to perceive an apparent conflict of interests, even

---

1. "McCallion: a 'real and apparent' conflict of interest," *Toronto Star*, October 3, 2011, http://www.thestar.com/news/mississauga/article/1063465--mccallion-a-real-and-apparent-conflict-of-interest.
2. For example, "Black v. United States," Wikipedia, http://en.wikipedia.org/wiki/Black_v._United_States.

though adequate controls are in place, the corporation should take additional measures to counter potential but unfounded concern. This could involve replacing the conflicted employee, or avoiding the conflict by not pursuing the transaction or by making sure that the public misperception is corrected. In a public setting, such as that facing Mayor McCallion, the conflicted person should declare the conflict publically as soon as it is identified, and refrain from voting on any related action. Needless-to-say, in the corporate or the non-profit world, the rigor of an employee signing a code of conduct annually that specifies the need to identify, announce such conflicts, and seek guidance, is now regarded as essential to manage and mitigate conflict of interest risks.

Corporate Conflicts of Interest

The subprime lending crisis exposed the fact that some companies are strategically in conflict with one or more of their stakeholders. For example, Goldman Sachs sold unsound securities to their clients, and then traded against these securities so that the market value was undermined (*see* case insert on page 142). In so doing, a company that was expected to act in the best interests of its clients, actually acted against those interests because of favouring their own profit and liquidity objectives.

Many financial institutions and professionals have similar temptations. They have to be continuously on guard against taking advantage of their clients for their own excessive corporate gains. The issues involved in being fair to clients while still being fair to company shareholders are strategic in nature, and should be overseen in a policy sense by the board of directors, and monitored carefully by company executives and the board.

Figure 9.1 summarizes this discussion of the nature of individual and corporate conflicts of interest, the extent of management, and the relative potential impact of each on matters of reputation and economics. It should be noted that a tarnished reputation can have a far larger, longer-term impact than most employees appreciate.

Main Aspects of Conflicts of Interest

Usually conflicts of interest arise when there is an opportunity for the self-interest of a decision maker to be placed ahead of the interests he or she should be representing. Most frequently, the main inducement for improper behaviour in conflict of interest situations is financial, but sometimes inducement comes from other beneficial arrangements for directors and employees, their immediate families, or other organizations with which their employer does business. An example of a financial conflict is a purchasing agent whose spouse is a major shareholder in a supplier. An example of a non-financial conflict is when a senior officer is part of a decision-making process on an issue involving an organization that employs a family member. In not-for-profit and charitable organizations, conflicts are potentially very sensitive issues because of the fiduciary responsibilities of directors, officers, and employees, to those who provide the funding.

Conflicts of interest also arise in relation to gifts and favours received and given. Conflict arises when a person who has the responsibility for hiring finds applicants who are family members or friends. Conflicts will frequently arise when considering promotions or selection of personnel for termination or downsizing.

Misunderstandings can also give rise to conflicts of interest. Sometimes employees don't understand what they should be doing. They may be so intent on making a profit that they take unfair advantage of customers, employees, or other stakeholders, or break rules they don't understand the significance of, or both, as in the case of RT Capital Management, Inc., or of selling probably unrealizable securities to unsuspecting investors during the subprime lending fiasco. Employees may be misled by errant managers, or by how things have been done previously. Clearly, directors and officers have a responsibility to make sure that there is clear guidance about important conflicts of interest, and a supportive ethical corporate culture of shared values to ensure guidance is followed and appropriate consultation on ethical questions take place. Directors and officers have a responsibility to determine and articulate the conflict of interest strategy that their organization will observe, and then they must ensure that it is adhered to.

The RT Capital Management fiasco is a case where an employee was manipulating stock market closing prices to the detriment of a client, and expecting other team members to falsify trade records to cover up. Clearly, the employees and traders involved were focussed on their own gains, or on misplaced loyalty to their colleagues, rather than on their fiduciary duty to the company's clients and to the company itself.

Fraud by Employees

Employee fraud[3] against an employer is relatively common, and is an example of a conflict of interest in operation. Employees may also commit fraudulent, or otherwise illegal acts on behalf of their employer – *institu-*

---

3. For purposes of this chapter, employee fraud consists of fraudulent acts by employees and directors, against their employer.

tional or organizational fraud – either because they believe they are acting in accordance with their employer's wishes (for example, paying a bribe to win a contract), or because they are instructed to do so. In both cases, an effective code of ethics that covers the issue should minimize the risk of occurrence, and in the latter case, a whistleblowing mechanism may be effective if used by the employee. When an employee commits a fraudulent act ostensibly on behalf of the company, but in reality to obtain recognition and possible reward or promotion, for example by increasing his or her sales volume, then this fraud becomes a more straightforward conflict of interest situation. Enron and other recent corporate scandals are examples of both employee fraud against the company (i.e. excessive stock option gains) and institutional fraud on behalf of the company against others (i.e. misleading investors). Not surprisingly, literature on the subject of fraud is extensive.[4]

While many managers may believe that their associates and employees would rarely engage in unethical behaviour, forensic experts indicate that their experience suggests that the general population can be divided into three groups:

- 10–20 percent would never bend the rules, steal or commit a fraud
- 80–60 percent would bend the rules if they thought they could get away with it
- 10–20 percent will seek to bend the rules, steal or commit fraud regardless of what controls are in place.[5]

The accuracy of these numbers is not as important as it is for management to realise that employee fraud is not rare, and that measures need to be taken to minimize the likelihood of its occurrence. That awareness, in itself, is an ethical action. It is unfair, for example, for a company to put unnecessary temptation in an employee's way by having poor internal controls.

---

4. For example, publications like the periodical *Report on Fraud* by Kroll Linquist Avey, now Navigant Consulting, published jointly by Navigant Consulting, the Canadian Institute of Chartered Accountants, and the American Institute of Certified Public Accountants.
5. The 20/60/20 rule is based on discussions and presentations by experienced experts to the Diploma in Investigative & Forensic Accounting Program at the University of Toronto. This rule is referred to in Chapter 2.

Identifying potentially harmful situations and likely perpetrators

Recognizing High Risk Situations: The Fraud Triangle[6]

Many forensic experts believe that the following three conditions need to exist before an employee will commit a fraudulent act against an employer. They refer to these as the elements of the *Fraud Triangle*.[7]

1. There must be a *need*. For example, an employee who has serious financial problems will be more likely to steal resources from his or her employer than one who does not.
2. There must be an *opportunity* to commit the fraud with a low risk of getting caught. For example, a high risk of fraud occurring exists when an employee has access to a valuable and marketable inventory over which there are poor controls.
3. There must be some way for dishonest employees to *rationalize*[8] their fraudulent behaviour. For example, the rationale for an employee stealing stationery or computer time might be, "everyone does it," or for padding an expense report, "my boss does it." A more general rationalization might be that the employee believes – sometimes with good reason – that his or her employer does not give a damn about its employees, or regularly cheats its customers or suppliers.

Removing Risk

The first element, need, is largely beyond an employer's control, although the presence of counsellors to provide confidential advice and assistance to employees in financial and other difficulties may reduce the risk somewhat.

The second element, opportunity, can be significantly reduced by a

---

6. The Fraud Triangle and Heath's 7 rationalizations are discussed in Chapter 7, *see* Figures 7.4 and 7.5.
7. Fraud Triangle – *see* CICA Handbook Section 5135 or the new CAS 240; *see also* W. S. Albrecht, C.C. Albrecht and C.O. Albrecht. *Fraud Examination*, 2e, (Mason, Ohio: Thomson South-Western, 2006), 31.
8. Joseph Heath, in his speech, "7 Neutralization/Rationalization Techniques" at the Centre for Ethics at the University of Toronto, April 9, 2007 (Later published as "Business Ethics and Moral motivation: A Criminological Perspective," *Journal of Business Ethics* 83 (2008): 595–614.) mentions the following rationalizations (*see* Figure 7.5):
    1. Denial of responsibility.
    2. Denial of injury.
    3. Denial of the victim.
    4. Condemnation of the condemners.
    5. Appeal to higher loyalties.
    6. Everyone else is doing it.
    7. Entitlement.

strong system of internal controls, particularly over cash and other valuable assets.[9]

The third element, erroneous rationalization, can be mitigated by having a comprehensive and effective code of conduct and supporting policies. The code or policies must cover the matter in question comprehensively, for example, regarding the use of company computers for personal purposes, or policy concerning use of airline reward miles earned on company business; and must be effective in that employees must be aware of the rules, and that they are in fact applied consistently. In general, it appears that employees will be significantly less motivated to commit fraudulent or other dishonest acts against the company if they believe its business is conducted on a high ethical plane.

Information Risks: Insider Trading Rules, Chinese Walls

Sometimes corporations are concerned that their employees will use, or be seen to use, information that is confidential, or that is to be kept confidential until a specific time. This is the situation that corporate insiders face when they know something before the stock market knows it, and therefore must not use it to their own advantage. Insider trading rules are set up to prevent employees from taking unfair advantage of this knowledge by delaying their use of information until appropriate disclosure has been made to the market. Corporations often lay down rules that extend the period during which insiders cannot trade to prevent the perception that insiders are misusing inside information.

"Chinese wall" is a term euphemistically used to describe barriers intended to prevent information from passing from one part of an organization to another, so as to prevent the misuse of that information. For example, a brokerage often will be involved in underwriting a new issue of securities, and the details of the pricing and timing are known in the underwriting department. This information would be of great value to the employees of the brokerage that serve the retail clients, because the clients could then buy or sell with perfect knowledge of the coming price of the securities. Obviously, this would be unfair to the other market participants, and therefore has been declared illegal. Great care is therefore taken to erect Chinese Walls to prevent such misuse of information – rules are put in place about who cannot be told, who has access to files, how personal trades are scrutinized, how sign-off declarations are used, and so on.

---

9.   For example, *Enterprise Risk Management – Integrated Framework: Executive Summary*, Committee of Sponsoring Organizations (COSO) of the Treadway Commission, September 2004, http://www.coso.org/publications.htm.

Agency Theory and Ethics

According to agency theorists, shareholders expect and hope that managers, and in turn, non-managerial employees will behave in line with the goals set for the corporation. In their terms, the principals or shareholders hope that their agents will be motivated to act as the principals wish. Incentive systems and punishment systems are created to try to influence the agents to stay on the right path and avoid situations involving *moral hazard*. Clearly, as the public's expectations for corporate performance now include ethical standards, the reward and punishment systems set up should also reflect ethical dimensions, or shareholders are going to be disappointed. In fact, the corporation's strategic plans should include ethical dimensions to ensure that their agents, both inside and outside the corporation, are properly influenced, and conflicts of interest are avoided.

Management to Avoid and Minimize Consequences

As indicated earlier, *conflicts of interest are almost impossible to avoid, so the emphasis should be on increasing awareness of the dilemmas involved, and on how to manage to minimize their impact.*

Awareness Training

The first step in the process of managing to defend against these influences is to ensure that all employees are aware of their existence and consequences. This can be done through mission statements, codes of conduct, and related training. One of the items that should be covered in the training is the *slippery slope problem* where an individual can be enticed into a relationship by a seemingly innocuous request for a small favour, and then a larger one, and then find themselves being told that unless they go along with a serious infraction, their past favours will be revealed. The start of the slope is too gentle for some to notice, but the slope becomes steeper and more slippery very quickly. In this area, it is important to set specific policies and communicate them. For example, personal use of air mile rewards earned on company business may be allowed or disallowed. If allowed, policies must include requirements to prevent employees taking unnecessarily circuitous routes to their destinations. The important thing is for employees, and their bosses, to know where they stand. The same applies to personal use of company computers. It may be totally forbidden, or it may be permitted, or even encouraged at designated times, and within certain limits of time and subject matter. Ford Motor Company attempted to resolve this matter imaginatively by giving their employees a personal computer of their own.

Understanding the Reasons Motivating the Training

The second step is to create an understanding of the reasons why the employer has developed guidelines to prevent conflicts of interest from occurring, their exploration though counselling if recognized, their reporting if they are identified as having occurred, and the penalties for their occurrence and non-reporting. These understandings can be reinforced by annual written confirmations of ethical behaviour and adherence to the employer's code of conduct that could include reference to conflicts of interest encountered by the signatory, and those identified involving others.

Guidelines and Consultation

The company's code of conduct should provide the rationale for avoiding conflicts of interest, what they are, how to avoid them, and what to do if an employee discovers that he or she is involved in one, or suspects that they might be. Consultation with a superior or an ethics officer is often warranted, and frequently used for clarification of issues of concern. Prior consultation is to be encouraged in order to avoid problems arising or becoming more serious.

Additional guidelines can be quite useful as supplements to codes of conduct. One helpful set of guidelines are those that clarify when it may be acceptable to give or accept a gift or preferential treatment. A useful series of questions to ask in this regard would be:

1. Is it nominal or substantial?
2. What is the intended purpose?
3. What are the circumstances?
4. What is the sensitivity (i.e. the real or apparent culpability) of the recipient?
5. What is the accepted practice for the company or the country?
6. What is the firm or company policy?
7. Is it legal?

As indicated in the section on ethical decision making, these questions can act as sniff tests. If a problem is identified, then the employee, senior officer, or ethics officer should conduct a full stakeholder impact analysis using one or more of the decision-making approaches outlined above based on consequentialism, and involving duty, rights, fairness and expected virtues.

Reinforcement, Monitoring and Compliance

Conflicts of interest can undermine an organization's values and reputation quickly and significantly. They must be featured in the company's reinforcement, monitoring, and compliance mechanisms on a regular basis, so that company employees, officers, and directors remain sensitized to potential conflicts of interest, and aware of the remedies and the penalties for involvement. Company personnel must appreciate that conflicts of interest are an important dimension of the annual sign-off and company monitoring mechanisms.

Useful References

Canadian Institute of Chartered Accountants. *Conflict of Interest: A Task Force Report*, (Toronto: September 15, 2000).

Navigant Consulting, *Investigations Quarterly (IQ), 2007–* , previously *Report on Fraud, published by Navigant Consulting, Kroll Linquist Avey, the CICA and the AICPA. 1999–2006.*

Additional Readings and Useful References will noted on http://www.ethicscentre.ca.

Checklist – Special Topics	
Conflicts of Interest	
✓	Training Program/Ethics Workshop
	• Includes conflicts of interest material identifying:
	○ Apparent Conflicts
	○ Potential Conflicts
	• Includes conflicts of interest material on the management of:
	○ Apparent Conflicts
	○ Potential Conflicts
	○ Actual Conflicts
	• Includes material on:
	○ Employee fraud

	○ Institutional or organizational fraud
	○ The Fraud Triangle
	○ Information risks
	• Insider training
	• Chinese Walls
	○ Agency theory
	○ Slippery Slope problems
Organizational Codes, Guidelines & Policies	
• Include:	
	○ Rationale for avoidance
	○ Management of risk
	○ Consultation with superior or ethics officer
	○ Guidance for gifts, bribes
• Reinforcement mechanisms	
• Monitoring mechanisms	
• Compliance mechanisms	

Special Topics

Chapter 10
Financial Services and the Subprime Mortgage Crisis
– A Special Case

The 2008 subprime mortgage collapse in the United States and its ramifications require special emphasis and consideration. It was caused by a mixture of bad policy, poor business practice, naivety and widespread highly unethical (and in some cases illegal) conduct. Sorting out the key corporate ethics issues is easy with respect to the most egregious cases of dealing in bad faith, conflict of interest and outright fraud. These occurred virtually throughout the financial services industry, from mortgage brokers, to intermediaries that packaged very high risk loans into products that they sold as relatively low risk investments, to the credit rating agencies that hugely inflated their ratings, to Wall Street traders and CEOs of major and not so major financial institutions. Other aspects are more nuanced. For example, to what extent is a home buyer behaving unethically when he or she signs a mortgage they know they will not be able to repay unless home prices keep rising? Most would say such people are victims, rather than unethical. For unsophisticated homeowners, this is probably accurate. However, for a speculator who buys several houses, one would tend to be less generous, even if the speculator was unsophisticated. And is a political system that espouses the impossible dream of every American owning a home unethical? Or is it just bad political policy?

Nevertheless, egregiously unethical conduct clearly occurred at all levels of the U.S. financial services industry, including at some of the largest corporations in the world, and to some extent among regulators as well. Books have been, and will continue to be, written about this fiasco, and a detailed description is well beyond the scope of this small chapter. So our focus will be to highlight a few of the ethical lapses within the industry and suggest some possible preventative measures. Legislation and regulation have been tightened somewhat, but the enormous political pressure that the American banks and other institutions can exert on Congress severely limits what is possible. The primary solution must be to insist on more ethical governance processes and internal policing within financial institutions, especially given that fundamental conflicts of interest have not been removed. Retail banks will still be allowed to trade on their own account in potential conflict with their depositors; and investment banks will still be allowed to trade in and underwrite investments that they advise their clients to buy, sell or hold.

Brief description of the 2008 crisis[1]

The immediate trigger of the crisis was a collapse in the U.S. housing market that rendered much mortgage debt uncollectible and related derivative securitized products virtually worthless. However, existing underlying conditions enormously exacerbated the problem. Mortgage lenders had sold mortgages that they knew would be never be collected up the line to larger financial institutions, larger institutions then packaged them, obtained AAA ratings from rating agencies that were conflicted, and sold them to unsuspecting customers (many of whom were supposed to be sophisticated), after which they were insured by credit default swaps issued by other large institutions. The entire process was oiled all the way up by copious fees and bonuses, enabling institutions to keep their fees but pass the risk on until the collapse. Some financial institutions even bet against their clients by selling short the securities they had earlier sold.

Furthermore, this scenario was superimposed on a financial system that was already well along the road to what is termed "casino capitalism." Trillions of dollars changed hands as derivative financial instruments in transactions that had virtually no connection to real economic activity. In this system, those in charge, and top traders, earned enormous commissions, salaries and bonuses for their roles in pushing uncollectible or toxic mortgages or in trading related securities such as credit default swaps that were, in reality, just sham transactions.

---

1. Wikipedia's entry under the title "Subprime Mortgage Crisis" is not only an excellent summary description of the crisis, but contains over 250 references and over 30 suggested readings and external links.

Credit Default Swaps (CDSs), Naked and Otherwise

Credit default swaps are financial instruments that were originally intended to manage the risk of default that arises from holding debt. A bank, for example, may hedge its risk that a borrower may default on a loan by entering into a CDS contract as the buyer of protection. If the loan goes into default, the proceeds from the CDS contract cancel out the losses on the underlying debt. CDS contracts are negotiable instruments, and can be extremely complex; they took on a life of their own and eventually traded in enormous volumes (reportedly over $26 trillion in 2010 – many times greater than any underlying debt, and way beyond the power of the issuers to pay out if the original debt defaulted). By buying a credit default swap, a lender such as a bank can lay off default risk while still keeping the loan in its portfolio. The downside to this hedge is that without default risk, a bank may have no motivation to actively monitor the loan and the counterparty has no relationship to the borrower.

A "naked" CDS (NCDS) is essentially a CDS issued by an institution that does not own, or have an insurable interest, in the loan that is insured, resulting in an almost unlimited volume of insurance that can cause financial havoc if a loan goes into default and the issuing party cannot pay. Trading in NCDSs is high risk gambling, with little or no benefit to anyone other than those who collect fees along the way. The winners, of course win big – the losers lose the same. The financier George Soros famously called for an outright ban on them, viewing them as "toxic" and allowing speculators to bet against companies or countries.

CDSs were a major contributing factor in the 2008 financial crisis and the subsequent government bail out because the issuing parties (notably AIG) were unable to pay out on the insurance losses incurred. This caused a liquidity crisis that affected banks and other financial institutions around the world.

Ethical lapses

It can reasonably be argued that a strong ethical culture throughout the financial services industry could have averted, or at least significantly ameliorated, the crisis. Examples of ethical lapses include:

- Making mortgage loans to people known to be unable to repay them, and compounding the problem by knowingly selling them up the line for a fee. This is not alleviated by the knowledge that the purchasing institutions will probably, in turn, market the loan to other investors, again for a fee.

- Falsifying or creating fictitious documentation to support foreclosure proceedings, or simply not documenting at all, with the result that some foreclosures were found to be illegal in retrospect.
- Packaging worthless mortgages as AAA rated paper (with the collusion of the rating agencies – also a serious ethical problem) and selling them to larger financial institutions and investors. Many of these investors were sophisticated, and should have known better, but were frequently given inaccurate information on which to base their decision.
- Generic conflicts of interest in financial institutions between their own interests (which include interests of shareholders and senior executives who profit through bonuses) and those of their clients. This occurs, for example, when:
  - banks and brokerage firms are allowed to trade on their own account as well as on behalf of clients, whether or not the conflicts are to the detriment of clients (which in fact happened)
  - investment banks underwrite stocks and provide advice to clients on whether to buy those stocks
  - bond rating agencies are paid by the companies they rate
- The fact that such generic conflicts exist is the fault of legislators and regulators who permit them. Within the industry, many do not manage them effectively. Payment of outrageous bonuses causes actions to be taken with the primary purpose of obtaining the maximum bonus possible. This is exacerbated when, as is often the case, bonuses are tied to trading volumes rather than the bottom line, so that bonuses are paid even when profits are down or non-existent. In short, many bonuses in the finance industry encouraged unethical, high risk behaviours.
- When the existence of conflicts of interest causes institutions to take advantage of them to the detriment of clients and investors, and at the same time enriches traders and executives. For example, when a company advises clients to make investments in instruments that it is short selling for its own account, such as was the case with Goldman Sachs.
- Unethical cultures within financial market institutions that result in clients being "fair game" or, as Goldman Sachs apparently referred to them internally, as "Muppets." In other words, there is a total lack of any fiduciary responsibility among senior management.

Examples of Values Gone Awry at Goldman Sachs and Merrill Lynch

The following cases illustrate what can happen when values go awry. Whatever codes of conduct and regulations might have existed, the influence of greed overwhelmed ethical conduct.

Resignation for Values Deterioration at Goldman Sachs (Goldman)

Allegations of serious impropriety and perhaps illegality surrounding Goldman's contribution to the 2008 crisis have been well publicized. Allegations included trading for their own benefit directly against the interests of its clients (e.g., the ABACUS deal involved deliberately stuffing collateralized debt obligations (CDOs) with inferior mortgage assets, selling them to clients, and then short selling them for their own account) and abusive practices generally).[2]

The underlying values associated with this kind of activity were obviously deficient. This was further illustrated in 2012 when Greg Smith, head of Goldman's U.S. equity derivatives business in Europe, Africa and the Middle East, wrote an Op-Ed piece in the New York Times (March 14, 2012) about his resignation,[3] due to the appalling deterioration of the firm's culture. Goldman's old culture had previously been recognized for its ethicality, that he describes as revolving around "teamwork, integrity, a spirit of humility, and always doing right by your clients." The new culture he describes as "toxic" and "destructive."

Here are some quotes from his article:

> To put the problem in the simplest terms, the interests of the client continue to be sidelined in the way the firm operates and thinks about making money.

> Leadership (in Goldman) used to be about ideas, setting an example and doing the right thing. Today, if you make enough money for the firm... you will be promoted into a position of influence.

> It makes me ill how callously people talk about ripping their clients off. Over the last 12 months I have seen five different managing directors refer to their own clients as "muppets"...

---

2. *See for example*: BBC News, "Goldman Sachs accused of misleading investors," April 14, 2011, a report based on testimony at the US Senate Permanent Committee on Investigations, http://www.bbc.co.uk/news/business-13077509.

3. Greg Smith, "Why I Am Leaving Goldman Sachs," *The New York Times*, March 14, 2012, http://www.nytimes.com/2012/03/14/opinion/why-i-am-leaving-goldman-sachs.html?pagewanted=all (accessed March 30, 2012).

He elucidates on what he believes to be the three quick ways to become a leader at Goldman:

a) persuading your clients to invest in stocks or other products that Goldman was trying to get rid of because they were not seen as being sufficiently profitable (described as the firm's "axes")

b) "Hunt Elephants", that is, persuade your clients to buy the products that are the most profitable for Goldman rather than what is best for the client

c) trade "any illiquid, opaque product with a three letter acronym"

Of course, Goldman disputes this view of its practice, but Smith's interpretation intuitively explains how it, and other firms with similar cultures, got so far off the rails. It is also worthy of note that this culture is said to exist in 2012, long after the 2008 crisis and subsequent fall out, suggesting that the lessons have not been learned and the problems are at least as bad as they were before the crisis.

Naked Short-selling –
Overstock.com Law Suit against Goldman Sachs & Merrill Lynch

Overstock.com, also known as O Co., is an online retailer of overstocked merchandise. In May 2007, O Co. successfully sued various brokers and hedge funds for colluding to damage its stock. Two of these suits, against Goldman and Merrill, are ongoing, alleging that these firms collusively urged their clients to take out naked short sales on the stock, thereby driving down its price. Much of the evidence presented by the defence is currently under a publication ban, but an error by legal representatives released some into the public domain in May 2012, as reported in *The Economist*,[4] and other sources. The result is further evidence of appalling ethical values, even if not illegalities. Much of the released evidence is in the form of e-mails.

E-mail excerpts show that stock deliveries on short-sale trades were being intentionally failed in both firms to the detriment of clients (even though the firms had millions of shares available) and that Merrill's compliance officers described some of this conduct as totally unacceptable (but were ignored). In theory, short selling is supposed to be done when the seller has made arrangements to deliver shares in order that the total shares sold should not exceed the number of borrowable shares.

---

4. "An enlightening mistake," *The Economist*, May 15, 2012, http://www.economist.com/node/21555472 (accessed May 22, 2012).

Naked short selling (without specific ties to shares) permits the number of shares sold to expand to any level thus driving down prices abnormally, and to the great disadvantage of existing shareholders. *The Economist* also reports that a Merrill senior executive, "responded to internal concerns about failed trades thus: 'F__k the compliance area – procedures, schmecedures'"

Short of wholesale firings, fines and jail terms, coupled with much stronger regulation, it is very hard to see how such egregiously toxic ethical cultures can be corrected, once entrenched. Time will tell, but as of 2012, there is little evidence of any major improvements. A total change in leadership at the very top would seem to be a prerequisite, but not necessarily enough to fix the problem.

What can be done?

By government and regulators

- Much of the problem can theoretically be solved, or at least mitigated by tougher legislation and regulation, but this is unlikely to happen because:
  - ○ financial market institutions oppose it tooth and nail, and have enormous political clout in the USA and, to a somewhat lesser extent, in other major countries
  - ○ any regulation has to be international to be effective, and is therefore even less likely to happen. This is exacerbated by the fact that some countries actively encourage shady transactions, although they will not openly admit it. Unless a company is in the tourism business, for example, or a supplier of goods or services to countries such as The Cayman Islands, there is usually no legitimate economic reason to have any dealings there. Governments could tax all such transactions at a punitive rate. They don't, possibly because too many influential people and corporations take advantage of the existence of such countries
- Examples of things that could be done by governments and regulators are:
  - ○ Prohibition of, or taxes on, financial transactions, especially those that are not directly related to real economic events
  - ○ Prohibition or punitive taxes on transactions with financial institutions in "rogue nations"
  - ○ Controls over trading in derivatives that parallel those over stock trades

○ Ban on naked credit default swaps, naked short selling, and similar instruments or transactions

○ An effective ban on institutions both handling funds on behalf of clients and trading on their own accounts (The *Dodd-Frank Act* in the USA was intended to do this, but has left loopholes, and no doubt more will be found)

○ Making rating agencies more independent and accountable

○ Further tightening the availability of mortgage loans (*Dodd-Frank* took some steps in this direction – see insert below – but not to the extent operative in most other developed nations, including Canada)

○ Legislating caps on fees, salaries and bonuses

○ Greatly increasing the quality and quantity of resources applied to enforcement, and the penalties for misfeasance; and finally

○ Recognizing that clever financial operators assisted by clever lawyers will find ways to get round specific regulations, draft regulations in such a way that they deal with values, rather than with transactions. This may not be possible in the U.S. because of its legalistic environment, but it may be possible in other countries and would therefore apply to business U.S. firms conduct in those countries. For example, instead of writing regulations to prohibit certain specific kinds of trading activity, have them state simply that companies may not take any position, undertake any transaction, or establish any process that is contrary to the interests of its investor clients. Unfortunately regulators may then try to write hundreds of specific prohibitions to "interpret" the values-based prohibition

Is regulation a solution? The Dodd-Frank Act[5]

After the subprime lending fiasco, many people asked: Can government legislation and regulation cleanse the ethical cesspool in the financial services industry? The answer is yes, partly, but not completely. It is the only option for controlling unethical behaviour in corporations or senior management that otherwise have no intention of cleaning up their own act (they simply do not believe ethical conduct is important enough to override activity to increase this year's bonuses). The advantage of good legislation and regulation is that it can:

---

5. The *Dodd-Frank Wall Street Reform and Consumer Protection Act* was signed by U.S. President Barack Obama on July 21, 2010.

- Put a stop to specified unethical and high risk activities
- Require financial cushions against unforeseen circumstances
- Improve transparency through disclosure
- Create properly controlled markets for financial instruments such as derivatives
- Ban certain kinds of instruments, such as naked credit default swaps
- Force corporations to divest specified conflict of interest activities

Unfortunately, there are severe limits to what can be accomplished by legislation and regulation:

- The financial services industry always uses its political clout to water down legislation and create exemptions (as happened with *Dodd-Frank* and ensuing regulation)
- The industry is usually smart enough to find ways around specific regulations
- Regulators themselves become subject to political influence, such that enforcement is spotty, particularly when resources and budgets are shrunk, as has been the case in many countries

In theory, regulation could be values-based, rather than prescriptive and in detail. In practice this is not possible in the United States, and difficult to enforce elsewhere, although Canada's approach to banking regulation through the Superintendant of Financial Institutions has been relatively successful. Even international initiatives to control risks in the banking sector are very detailed and prescriptive.

The primary American regulatory response to the 2008 financial crisis has been the so-called *Dodd-Frank Act*, which incorporates the so-called Volker Rule intended to prohibit depositary banks from risking funds in proprietary trading. This was signed into law in July, 2010.

This legislation is comprehensive, complex,[6] and covers many areas beyond the interest of this book. The main components are:

1. A somewhat watered down version of the Volker Rule, such that banks are permitted to perform certain limited proprietary trading (e.g., for hedging purposes).

---

6. There are thousands of regulations, mostly dealing with various provisos and exemptions inserted due to the lobbying of the financial services industry and politicians beholden to them.

2. Tighter reporting of, and shareholder input to, executive compensation and "golden parachutes."
3. Empowerment of the Federal Reserve to impose risk based capital requirements.
4. Measures aimed at preventing predatory lending practices, particularly for residential mortgages.
5. Establishing a derivatives Exchange (although its effectiveness was significantly watered down).
6. Some restrictions on the creation of asset backed securities and securitization processes generally.
7. Certain controls on the activities of investment advisors, hedge funds and private equity firms.
8. More onerous requirements for credit rating agencies.

However, corporate conduct coming to light subsequent to implementation shows that opportunities for excessive greed and unethical conduct still abound.[7] Perhaps the most optimistic aspect is that many investment institutions strongly opposed it, which means that it must have some merits. Nevertheless, some Wall Street advocates have supported it, but perhaps because they feel that something worse (for them) could have happened.

Specifically, *Dodd-Frank* shied away from abolishing certain toxic financial transactions that amount to pure gambling, with little or no connection to real economic activity. Certain derivatives fall into this category – e.g., naked credit default swaps, see the insert box.

In conclusion, sound regulation and enforcement thereof can be positive for corporate ethical behaviour. *Dodd-Frank* helps; perhaps it helps a lot. It should help those in charge of governance who genuinely wish to maintain high ethical standards, but it is not a substitute for internally developed values and conduct that reflects those values.

Actions by educational institutions

- In the most basic sense, public attitudes towards consumption and debt led in some respect to the crisis. Better public education might have some benefit in reducing the possibility of recurrence of this crisis. The public and private school systems could be required to include basic financial literacy courses. However, getting people to curb their own desires is unlikely, so the best that can be hoped for

---

7. For example, the failure in 2012 of JPMorgan Chase to prevent a $2 billion loss (and maybe more) on a position taken by its investment office (*The Economist* May 19–25 2012, p. 79)

is an improved recognition by the general public of financial scams and other frauds. Nevertheless, many of those who were duped were sophisticated investors, not to mention regulators, so this approach is an inadequate solution at best.

- Business schools, on the other hand, educate the people who are likely to become key players on Wall Street, whether as CEO, CFO, CCO or another managerial position. It is therefore incumbent on these schools to attempt to instill into their charges an attitude of integrity, service to clients and ethics.
- This may require a change in approach, as pointed out by Peter Henry, Dean of NYU Stern.[8] He said, "Every economic crisis seems to evoke a renewed call for business schools to redouble their emphasis on ethics. The repeated nature of these exhortations suggests that the problem may not be a lack of attention to the issue but the need for thoughtful new approaches." He plans to bring his knowledge to bear upon questions of design for ethical business systems.

By financial institutions themselves

Whatever can be done by governments, regulators and educational institutions, no solution is possible without major changes in the ethical conduct of the financial market institutions themselves. Since there is very unlikely to be much help from governments and legislators, at least in the USA, the burden is placed on those in charge of governance in these financial institutions.

What might Boards of Directors and CEOs do to improve ethical conduct in their industry? There is, of course, reason to question if those in charge of governance want to behave more ethically. There is evidence that they do not, as the Goldman and Merrill cases above demonstrate, and the insert below on corporate psychopaths suggests. It may even be that effective governance will make things worse (i.e. miscreants will become more effective at being unethical!). However, this chapter takes an optimistic view about ethical intent, and focuses further commentary on improved governance for large and medium sized financial institutions. There are also issues of governance for smaller players, such as mortgage brokers, real estate agents, small banks, and other loan institutions, but they are too diverse to generalize, and heavily dependent on the ethical bent of the CEO.

8. "Renowned Social Psychologist Jonathan Haidt Joins MY Stern School of Business", Press Release, New York Stern School of Business, May 9, 2012, http://www.stern.nyu.edu/experience-stern/news-events/haidt-joins-stern (accessed May 31, 2012).

Corporate psychopaths

(Source: *Journal of Business Ethics*, Spring 2011 article by Clive R. Boddy)

The Spring 2011 issue of the *Journal of Business Ethics* contains a short theoretical article that presents a plausible theory about the Global Financial Crisis and the role of senior financial corporate directors in that crisis. It argues that psychopaths working in financial corporations have played a major role in causing the crisis. The paper discusses significant ways in which they may have caused havoc and refers to a growing body of academic research on the issue.

The question raised is how traditional financial institutions with decades-long sterling reputations end up with leaders who appear devoid of ethical values and who demonstrate poor leadership that enables unethical and high risk conduct by management employees. This can occur when the primary motivating force within an organization is bonus maximization, even at the expense of the interests of long-standing clients.

The following quote sets out the subject of the article and a definition of the term:

> In watching these events unfold it often appears that the senior directors involved walk away with a clean conscience and huge amounts of money. Further, they seem to be unaffected by the corporate collapses they have created. They present themselves as glibly unbothered by the chaos around them, unconcerned about those who have lost their jobs, savings, and investments, and as lacking any regrets about what they have done. They cheerfully lie about their involvement in events, are very persuasive in blaming others for what has happened and have no doubts about their own continued worth and value. They are happy to walk away from the economic disaster that they have managed to bring about, with huge payoffs and with new roles advising governments how to prevent such economic disasters. Many of these people display several of the characteristics of psychopaths and some of them are undoubtedly true psychopaths. Psychopaths are the 1% of people who have no conscience or empathy and who do not care for anyone other than themselves. Some psychopaths are violent and end up in jail, others forge careers in corporations. Members of the latter group are called Corporate Psychopaths and, it is argued, are highly attracted to financial institutions.

Expert commentators on the rise of Corporate Psychopaths

within modern corporations have also hypothesized that they are more likely to be found at the top of current organizations than at the bottom. Further, that if this is the case, then this phenomenon will have dire consequences for the organisations concerned and for the societies in which those organisations are based.

There is also some evidence that they may tend to join some types of organisations rather than others and that, for example, large financial organisations may be attractive to them because of the potential rewards on offer in these organizations. (Boddy, 2010a).

The Corporate Psychopaths Theory of the Global Financial Crisis is that Corporate Psychopaths, rising to key senior positions within modern financial corporations, where they are able to influence the moral climate of the whole organization and yield considerable power, have largely caused the crisis. In these senior corporate positions, the Corporate Psychopath's single-minded pursuit of their own self-enrichment and self-aggrandizement to the exclusion of all other considerations has led to an abandonment of the old fashioned concept of noblesse oblige, equality, fairness, or of any real notion of corporate social responsibility. The Corporate Psychopaths Theory of the Global Financial Crisis argues that changes in the way people are employed have facilitated the rise of Corporate Psychopaths to senior positions and their personal greed in those positions has created the crisis.

To the extent that this theory holds true (and there are those who do not agree with it), the only solutions would appear to be vigilantly monitoring such people, or keeping them out of senior management positions in any institution that owes any fiduciary duty through managing other people's money, or which can do severe damage to an economy through excessive risk taking. Obviously, the most effective way of achieving this is to not hire them in the first place. Therefore, Directors and Hiring Committees need to be aware of this issue and take steps to assess the moral character of applicants, perhaps employing experts to help in the assessment. Another deterrent is to establish reward mechanisms that do not encourage psychopaths. For example, bonuses should:

- discourage excessive risk-taking
- focus on long-term success
- be able to be clawed back if those already paid, payable or accrued can be linked to inappropriate conduct
- link bonuses to success for all key stakeholders, not just the bottom (or, even worse, the top) line

Also, so-called "golden parachutes" should not be payable when an employee is terminated for cause or resigns. In fact, it may be prudent for companies to eschew such parachutes altogether.

If all else fails, and corporate psychopaths are already entrenched, Directors and senior management should have the means to identify them and fire them, or at least keep them on a very short leash (at which point they might well leave of their own accord). All these steps are made more difficult by the fact that these people are likely charming and very persuasive.

In short, Directors and senior management should be on the look out for key individuals in any organization who appear to have no moral compass at all. At present, it is unlikely that this is happening except rarely and episodically.

There are several recommendations that hold promise for Boards of Directors who wish to avoid ethical catastrophes and business and reputational risk such as were faced during the subprime mortgage crisis. Most of these recommendations are prudent business steps, as well as ethical ones:

- Make sure the CEO constantly reinforces and exemplifies the need for ethical conduct and in particular, fair treatment of clients. Among other steps, this must be built in to the performance appraisal and reward system.
- Make sure that the code of ethics is comprehensive in terms of basic principles and specific for trading activities. The principles in the rest of this book concerning developing, maintaining and enforcing a code should be applied with rigour. In particular, an effective whistleblowing mechanism needs to be in place, with timely reporting to the Board.
- Make sure management can explain, in terms all the directors understand, the nature of all financial activities undertaken by the firm, especially the more esoteric derivates and other financial instruments.
- Make sure the CEO, senior officers and internal auditors fully understand all the financial activities of the institution.
- All activities should have a purpose and execution that is sound economically and ethically.
- Exhaustively examine all bonus provisions to ensure that they are not linked to, or encourage, high risk or unethical activities. Approve all bonuses and ensure that they are fair to investors and clients. Preferably have an overriding clause in bonus agreements to

prevent large bonuses that deplete the value of the company in hard times.

- Exhaustively examine all new major internal, and especially external, appointments. Directors should explicitly sign-off that they have carefully considered the ethical values and mindset of the applicants and are completely satisfied. For example, an applicant's CV that contains any untruths or egregious mistakes should be an automatic disqualification, irrespective of their technical qualifications and experience. Is there evidence that applicants have demonstrated a willingness to champion values congruent with the company's policies and strategy, and/or have they been specifically considered for any evidence of psychopathic tendencies? Outside expertise would be appropriate here.
- On the same basis, re-examine all senior appointments on a regular basis (say every three years).
- Appoint a sub-committee to oversee high-risk activity on a daily basis, and have personal contact with individuals conducting such activity. Rotate personnel conducting these oversight activities so that they do not become too close to those they are overseeing.
- Identify all potential conflict of interest situations and ensure that they are not being improperly used to the advantage of the company or individuals within it. If there are so-called "Chinese walls," make sure they work in practice to the extent possible.
- Give wide-ranging powers for an ethics or values audit to the internal audit department to investigate and have access to all activities, and report regularly to the Board.
- From time to time survey the Boards of the company's primary counterparties to see if there is important feedback concerning trading activities. This could be done by the internal and external auditors.
- Have the Chief Compliance Officer (CCO) report directly to the Board and approve any transactions that are undertaken against the advice of the CCO.
- Via the audit committee, make sure that the external auditors fully understand all financial transactions and require them to report in writing whether they have found breaches of laws, regulations, the internal code of ethics or any other suspicious transactions or practices.
- Consider meeting with the company's regulators to discuss outstanding issues and assess whether the regulator has any concerns about the company's activities or particular personnel.

- As part of normal risk management procedures, require the preparation of an annual report on the nature of customer and employee complaints received, to be submitted to the Board, with an analysis of the ethical values involved and needing redress.

The most important role for the CEO is to show by leadership that he or she insists on integrity, fairness and transparency throughout the company and, in particular, scrupulously fair treatment of, and respect for, the interests of clients and other stakeholders (e.g., counterparties to financial transactions). The CEO should be heavily involved in salary and bonus determinations and should ensure that unethical conduct is monitored and not rewarded. Employees who transgress should be visibly disciplined and reasons why they are penalized explained. The CEO should meet regularly with key trading personnel and others in a position to create significant risk for the entity. In these meetings (collective or one-on-one) he or she must always, without exception, cover the importance of unethical conduct.

Concluding Thoughts

The Subprime Lending fiasco was due to a failure of ethics on many dimensions. It showed how interrelated all capital markets are now globally, and how important improved ethical behaviour is worldwide. It also revealed the propensities of the financial services industry toward unethical behaviour and exposed its aversion to tight regulation so that such behaviour could continue legally unbridled. Given that clever determined people will look for and find loopholes in regulations, they are only a partial remedy. Corporate self-regulation through good governance, in the form of development and maintenance of a culture of integrity, is much more likely to produce responsible, ethical behaviour in the future. Education of all – from directors, to executives, managers and particularly potential shareholders – is essential to fostering an ethical future.

Special Topics

Chapter 11
International Operations

When a corporation operates outside its domestic market, the guidance offered employees should include:

- How their usual operating practices will impact on the local economy and culture
- How to react to requests for bribes, facilitating payments and other special favours
- How to react to improper operations and bribes or facilitating payments by domestic stakeholders, particularly by primary stakeholders,[1] including major customers and capital markets

Impacts on local economies and their cultures

Multinational corporations may have a significant impact on local cultures that they would not have domestically. For example, they may have significant impacts on local:

- Labour markets including wage rates and supply
- Raw material and other input markets
- Political and legal processes
- Environmental conditions
- Religious and social customs

---

1. According to current thinking about the role of stakeholders (*see* Chapter 2), the support of the corporation's primary stakeholders is necessary for the corporation to achieve its medium– and long–term strategic objectives.

If a multinational ignores local religious or social customs, it and its workers may be accused of *cultural imperialism*, and may find it difficult to obtain cooperation for future activities. Similarly, by virtue of its size, a multinational may so dominate the locale that there may be an unintended domination of local governments, courts, or elections that again may produce a backlash at some point.

Conflicts between domestic and foreign cultures

Perhaps the most difficult problems arise when the values of the primary corporate stakeholders differ from those in the local foreign country. Differences noted in the media in recent years have included:

- Bribery. Although bribes are illegal virtually everywhere, they are accepted in practice in many countries, but only as long as they receive no publicity. Facilitating payments (see below) are accepted even more widely, and some regard them as akin to tips that are paid to service providers in most Western cultures.
- Use of child labour. This is viewed as an essential component of the economy in many poorer countries, yet it is considered as unacceptable by many in developed nations.
- Use of prison labour. This has been an issue in China, although some states in the U.S. and at least one Canadian province use, or have recently used, prison labour.
- Unhealthy labour conditions. Fatal fires in Thai toy factories resulted in widespread publicity.
- Treatment of women. Attitudes towards women in the workforce differ significantly across different cultures.
- Support of repressive regimes through location of operations. There are arguments within the developed world as to whether or not there is a net benefit to those who live under oppressive regimes as trade and investment increase. The United Nations and individual governments establish boycotts of certain countries for human rights abuses, and consumers now boycott companies that do not avoid such abuses. Companies need to be careful to look beyond the local labour laws in a foreign country, and respect international and home government directives. It is also wise to consider adopting a policy to strive at all times to improve the lot of those they employ or deal with, or at least to not take a direct part in the repressive aspects of a regime's practices.
- Respect for environment. Environmental standards may be lower

in undeveloped countries, or the standards are not effectively enforced.
- Dealings with family members. What in the West could be called
nepotism may be regarded in some countries as acceptable, or even
desirable.

Operating in foreign jurisdictions can lead to unexpected ethical dilemmas, and the need to modify application of an organization's code to take
account of these circumstances. An illustration of this follows.

Illustrative Case: Making the Best of Bad Choices

This case illustrates that it is sometimes necessary to temporarily aban-
don established ethical principles to bring about a greater good. But this
needs to be done rarely, and must be well-thought out and justifiable.

Some years ago a multinational company wished to operate a mine
in a Third World country. To get permission, they had to come to terms
with the needs of the native tribe that lived in the area. The company
was convinced that the benefits in infrastructure and income to the local
population were positive, and the locals agreed and were enthusiastic.
After much negotiation they reached an agreement. In due course, the
signing ceremony was arranged, with dignitaries from the company,
the host government, and the local tribe present. Then, at the very last
minute, the chief approached the head negotiator for the company with
an extra demand – that the company should agree that it would not employ anyone on the project from the next tribe down the river!

How was the company to deal with this? It had a firm principle that
it would not discriminate in employment on grounds of, among other
things, ethnic origin. Agreeing to this would clearly breach that principle.
On the other hand, holding up the signing ceremony, and potentially the
project, on this issue would do enormous harm to a range of stakeholders. So a decision was made, and subsequently carefully documented, to
agree to this change on the grounds of supporting the greater good. At
the same time an internal commitment was made to try to persuade the
tribe to change their attitude during the course of the contract, or as soon
as possible. There was of course a risk that this would not succeed, but
on the other hand there was the possibility that, if they were successful
in changing their minds, the company might achieve an improvement in
relations between two tribes with currently hostile relations.

This case illustrates that companies may consider acting contrary to
specific principles when to do so would result in a greater good to most
stakeholders and do no serious harm to others. When this is necessary,

however, it is essential that the decision be made with the *utmost care and consideration*. In the above example, the decision was relatively easy because the alternative would have potentially been catastrophic for all concerned. The company may also choose to benefit the disadvantaged tribe in another way. In other cases, the decision will be more nuanced, but the principles remain the same.

Corporations may locate operations in a country primarily because they want access to cheap labour, lower environmental protection costs, or less governmental red tape, and they are often invited to come by local politicians who offer what they can by way of inducements. Why then should businesspeople worry about taking advantage of these opportunities when they find them? The reason lies in the new broader and *global accountability* that stakeholders expect and demand of corporations. Putting it simply, influential stakeholder groups have made it very difficult for corporations caught offending their values anywhere in the world. The most obvious examples relate to the clothing, sports gear, and toy industries. Major retailers and manufacturers have been compelled by public pressure to ensure that abusive labour practices that have occurred in the past have been eliminated. This has happened even when the company had been previously unaware of the abuses.

The growth of the internet in recent years has made it virtually impossible for any multinational to isolate, or keep secret, knowledge of the conditions of local communities. If abuse is occurring, and a company has no processes for discovering it, the risk is that they will first hear about it over the internet, at the same time as thousands of others, and not be able to prevent or minimize resulting damage.

In addition, environmental and personal disasters such as at Bhopal, caused by Union Carbide's poorly maintained plant; and in Ecuador, caused by oil spills from a pipeline built by Texaco; have resulted in lawsuits launched or endorsed by the same foreign governments that had invited the companies in, and even entreated them to stay in adverse circumstances. In addition, in response to such disasters, lawsuits have also arisen in the jurisdictions where the offending company's stock has been traded (in the U.S.A.) or the company has assets (in Canada)[2] because of investors' claims that management was negligent and should have issued warnings of heightened risk caused by reduced safeguards. While it seems that some customers want cheap goods, and some investors rejoice in high profits,

2. Drew Hasselback And Julia Johnson, "Giant suit hits Chevron Canada," *Financial Post, May 31, 2012,* http://www.canada.com/business/Giant+suit+hits+Chevron+Canada/6705109/story.html.

there are others who care about how these are produced, or are willing to sue if an opportunity presents itself.[3]

More important than the costs of a trial in terms of time lost, fines, and legal fees paid, companies should realize that the damage to their reputation is usually the largest impact they suffer. The impact of lost reputation may not be seen for some time, but there is no doubt that it can translate into lost future revenues of very large magnitude.

Finally, engaging in unworthy practices has an impact on the morale of domestic employees that should be considered. Their desire to be productive, and to produce at high levels of quality may be undermined, with serious consequences.

An example of a case with global impact, Google vs. China is provided below.

Illustrative Case: Google vs. China[4]

In 2006 Google, the world's largest search engine, began operations in China as Google.cn, based on an agreement with the Chinese government that Google would censor information on topics that had been banned by the Chinese government. But in January 2010, Google threatened to pull out of China after Google claims that it, and some twenty other large companies, had been subjected, in December 2009, to, "a highly sophisticated and targeted attack,"[5] designed to steal software codes. The alleged purpose of the attack was so that the Chinese government could break into the Gmail accounts of Chinese human rights activists. Although the attack was unsuccessful, Google decided it should review its operations in China. "We have decided that we are no longer willing to continue censoring our results on Google.cn, and so over the next few weeks we will be discussing with the Chinese government the basis on which we could operate an unfiltered search engine within the law, if it all. We recognize that this may well mean having to shut down Google.cn, and potentially our offices in China."[6]

Three months later, in March 2010, Google closed Google.cn and began directing its Chinese customers to a search engine in Hong Kong, Google.com.hk. Hong Kong is a special administrative region and so the Google.com.hk search engine is not subject to Chinese government

---

3. Texaco's website, http://www.texaco.com/sitelets/ecuador/en/.
4. This is an edited version of a longer case of the same name that appears in L.J. Brooks & Paul Dunn. *Business & Professional Ethics for Directors, Executives & Accountants*, 6e, (South-Western Cengage Learning, 2012).
5. Drummond, David, "A new approach to China," *The Official Google Blog*, January 12, 2010, http://googleblog.blogspot.com/2010/01/new-approach-to-china.html.
6. Ibid.

censorship. The Chinese government complained that this was a violation of the written promise Google had made when it began operations in China in 2006.

The licence for Google to operate in China was up for renewal on June 30, 2010. Without the licence, "Google would effectively go dark in China."[7] In July, a compromise was reached. The Chinese government renewed Google's licence to operate in China, and Google said that it would not automatically redirect its Chinese users to the uncensored Hong Kong site. Instead, users would go to a landing page on Google. cn that is linked to Google.com.hk. In other words, users would have to double-click in order to get to the Hong Kong site. This solution saved face. Google agreed to obey Chinese laws, while at the same time, by providing access to the Hong Kong site, the company would be able to say that it was maintaining its anti-censorship policies. "As a company we aspire to make information available to users everywhere, including China. It's why we have worked so hard to keep Google.cn alive, as well as to continue our research and development work in China. This new approach is consistent with our commitment not to self-censor [sic] and, we believe, with local law."[8] After the announcement that Google's Chinese licence had been renewed, the company's stock rose 2.8 percent.

Was Google acting ethically in 2006? Was their resolution of the dispute in 2010 ethical? Was there a better resolution to be considered for either?

Additional Sources

The factual information in this case has been drawn from various newspapers, including:

- "Google and China work it out," *RedHerring.com*, July 14, 2010, http://www.redherring.com/home/26359.
- "Google says China licence renewed by government," *BBC News Business*, July 9, 2010, http://www.bbc.co.uk/news/10566318.
- "Google vs. China," *The Washington Post*, January 14, 2010, http://www.washingtonpost.com/wp-dyn/content/article/2010/01/13/AR2010011302908.html.
- Helft, Miguel, and Barboza, David, "Google shuts China site in dispute over censorship," *The New York Times*, March 22, 2010, http://www.nytimes.com/2010/03/23/technology/23google.html.

---

7. Ibid.
8. Drummond, David, "An update on China," *The Official Google Blog*, July 9, 2012, http://googleblog.blogspot.com/2010/06/update-on-china.html.

Child and Sweatshop Labour Issues

Companies that manufacture in developing countries, or purchase product from such countries, will inevitably run into the issue of the use of child labour or so-called "sweatshop labour," especially if they are retailers. This issue has immense ethical implications for producers, retailers, and consumers, and there is no easy answer to it. Ethical models set out in this book will not provide ready answers, or answers at all. However, they may help a particular company at least consider the most important aspects of the issue, so they can demonstrate that they are operating on a duly considered and ethical platform, even if others may disagree with it. Unfortunately, the issue is intertwined with the emotional views of various NGOs that have their own agendas, with media attempts to overdramatize particular aspects of the issue, with political and union pressure to preserve jobs locally, and with pure xenophobia. Consequently, making a sound ethical decision may not be the right thing to do to protect the interests of stakeholders. Whatever approach is taken will likely subject the company to criticism from some quarters, which might cause some companies to take the easy way out and simply go out of business. Nevertheless, the worst possible approach for companies in this situation is to ignore the issue and hope that problems will not occur. This is unethical, because there are important ethical issues at stake, and they are potentially disastrous for business.

There are a huge number of organizations that operate in this field. Most of them have strong views. They all base their views on ethical principles. They all present different, even conflicting, approaches. So what is a company to make of all this? How should its decisions be made? What principles should apply?

To highlight the fundamentally contradictory ethical issues that can arise, consider the following:

- A company may decide that, to compete and survive, it must move some of its manufacturing operations offshore to a low-wage country. One of the key issues likely to be raised by existing employees, and local communities, is that it is unethical to fire the existing employees, or to fail to provide them with new employment opportunities. On the other hand, a moral argument can be made that workers in developing countries need the jobs more than workers in North America, where there is more of a social safety net.
- Using cheap labour permits consumers to benefit from low prices, and most consumers would not willingly forego their bargains for the sake of employing local people. On the other hand, laid off

or otherwise unemployed local people do not have the economic wherewithal to pay even the cheaper prices, so the companies will lose business. As with all things, a balance is needed.[9]

- While most people will agree that child labour is immoral, the actual morality issues are highly complex. If the alternative to child labour is, in practical terms, total destitution or the enticement of children into the sex trade, child labour may be preferable to the alternatives, provided it is not abusive or unsafe. Unduly sanctimonious refusal to contemplate child labour for, say, twelve-year-olds can lead to legitimate arguments that we in the west allow child labour, for example, on farms where family members work the harvest, or summer camps where some counsellors are under age. On the other hand, one can argue that children should be in school, not working at full-time jobs.

The remainder of this section deals with sweatshop labour. Child labour is dealt with as a separate issue at the end.

Some principles follow that may be applied when considering taking advantage of low wages paid in developing countries. The key is to consider all stakeholders.

- Why are we manufacturing or purchasing in a low-wage country? Is it necessary for survival? Is it from a genuine belief that quality will improve and benefits will accrue to workers in those countries, and to the countries themselves? Or is it simply to gain a competitive advantage over other companies that employ locally? All may be acceptable, but should be consciously decided and supported.
- Are we treating existing employees fairly if any are to be laid off? Have there been appropriate consultations and alternatives offered, for example, pay cuts? Has compensation been established, and help in finding new employment provided?
- If there are lay-offs, has the effect on the community been considered, and dealt with as fairly as possible?
- Are we paying at least a living wage? There is no standard definition of a living wage, but estimations can recognize such costs as a nutri-

---

9. An interesting example of this conundrum took place recently in Toronto, where the City Council awarded its order for new street cars to a Canadian company that would build them locally, thus providing employment, tax revenue for the government, and all kinds of other spin-off benefits that would not occur if the contract had been put up for tender and won by the foreign company that had expressed a strong interest. On the other hand, some noted that the Canadian company itself would be devastated if cities in other countries took the same approach, since the company is a major supplier of transportation equipment to foreign countries.

tious low-cost diet, basic acceptable housing, clothing and footwear, and other costs of a decent life; as well as the household size to be supported, the number of full-time equivalent workers in the household, and possibly some discretionary expenditures, savings, or funds for emergencies.[10] The wage computed will vary significantly from one location to another, but information will usually be available from local sources or international studies.

- Are employees treated on a non-discriminatory basis? For example, are pregnant women treated fairly and given appropriate pregnancy and maternity leave with the right to return to work?
- Are working conditions safe?
- Are reasonable facilities provided, when needed, for accommodation, child care, training, education and meals, all at reasonable and affordable prices?
- Is there a system in place whereby serious abuse of employees can be reported without fear of intimidation?
- Are the conditions actively monitored on a regular basis by organizations or people who are free from bias, and competent to detect abuses? Employees are sometimes intimidated to not report abuses. There are several organizations that perform audits of operations for these purposes.[11]
- Is environmental damage minimized?

Additional considerations apply when a company finds that its subsidiary, partner, or supplier employs child labour, or plans to do so.

- Is the employment of child labour the norm in that location? It is particularly problematic if child labour is illegal but universally tolerated.
- What would be the result on the children, their families, and their communities if child labour were to be immediately terminated? If the damage would be significant, are there means of ending child labour over a period of time without such damaging results?

And if child labour is to be used on a temporary or permanent basis:

---

10. Figure 1: Flow chart on how to estimate a living wage, Richard Anker, *Estimating a living wage: A methodological review*, Conditions of Work and Employment Series No. 29, International Labour Organization, 2011, p. 6., http://www.ilo.org/wcmsp5/groups/public/---ed_protect/---protrav/---travail/documents/publication/wcms_162117.pdf, (accessed on September 14, 2012).
11. *See for example*: Social Accountability International (SAI), http://www.sa-intl.org/.

- Are working hours sufficient that the children have time to attend school? Better still, can the company provide education for its workers?
- Are the physical aspects of the work unduly onerous for children?
- Is the minimum age reasonable? Five years old, for example, is not reasonable under any circumstances. There is no consensus on an acceptable minimum age, even by those who believe child labour is never justified.
- Do the children have adequate family time? This means travel time between home and work must be considered.

Overall, operating in low-wage countries and employing child labour is fraught with many pitfalls and will inevitably upset some stakeholders. This does not mean that companies should not do it. Economic necessity may make it necessary or desirable. It is critical for the company to consider all its options, and demonstrate that it has considered all the ethical implications and truly believes that on balance it is doing good in the process, and no egregious harm.

Bribery and facilitating payments

In their foreign operations, multinational corporations are likely to be asked for facilitating payments or bribes. A facilitating payment is usually nominal in value and made to speed up a result that would have happened anyway given enough time, for example, a small payment made to customs officials that all importers pay to facilitate movement of goods. Such payment usually provides no competitive advantage. A bribe is usually larger than nominal, usually paid to gain a competitive advantage, and without the payment the desired result would not occur. Both payments are intended to influence outcomes, but some observers believe that a facilitating payment is of lesser ethical consequence than a bribe. Others do not make this distinction.

Most business leaders understand that there is nowhere in the world where bribing government officials is legal in the country where the bribe is paid. Yet at the same time they know that bribery is the normal way of doing business in some regions, and the laws are enforced only sporadically, or not at all. But in all OECD member countries it is now illegal to pay a bribe to a foreign government official. In the United States, the *Foreign Corrupt Practices Act (FCPA)* is widely known, because it has been on the books since 1977 and is enforced by the SEC, which has imposed serious penalties from time to time. However, there are many who are unaware

**Figure 11.1
Anti-bribery Developments: 1975-2011**

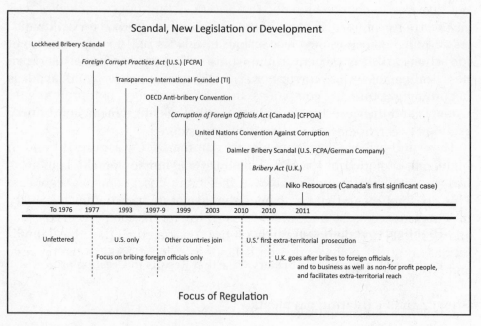

Canada has an almost exactly identical law called the *Corruption of Foreign Public Officials Act*,[12] passed in 1999, although Canada has been criticized for being lax on enforcement. Basically, senior officials of a Canadian company that cause bribes to be paid to a foreign government official could finish up in jail. In some countries, local employees caught paying or receiving bribes may be severely punished, including the death penalty in a few cases, for example in China.

More importantly, since 2010 the FCPA has been enforced globally, not just in the U.S., and in 2010 the U.K. followed suit on an even broader scale by passing the *Bribery Act*. The *Bribery Act* applies to any company – and indeed any non-profit organization – with a presence in the U.K. (i.e. even if not headquartered there) *for the bribery of business people or government officials,* not just the latter. Moreover, there are *penalties for the company or person giving a bribe as well as the company failing to guard adequately against the receipt of a bribe.* In addition, *the exception allowed for facilitating payments under the*

---

12. *Corruption of Foreign Public Officials Act* (Canada), http://www.justice.gc.ca/en/dept/pub/cfpoa/ guide5.html.

FCPA is not available under the Bribery Act, although reasonable expenses (which will require continuous scrutiny and interpretation) will apparently not give rise to charges. Finally, the *Bribery Act* introduces *unlimited fines and imprisonment up to 10 years* – both of which far exceed the FCPA limits. As a result, businesses now face serious fines with jail times for executives for actions taken anywhere in the world with regard to bribery in business dealings, as well as corruption of government officials. Even Canada is beginning to prosecute companies. In short, companies, non-profit organizations, and their executives, are now facing an entirely new anti-bribery regime.

These anti-bribery developments are summarized in Figure 11.1 and in highlights provided of the SNC-Lavalin, Wal-Mart in Mexico, Lockheed, Daimler and Niko Resources cases.

Highlights of Significant Bribery Cases

Lockheed Corporation – Bribery Case that Results in Creation of U.S. FCPA

In 1976, a sub-committee of the U.S. Senate decided that Lockheed Corporation had paid foreign government officials, and others, millions of dollars to guarantee purchases of planes, including:

- Japan   – in the 1950s for the F-104 Starfighter
            – in the 1960s for the L-1011
            – in the 1970s for the L-1011
- West Germany – in the 1970s for the F-104 Starfighter
- Italy – in the 1970s for the C-130
- Netherlands – in the 1970s for the F-104 Starfighter
- Saudi Arabia – in the 1970s, $106 million in commissions to an arms dealer.

Nonetheless, Lockheed was in such financial difficulty in 1971 that the U.S. government had to guarantee repayment of $195 million of its bank loans. The resulting public outcry and investigation gave rise to the U.S. *Foreign Corrupt Practices Act* (FCPA) of 1977 that prohibited the corruption of foreign officials.

Daimler AG – FCPA's First Significant Extra-territorial Bribery Case

Although Germany had outlawed bribery of foreign officials in 1999, David Bazzetta learned at a corporate audit executive committee in 2001, in Stuttgart, Germany, that units of DaimlerChrysler continued to do so, and that the company was conspiring to continue. Since the company raised funds in the U.S., it was an SEC registrant in the U.S., and was therefore subject to U.S. FCPA legislation and regulation. Mr. Bazzetta blew the whistle, as is possible under the FCPA, which led in early April 2010 to guilty pleas in the U.S. to charges of bribery by German and Russian business units and to the failure to maintain books and records, and of internal controls, as required under the FCPA. The investigation of the whistleblower's allegations focussed only on 51 transactions, but revealed that bribes had been given in 22 countries. Daimler settled the case in 2010 by paying the SEC $91.4 million as disgorgement of profits, and $93.6 million to the U.S. Department of Justice for related criminal charges, for a total of $185 million for bribes made outside the United States.

Niko Resources – Canada's First Significant Bribery Prosecution

In June 2011, Niko Resources plead guilty to bribing an official of the government of Bangladesh, by giving him a $190,000 vehicle, among other inducements (travel, etc.), to levy a low penalty for faulty and negligent drilling operations that resulted in unsafe conditions and an explosion. The company agreed to pay a fine of $9.5 million for the bribery. This was the second Canadian prosecution under the CFPOA. The first involved the bribing of a U.S. customs inspector for $28,299.88, by officials of Hydro Kleen Group Inc.. Hydro Kleen was fined $25,000 in 2005.

SNC-Lavalin Missing Funds Topples CEO & Triggers Investigation

Pierre Duhaime "retired" as CEO of SNC-Lavalin on March 26, 2012, a post that he had held since 2009, following over 20 years of employment at the company. He did so, because of his role in approving $56 million in payments, in contravention of the company's policies.[13] Police were called in to help trace and recover the payments, following an Independent Review by Stikeman Elliott LLP, a prominent law firm. The story originated at a news conference by Board Chair, Gwyn Morgan, and a Press Release[14] by the company on March 26th.

According to the Press Release, two payments were initiated by Riadh Ben Aissa, the Executive VP of Construction, for which, "the nature of the services or actions undertaken by, or the true identity of any

---

13. Paul Waldie and Sean Silcoff, "Mystery funds put CEO out, police in," *The Globe and Mail*, March 27, 2012, https://secure.globeadvisor.com/servlet/ArticleNews/story/gam/20120327/RBSNCLAVALINPAPER0327ATL (accessed March 27, 2012).
14. "SNC-Lavalin Reports on Results of Voluntary Independent Review," Press Release, SNC-Lavalin, March 26, 2012, http://www.snclavalin.com/news.php?lang=en&id=1707&action=press_release_details&paging=1&start=6 (accessed March 27, 2012).

presumed agent," could not be established. One payment, made in 2011, was for $33.5 million. When the required signatories (the Chairman of SNC-Lavalin International and the CFO) refused to sign the required authorization, the CEO, Mr. Duhaime, was approached, and he signed the authorization based upon the understanding that, "it would help secure work in respect of Project A." Project A was not identified in the Independent Review. For the second payment incident, regarding Project B, the story is much the same, except that it was initiated in 2009, for $30 million, with payments aggregating $22.5 million being made in 2010 and 2011. Mr. Aissa, and someone in his division, improperly approved these expenditures. "In 2010, the CFO was told at a meeting with the CEO and Mr. Aissa that an agent had been hired on Project B and that its fees would be charged to other projects. The CFO objected to this at the meeting." These payments were detected as anomalous in an analysis in February 2012, and were then, "reported to the Senior Vice-President and Controller of the Company," who objected to them.

The Independent Review concluded that the company's Code of Ethics and Business Conduct, and its Agent's Code, had been breached, but neither code required reporting of a breach or suspected breach, nor did it find the failure to report a breach of the code. The company's Whistle-blower Policy did not impose any obligation to report either. Not surprisingly, the Review recommended changes to these codes, and increased attention to management override and improvement, and enforcement of controls.

From a governance perspective, the Board failed to ensure that company policies were adequate to ensure ethical and legal conduct, and that the actions of Mr. Aissa and Mr. Duhaime speak to a lack of ethical tone at the top.

The full story of SNC-Lavalin corruption of foreign officials is still unfolding. There are reports of the company's personnel being involved with the former Libyan ruling Gadhafi family. The company reportedly hired Cyndy Vanier to go on a fact-finding mission to Libya, and bring Gadhafi's son Saadi to Mexico. [15] She is presently incarcerated in Mexico. On March 28th, it became known that, when the company left Libya before the revolution in 2011, it left $22.9 million in cash in Libyan banks, and it hopes the money will be available if, and when, it returns to Libya.[16]

Time will tell if the company or its officers or directors will face legal action from the *Canadian Corruption of Foreign Public Officials Act* or the U.S. FCPA.

---

15. Alyshah Hasham, "SNC-Lavalin players: Who's who as CEO steps down amid ethics probe," *thestar.com*, March 26, 2012, http://www.thestar.com/business/article/1151980--snc-lavalin-players-who-s-who-as-ceo-steps-down-amid-ethics-probe (accessed March 27, 2012).
16. Paul Waldie, "SNC's Libyan mystery deepens: It left $23-million behind," *Globe and Mail*, March 28, 2012, pp. B1, B4.

Wal-Mart Bribery in Mexico Triggers Brand Damage and U.S. FCPA Investigation

Wal-Mart has a brand image that triggers strong reactions in North America, particularly from people whose businesses have been damaged by the company's overpowering low price–vast selection competition, and by those who value the small business–small town culture that has been supplanted. The company doesn't need more controversy, and has taken on causes such as environmental sustainability and rushing aid to hurricane victims, partly to build brand support. Consequently, from September 2005, when a report of significant bribery in Wal-Mart de Mexico was received, according to a report[17] in *The New York Times*, senior officers in Mexico and then the U.S. sought to keep the matter quiet, impede company investigations, blunt the efforts of qualified investigators, refer the matter to senior company lawyers implicated in the scandal for investigation and resolution, weaken company protocols for investigation and reporting, and promote executives involved. As is often the case nowadays, the bribery scandal could not be hushed-up, and now the company faces prosecution under the *U.S. Foreign Corrupt Practices Act* (FCPA) as well as significant damage to the Wal-Mart image and credibility. Wal-Mart issued an immediate response[18] to the article, indicating non-tolerance for bribery, committing to get to the bottom of the allegations, as well as disclosing that they had requested and met with the U.S. Department of Justice and the SEC about the matters raised, and had disclosed the investigation in the company's 10-Q filing in December 2011. Unfortunately, dealing partially with the matter six years after it was first raised, did little to appease the company's critics.

In September 2005, a senior Wal-Mart lawyer received an email from a former Mexican executive, a lawyer, who had been in charge of the bribery payments process, using "gestores" (trusted fixers) to speed up permits for store construction, obtain confidential information, or eliminate fines. Investigators were sent immediately from the U.S., who established the veracity of a paper trail, for $24 million in payments. When they wanted to expand the investigation, U.S. executives shut it down. According to the *New York Times* article, senior executives were, "(U)nder fire from labor critics, worried about press leaks, and facing sagging stock prices.... recognized that the allegations could have devastating consequences." No one was disciplined, an executive involved was promoted to a senior post at Wal-Mart headquarters, and investigators

---

17. David Barstow, "Vast Mexico Bribery Case Hushed-up by Wal-Mart After Top-Level Struggle," *The New York Times*, April 21, 2012, http://www.nytimes.com/2012/04/22/business/at-wal-mart-in-mexico-a-bribe-inquiry-silenced.html?pagewanted=all (accessed April 23, 2012).
18. "Walmart Statement in Response to Recent New York Times Article About Compliance with the U.S. Foreign Corrupt Practices Act," Walmart Corporate Press Release, April 21, 2012, http://www.walmartstores.com/pressroom/news/10879.aspx (accessed April 23, 2012).

were criticized for being overly aggressive by H. Lee Scott, Wal-Mart's Chief Executive. Responsibility for the investigations was shifted, investigators were confined only to "significant" matters, and administrative oversight and approvals were increased. In time, a law firm was hired and a full investigation was recommended. This was rejected by senior Wal-Mart executives and a special in-house, major corruption investigations unit was created, but the unit was under-resourced, and senior executives were allowed to transfer some sensitive cases involving themselves, or their people, to other units and individuals. The Mexican bribery investigation was reassigned. Ms. Munich, the General Counsel of Wal-Mart International, who had received the original email, and had triggered the original investigation, complained about these changes, and ultimately resigned in 2006.

In an interesting twist, the bribery investigation was ultimately assigned to a lawyer, José Luis Rodríguezmacedo Rivera, the General Counsel of Wal-Mart de Mexico, who had been identified as a person who had redacted a 2003 report on the company's FCAP compliance by an auditor who had red-flagged gestore payments. The auditor was fired. Rivera dealt with the matter as follows; he asked his colleagues if they had bribed anyone, which they denied doing, and he cast aspersions on the whistleblower, Mr. Cicero, inferring that the bribes were meant to enrich Cicero, who had been passed over for promotion, and whose wife was a partner at the law firm, where one of the gestores was also a partner. Rivera further claimed that Cicero had been fired for failing to report his wife's potential conflict of interest, although he had personally negotiated with Cicero for his resignation bonus package. He also claimed that because Cicero had triggered the payments to enrich himself, the money was therefore stolen, and the bribes were not attributable to Wal-Mart – it was a case of employee theft, not company bribery. Rivera, it should be noted, was an instructor at Wal-Mart's in-house seminar on FCPA compliance.

There is much more to the story, and a close reading of *The New York Times* article, and Wal-Mart's response, is very worthwhile. Some of Wal-Mart's senior officials did know about and take action on the problems, but not in ways that led to sound results. Whether the Board of Directors knew about the allegations is much more in doubt, but theirs is the responsibility to ensure that systems and internal controls are in place so that they are informed. The Board should also ensure that the tone at the top, and the hiring processes, do not subvert proper governance objectives and the achievement of the company's long-term strategic objectives.

Transparency International (TI) has been a major driving force of increased bribery awareness, and the stimulation of governments to enact

Table 11.1
Comparison of U.S. FCPA and U.K. Bribery Act

Source: http://www.transparency-usa.org/documents/FCPAvsBriberyAct-forboard.pdf

 TRANSPARENCY INTERNATIONAL | USA

The U.S. Foreign Corrupt Practices Act v. the new UK Bribery Act:
A snapshot comparison of key provisions

PROVISION	FCPA	UK BRIBERY ACT
Who is being bribed	Only bribes ("anything of value") paid or offered to a "foreign official" are prohibited	Prohibits bribes paid to *any person* to induce them to act "improperly" (not limited to foreign officials)
Nature of advantage obtained	Payment must be "to obtain or retain business"	Focus is on improper action rather than business nexus (except in case of strict corporate liability)
"Active offense" vs. "passive offense"	Only the act of payment, rather than the receipt/acceptance of payment, is prohibited	Creates two offenses: (1) offense of bribing another ("active offense") and (2) offense of being bribed ("passive offense")
Corporate strict liability	Strict liability only under accounting provisions for public companies (failure to maintain adequate systems of internal controls)	Creates a new strict liability corporate offense for the failure of a commercial organization to prevent bribery (subject to defense of having "adequate procedures" in place designed to prevent bribery)
Jurisdiction	U.S. companies and citizens, foreign companies listed on U.S. stock exchange, or any person acting while in the U.S.	Individuals who are UK nationals or are ordinarily resident in the UK and organizations that are either established in the UK or conduct some part of their business in the UK
Business promotion expenditures	Affirmative defense for reasonable and bona fide expenditure directly related to the business promotion or contract performance	No similar defense (but arguably such expenditures are not "improper" and therefore not a Bribery Act violation)
Allowable under local law	Affirmative defense if payment is lawful under written laws/regulations of foreign country	No violation if permissible under written laws of foreign country (applies only in case of bribery of foreign public official; otherwise a factor to be considered)
Facilitating payments	Exception for payment to a foreign official to expedite or secure the performance of a routine (non-discretionary) government action	No facilitating payments exception, although guidance is likely to provide that payments of small amounts of money are unlikely to be prosecuted
Civil/criminal enforcement	Both civil and criminal proceedings can be brought by DOJ and SEC	Criminal enforcement only by the UK Serious Fraud Office (SFO)
Potential penalties	Bribery: for individuals, up to five years' imprisonment and fines of up to $250,000; for entities, fines of up to $2 million Books and records/internal control violations: for individuals, up to 20 year's imprisonment and fines of up to $5 million; for entities, fines of up to $25 million	For individuals, up to 10 years' imprisonment and potentially unlimited fines; for entities, potentially unlimited fines

Prepared May 2010 by Rob Walton of TI-USA and Michael Whitener of VistaLaw International LLC

anti-bribery statutes and increased regulation. Founded in 1993 in Germany, to do just that, TI has developed chapters in many countries around the world. Their websites are significant sources of information, such as the Table reproduced opposite, that compares the U.S. FCPA to the U.K. *Bribery Act*.

Faced with a much more comprehensive, and high risk environment, companies need to build anti-bribery risk identification and management techniques into their strategic planning, training, assessment and incentive systems. A number of anti-corruption tools are available, including the *TI-Canada Anti-Corruption Compliance Checklist*, First Edition (Revised), 2011, which is downloadable from http://www.transparency.ca/New/Files/TI-Canada_Anti-Corruption_Checklist_2011R1.pdf. It provides a comprehensive overview of the subject, with practical suggestions, background on major developments, and references to additional resources.

TI, along with its national chapters, is the primary source for authoritative information on international bribery and corruption. Every couple of years, TI publishes its *Bribe Payers Index (BPI)*, which ranks the likelihood for companies from 28 countries to bribe,[19] and every year it publishes its *Corruption Perceptions Index (CPI)*, which ranks the perceived levels of public sector corruption in 183 countries.[20] In 2011, according to the *BPI*, companies from the Netherlands and Switzerland tied at 8.8 out of 10 for the least bribery out of the 28 countries, whereas Russian companies were worst at 6.1, followed by Chinese companies at 6.5 out of 10. In 2011, the lowest perceived incidence of bribery (in the CPI) of government officials was in New Zealand at 9.5, followed by Denmark at 9.4, while the worst scores were for Somalia and North Korea at 1 out of 10. In 2011, Canadian and American companies were ranked at 6th and 10th in the *BPI*, and their perceived incidence of corruption at 10th and 24th in the *CPI*. *BPI* and *CPI* rankings are available on all TI websites, and can be valuable tools for companies in assessing their operational risks in foreign countries, particularly in countries near the bottom of the list. The following TI websites are gold mines of information and guidance:

- http://www.transparency.org – the worldwide site, based in Berlin
- http://www.transparency.ca – the Canadian site
- http://www.transparency-usa.org – the U.S. site

Of course, bribery and corruption are also dangerously improper on

19. TI *2011 Bribe Payers Index*, http://bpi.transparency.org/.
20. TI *2011 Corruption Perception Index*, http://cpi.transparency.org/cpi2011/.

purely ethical grounds. They can have a devastating effect on development, and create injustices for those not in a position to benefit or who have to pay the bribes. They are also damaging to reputations, as was discovered by Acres, a major Canadian engineering consulting firm that was convicted in Lesotho of paying bribes. Even though Acres denied guilt, it was essentially forced out of business. Enron and Siemens are recent examples of companies that have also taken a reputational hit.

Rather than leaving employees to make up their own minds as to when payment is appropriate, the corporation should have a policy concerning non-payment of bribes, and conditions under which facilitating payments might be paid. For example, it may not be sufficient to simply say that no bribes shall be paid; it is important to provide guidelines to employees concerning what to do if they are asked for them. If a company permits facilitating payments, it needs to have very strict and clear policies surrounding them. Facilitating payments should be defined, there should be limits and approval processes, and they should be properly recorded in the accounts.

It should be clear that facilitating payments or bribes are problematic for reasons other than illegality, including:

- Adding to the cost of the operation, good, or service
- Undermining the practice of purchasing based on merit in a country or firm
- Risking possible negative consequences from stakeholder groups should they find out
- Impossibility of enforcing performance, or obtaining a contract, after bribes are paid
- Impossibility of assessing sales force effectiveness
- Indicating to employees elsewhere in the multinational that bribes are permitted in spite of what codes of conduct say
- Indicating to seekers of bribes elsewhere that bribes are possible if they ask for them
- Risk to local employees and expat personnel should the bribes come to light
- Risk that a change in political control, particularly by revolution, could bring past practices to light, and have serious consequences for the company and local employees
- Undermining internal control. Usually, bribes paid are untraceable (e.g. frequently in cash) and management cannot know for sure that the real beneficiary was as reported. The recipient may in fact be an employee of the company who pretended that a bribe needed to be paid, or even the CEO.

Some multinationals have banned the giving of bribes or facilitating payments and have continued to operate profitably in the countries concerned. On the other hand, some claim they have lost business to companies who do not have similar scruples. Because of their lower economic power and influence, smaller companies may find it more difficult to resist pressure. The OECD treaty, and resulting legislation, helps to level the playing field, but it remains to be seen how helpful this will be to small companies.

In some cultures, particularly in Southeast Asia, China and Japan, there is a long tradition of gift giving to cultivate long-term relationships that facilitate business dealings. In these situations, corporations may be best advised to have a permissive policy where employees would be required to consult a corporate ethics officer to make sure that cultural niceties are observed without breaking laws at home or abroad. Gift giving might cover such items as an iPad but would certainly not stretch to a Mercedes.

This is a good example of an issue that has moved from being a business aggravation, to an ethical issue, and then to a legal issue. But it is still an ethical issue. It needs to be covered in corporate codes of conduct, and in business policies and practices, when a company is in a position to be asked for a bribe. Policies, especially for decision makers in the field, need to be clear and unequivocal. Canadian or U.S. management will not be saved by ignoring the issue, or taking steps to ensure that they do not know what goes on locally in high risk countries. In particular, employing an agent to deal with business abroad does not get management off the hook. They are still responsible for providing appropriate instructions to agents not to pay bribes, and to monitor their expenditures to be alert for any indication that bribes have been paid. An excellent article on this issue may be found in the October 2006 issue of *CAmagazine* by James Miklotz, "Not Seeing is no Defence," http://www.camagazine.com/3/3/9/9/2/index1.shtml.

Several additional articles have recently appeared that provide useful background information about the fine line between gifts and bribes, including:

- Matthew McClearn, "What is a Bribe in 2011?" *Canadian Business*, October 19, 2011 & November, 7, 2011, http://www.canadianbusiness.com/article/51851--what-is-a-bribe-in-2011
- Greg McArthur, "A Gift for Mr. Hossain," *Report on Business*, September 2011, [Niko Resources bribery case] https://secure.globeadvisor.com/servlet/ArticleNews/story/gam/20110826/ROBMAG_SEPT2011_P38_39_40_41_42_43_44

Boards, audit committees, and management of companies operating in high risk parts of the world, should expect their auditors to be aware of the associated risk that illegal bribes may have been paid and to take the risk into account in their audits.[21]

Moral Imagination

In some corporations, managers have used their *moral imagination* to devise alternatives that answered needs in the host culture but conformed to North American norms for acceptable behaviour. For example, a manager in China refused to pay an official of a potential customer, citing company policy. When the official insisted repeatedly, the manager sought and received approval for a corporate contribution toward the establishment of a community centre in a local park that would offer services to senior citizens. This appealed to Chinese cultural values, allowed them to save face, and was in line with the corporation's North American policy of community support. It was differentiated from a bribe in that no payment was made to an individual for his or her personal benefit, and all payments were made in public rather than in secret.

Guidelines for ethical practice

Two authors have made an extensive study of the ethics of foreign operations, and have written excellent books on the subject. They are Tom Donaldson[22] and Richard DeGeorge,[23] and they have each put forward guidelines that may be useful for corporations. Their views are summarized in an article by Nancy Roth[24]. Tom Donaldson's excellent article on bribery and foreign cultures is also referenced.

Corporations should also compare their values, codes, and practices to the Principles for Business that have been developed for worldwide application by the Caux Round Table in Geneva. These practices are available online at the Caux Round Table's website.[25]

---

21. This is a requirement of Canadian, U.S. and International auditing standards (CICA Handbook Section 5136, AICPA Au 317 and ISA 250, respectively).
22. Thomas Donaldson. *The Ethics of International Business* (New York: Oxford University Press, 1989).
23. Richard T. De George. *Competing with Integrity in International Business* (Oxford University Press, 1993).
24. Roth, N. et al, "Can't We All Just Get Along: Cultural Variables in Codes of Ethics," *Public Relations Review* 22 (1996): 151–161.
25. Principles for Business, Caux Round Table, http://www.cauxroundtable.org/documents/Principles%20for%20Business.PDF

Reading *located at the end of the book*

David Selley, "Bribing foreign government officials now illegal," *management ethics* (February 1999): 1–3, http://www.ethicscentre.ca/EN/resources/February%201999%20methics.pdf.

Useful References

Richard T. De George. *Competing with Integrity in International Business* (Oxford University Press, 1993).

T. Donaldson. *The Ethics of International Business* (New York: Oxford University Press, 1989).

T. Donaldson, "Values in Tension: Ethics Away from Home," *Harvard Business Review* (September–October 1996): 48–62.

Roth, N. et al, "Can't We All Just Get Along: Cultural Variables in Codes of Ethics," *Public Relations Review* 22 (1996): 151–161.

Transparency International website, http://www.transparency.ca

Additional Readings and Useful References will noted on: http://www.ethicscentre.ca

	Checklist – Special Topics
	International Operations
✓	Do Policies, Codes, Guidelines & Practices consider:
	• Impacts on local economies & their cultures, including:
	○ Labour markets including wage rates and supply
	○ Raw material and other input markets
	○ Political and legal processes
	○ Environmental conditions
	○ Religious and social customs
	• **Conflicts between domestic and foreign cultures**
	○ Bribery
	○ Use of child labour
	○ Use of prison labour

	○	Unhealthy labour conditions
	○	Treatment of women
	○	Support of repressive regimes
	○	Respect for the environment
	○	Dealing with family members
•	Bribery & facilitating payments	
	○	Do policies require compliance with highest legal requirements?
	○	Do employees receive adequate training?
	○	Do senior executives speak out in favour of company policies?
	○	Are payments carefully monitored, and problems reported?
	○	Is there an annual sign-off covering bribery and facilitating payments?
	○	Are penalties such as termination assessed?
•	Use of moral imagination	

Special Topics

Chapter 12
Not-for-profit Entities & Small Owner-managed Enterprises

Not-for-profit Organizations

Not-for-profit entities represent a huge segment of our economy. They include very large public institutions such as universities, schools and hospitals; large charitable organizations such as the United Way; large non-governmental organizations (NGOs) such as Greenpeace; and small and very small charities and NGOs.

Most of these entities have a number of features in common that make them vulnerable to employee fraud or unethical acts, for example:

Smaller Charitable Organizations and NGOs

- They are frequently parsimonious in monetary rewards and benefits to employees, often because they wish to minimize administrative expenses to improve their image. Because of this, they do not always attract the most competent people into financial management and other responsible positions. Worse still, this parsimony may increase the likelihood that employees will find themselves in financial difficulties, and therefore be motivated through need to improve their finances by unethical means. In some charities, it is difficult to anticipate incoming donations, thereby making it harder for any diversion of funds to be noticed.
- Boards of Directors may be inadequately compensated; frequently they are only reimbursed for expenses, and may be largely comprised of people able to make a financial contribution, rather than those with good oversight skills.

- Need for funding may tempt management to be less than fully honest and transparent in applying for government or other grants.
- Stakeholders, in the form of donors, may have even higher expectations than shareholders in profit-oriented enterprises.
- There is usually little or no oversight equivalent to the role market analysts perform for public corporations. Regulation is frequently non-existent or lax.
- Charitable organizations attract very highly principled and committed people. But such people may be so committed to their cause that they may be prepared to step over the line of what is ethical in order to help the organization meet its goals.
- Some organizations contract out fundraising without paying adequate attention to the ethical conduct of the organizations they contract it out to.

Larger Public Institutions, including Charities and NGOs

Large public institutions may have hierarchical executive and management structures similar to for-profit companies, and the same ethical considerations generally apply. But other factors come into play, such as a perceived obligation to protect the organization's reputation and "brand" at any cost. This appears to have been the case in the Penn State scandal and the various scandals suffered by the Roman Catholic Church, even when egregious acts like sexual abuse of minors is involved. They were tempted to think that the risk of reputational damage was of greater importance than honesty, transparency, and even illegality. These institutions may be very large and have a high public profile, making damage to their reputation as consequential as in a large public company. Penn State football was effectively an enormous business that yielded tens of millions of dollars for the university, and the salaries paid to officials were hardly parsimonious. This increased the motivation of those involved to hide what was occurring, and increased the damage should it be revealed, as indeed it was.

When seemingly exaggerated remuneration is paid to executives in public interest organizations, their "brand" may be damaged as well. Such remuneration is increasingly likely to come to light, as was the case when the remuneration of hospital CEOs came into question in Ontario in late 2011 and early 2012.[1] It is imperative for a publicly funded organization to very

---

1. See for example: "Generous Perks given to Ontario hospital executives, contracts reveal," *Toronto Star*, Wednesday Jan.4, 2012, http://www.thestar.com/news/article/1109999--generous-perks-given-to-ontario-hospital-executives-contracts-reveal (accessed January 18, 2012).

carefully consider the remuneration it pays to senior executives, and to be transparent.

So in all these organizations, tone at the top and a code of conduct are at least as important as they are in a public corporation, perhaps even more so. Virtually everything in this book applies to such organizations. In particular, organizations should:

- Develop, properly implement, and maintain a code of conduct as set out in this book, insist that all employees act honestly and transparently, and focus on an ethical tone at the top.
- Observe good board of director governance principles, including monitoring of ethical conduct.
- Establish the best possible financial internal controls to minimize the temptation for employees, especially those with the ability to intercept incoming funds. Even the smallest organizations, with limited resources to establish sophisticated internal controls, should insist that two signatures be required on all cheques, and require the second signer to perform due diligence on the payments, see the supporting documentation, and so forth. Frequently the second signature is that of the treasurer – a volunteer board member. This is an excellent practice, but only if the treasurer is diligent in understanding what he or she is approving.
- Ensure that compensation and benefits are reasonable for the sector, and be alert for financial distress among employees with financial responsibility. Also, insist such employees take vacations.
- Maintain scrupulous honesty in grant applications and fundraising activities. If contracted out, insist that fundraisers take an honest and transparent approach, and monitor their actions.
- Be transparent in financial reporting and ensure that annual financial statements are audited. In large organizations, establish an internal audit function.
- In larger organizations, consider establishing a whistleblowing process.
- In all cases, recognize that unacceptable or illegal conduct is very damaging, but trying to cover it up afterwards is even worse.

Small Owner-managed Businesses

In small owner-managed businesses, the ethical focus of the owner is critical to success. A formal code of conduct may not be necessary, but only if the owner has hands on contact with the entity's day-to-day activities. This provides him or her with the opportunity to convey an ethical tone at the top in both word and deed. This is not a guarantee that unethical conduct or fraud will not occur, but it certainly minimizes the risk. The owner manager needs to demonstrate his or her criteria for ethical treatment of customers and suppliers, employees, as well as all other stakeholders. Note that although small, a small business may nevertheless be the largest employer in its community. Small business owners have certain advantages over public company CEOs because they are not under constant pressure from the market to produce quarterly earnings. Unless under serious financial strain from lenders, the small business owner can afford to take a longer-term view and focus on establishing the reputation of the business for quality, value for money, and most importantly, integrity and fairness to primary stakeholders, particularly customers and employees.

In southwestern Ontario, every year a large number of farm workers are imported from Mexico for the summer and fall harvest. These workers are paid minimum wages and work hard. But what they earn is, for them, an opportunity to build a family nest egg that they could not do at home. Many stories have surfaced about the friendly reception these Mexican workers get from the farmers and the community. They are provided with basic but comfortable accommodation, and are treated with dignity. The benefit to the farmers, truly owner-managed businesses, is pervasive. They are perceived to be acting ethically, which is good for their standing in the community, and therefore their business.

Owner managers need to take specific steps to ensure that their ethical standards are actually implemented and that fraud is deterred. For example, owner managers should:

- Ensure that employees are aware that honesty is a cornerstone of the business and dishonesty towards customers, suppliers, lenders, and other stakeholders will not be tolerated.
- Ensure that honesty towards the company and stakeholders is built into operating instructions and performance evaluations, taking into account known risks.[2]
- Approve all significant transactions and review all other transactions after the fact.
- Sign all cheques.
- Obtain bank statements directly from the bank, and review them

---

2. See the case in Chapter six concerning the need to operationalise the prohibition of kickbacks to purchasing agents.

to ensure they recognize all the content. Every now and then they could perform the bank reconciliation.

- Keep a list of all sales, and cross-check them on a regular basis to incoming funds.
- Unless absent, make it a point to talk to all employees at least once per week and to senior employees on a daily basis.
- Ensure that all senior people take vacations.

Owner managers should also be sensitive to the example set by their own conduct. For example, if they habitually charge personal expenses to the company, such as rebuilding their own swimming pool, they are not sending a good message to their employees, who will quickly perceive a lack of honesty and may be tempted to imitate when the opportunity arises.

In short, an owner manager will find it significantly easier, with a modicum of diligence, to instill his or her ethical values into the way the business is run. However, to be successful, this requires constant communication and hands on involvement in the day-to-day activities of the business. And of course, any ethical lapse by the owner manager may have an equally negative effect on the conduct of other employees.

Useful References

Business Ethics for SMEs, Business Ethics Briefing, Institute of Business Ethics, December 2007, Issue 6, http://www.ibe.org.uk/BusinessEthicsforSMEs.pdf.

The website includes other useful readings and links to further websites.

J.J. Quinn, "Personal Ethics and Business Ethics: The Attitudes of Owner/ managers of Small Business," *Journal of Business Ethics* 16:2 (1997): 199–127.

L.J. Spence. *Practice, Priorities, and Ethics in Small Firms*, (London: Institute of Business Ethics, 2000). Available online at: http://www.ibe.org.uk/PPE.html.

	Checklist – Special Topics
	Not-for-profit Entities & Small Owner-managed Enterprises
✓	Does the organization consider or have:
	• Exemplary tone at the top
	• Code of conduct featuring:
	○ Honesty
	○ Transparency
	• Training & notification to ensure employees know expectations
	• Ethical Governance Principles including monitoring
	• Internal controls to remove temptation for employees
	• Dual cheque signing with a second knowledgeable signatory performing due diligence
	• Prior review of all significant transactions
	• Review & reconciliation of Bank Statements
	• Review reports for significant transactions
	• Monitoring for financial distress of employees
	• Scrupulously honest grant or fundraising procedures
	• Transparent financial reports
	• Audit of financial statements
	• Internal audit function if needed
	• Whistleblowing mechanisms in place
	• Ongoing contact and chats with employees
	• Compulsory vacations for all senior employees

Concluding Comments

Most would agree that reputation is absolutely critical to success in any organization; not only for businesses, but also for not-for-profit organizations of all types. Reputation is earned primarily through the use of quality processes, and the provision of quality products and services at an appropriate price. It can be destroyed, or at least badly tarnished, by perceived ethical lapses, and failure to properly deal with such lapses, when they do occur.

There was a day when ethical lapses could be kept hidden. Today this reactive approach to damage control will not work. Bear in mind that almost everyone now has a camera embedded in her or his cell phone. Instant global communications, and the growth of the internet and its offshoots, such as YouTube, mean that what would previously have been hidden or given limited circulation may be broadcast almost instantaneously to the whole world. A preventive, forthright approach to the management of ethics risks is more important than ever.

Maintaining the ethical integrity of any organization, comprised of human beings with all their frailties and mistakes, can be a daunting challenge. It is hard work, requiring constant vigilance and increasing expertise. In response, this book offers practical help to those with primary responsibility for developing and maintaining an ethical culture in their organization, and to upper and middle management personnel who are responsible for implementing it. The book emphasizes that it is a necessary, but not sufficient, condition that an organization's leadership and those charged with its governance behave ethically and communicate the need and expectations for ethical culture to all employees and agents. That culture must be lived every day, throughout the organization, and must be built-in to all key processes.

To achieve this objective, this book provides practical guidance, examples, and readings on the key aspects of developing and maintaining an ethical corporate culture. Guidance is provided on:

- Understanding what it means to have an ethical culture, to be a good corporate citizen, and to keep the support of stakeholders (Chapter 2)
- How to provide the leadership necessary to develop, and instill, a culture of integrity throughout the organization (Chapters 3 and 5)
- How to effectively communicate the organization's culture to those who need to live by it (Chapter 4)
- How to constantly reinforce the culture, so that it does not become a "flavour of the month" – a frequent fate of many management initiatives that are not constantly reinforced and do not achieve the necessary buy in from employees (Chapter 6)
- How to continually monitor actual performance, so that process improvements can be identified, and successes (and failures) measured (Chapter 7)
- How leaders and management can make good ethical decisions, including some "rules of thumb," and commentary on a range of ethical conceptual frameworks (Chapter 8)
- Specific topics such as conflicts of interest, so-called "whistle-blowing" processes, ethical international operations (including bribery and corruption issues), and ethics for not-for-profit organizations ranging from large organizations with public accountability, such as hospitals, schools and universities, to large and small charitable organizations (Chapters 6, 9, 11 and 12)
- How to understand the ethical failures that led to the Subprime Lending Crisis of 2008 and its aftermath, and the ethical problems facing financial services companies and those that deal with them (Chapter 10).

The cliché that business ethics is an oxymoron, and the notion that an organization cannot, by its nature, be ethical are now both generally viewed as completely obsolete. Public expectations of all organizations will continue to grow, fueled by insights stimulated by new information and misinformation, and fresh examples of unfortunate, as well as exemplary, behaviour.

What will the future bring? Today's hot button issues, such as concern for the environment, bribery and corruption, abuse of investors, and unfair practices, will not diminish. New hot button issues will emerge as stakeholder interests are sharpened by new information and by understanding better the potential for successful influence on organizational activities. The price to be paid for failing to anticipate problems or not meeting performance expectations will continue to grow, not diminish. The recent past offers many examples of corporations and individuals who failed tragically, not because they didn't have a great product or service, or because they didn't have a respected governance system, but because they failed to fully embrace a culture of integrity. This book is dedicated to helping those charged with developing and maintaining an ethical culture in their organization to navigate successfully through the intricacies of making it happen.

Appendix A:
CSR & Sustainability Reports, Indexes, & Rankings

Evidence of the pervasiveness of stakeholder interest in an organization's practices can be found in the following examples of company lists, indexes, and rankings. Further information is available on the accompanying website, http://www.ethicscentre.ca.

- **Global Reporting Initiative (GRI):** 30+ organizations with recent CSR reports on the GRI website, http://www.globalreporting.org.
- **Jantzi Social Index®:** Top 10 (by assets held) of the 60 companies in mutual funds patterned on the Jantzi Social Index® in 2012
- **FTSE4Good® Index Series:** Top 10 North American and Global companies based on an overall Environmental, Social, and Governance (ESG) rating by the FTSE
- **Dow Jones Sustainability World Index:** Top 10 companies in the Dow Jones Sustainability World Index in 2012
- **Examples of Corporate Social Responsibility Reporting**

Global Reporting Initiative (GRI)

Following an "Application Level Check" – evaluating the degree to which GRI reporting standards are covered in a CSR report – companies pay a fee to have their reports featured on the GRI website, http://www.globalreporting.org, and listed in GRI's Sustainability Disclosure Database. The 30+ organizations with reports featured in June 2012 include:

Organization Name (Alphabetical)
Ability Options Limited
AEGON
Akbank
American Electric Power (AEP)
Australian Paper
Ball State University
Clorox
Coloplast
Dubai Customs
EVVA
Fonds de solidarité (FTQ)
Gildan
Givaudan SA (Switzerland)
GLOBUL
Hydro-Québec
JSW Steel
La Trobe University
L'Oréal France
Mahindra Group
Mexichem
Munich Airport
Nestlé
Nordic Choice Hotels Rabobank
Royal Dutch Shell
RWE
Santander
Snam Rete Gas
Spectra Energy
Sulzer
VidaCaixa
Xella

Jantzi Social Index® (JSI®)

Companies in the in 2012 JSI® are chosen by the company Sustainalytics, http://www.
sustainalytics.com, by *inclusionary* criteria to meet broad environmental, social and
governance (ESG) criteria, and *exclusionary* criteria – related to military weapons, nuclear
power, and tobacco – that make associated companies ineligible for inclusion in the
index.[1] Two companies have created mutual funds that include, with some alterations, the
60 companies that comprise the index. These are Meritas Mutual Funds[2] in the Meritas
Jantzi Social Index Fund, and iShares, http://www.ishares.ca, in its Socially Responsible
Exchange Traded Fund (ETF).[3]

Ten companies account for approximately 60 per cent of each fund's assets. These
companies are:

Company	Sector
Royal Bank of Canada	Financial Services
Toronto Dominion Bank	Financial Services
Bank of Nova Scotia	Financial Services
Suncor Energy	Energy
Potash Corp of Saskatchewan	Basic Materials
Bank of Montreal	Financial Services
Canadian National Railway	Industrials
Canadian Imperial Bank of Commerce	Financial Services
Cenovus Energy	Energy
Enbridge	Energy

Source: OceanRock Investments Inc. (2012, April 16). *Fund Facts* "Meritas SRI Funds, Meritas Jantzi Social Index® Fund –
Series A," http://www.qtrade.ca/_pdfs/oceanrock/regulatory/Meritas_FFD_JSI_Series_A.pdf, (accessed June 7, 2012).

1. Sustainalytics, Jantzi Social Index Methodology, http://www.sustainalytics.com/sites/default/
    files/updated_jsi_methodology_sept_21_2011.pdf, 2011.
2. Meritas Mutual Funds, now a part of OceanRock Investments Inc., http://www.qtrade.ca/
    oceanrock/aboutus/about_meritas.jsp
3. Named iShares CDN Jantzi Social Index® Fund, http://ca.ishares.com/product_info/fund/
    overview/XEN.htm

FTSE4Good® Index Series

The top 15 North American and top 10 Global companies based on an overall Environmental, Social, and Governance (ESG) rating by the FTSE[4] are provided here. (Only companies that have passed the FTSE4Good criteria are presented.) In 2012, FTSE had five responsible-investment indices and data tools, compared to just one – FTSE4Good® Index Series – in 2001.

North America

Company	Country	FTSE's Industry Classification Benchmark (ICB) Supersector
Intel Corp	USA	Technology
Hewlett-Packard	USA	Technology
Telus Corporation	CAN	Telecommunications
BCE	CAN	Telecommunications
Canadian Pacific Railway	CAN	Industrial Goods & Services
Ford Motor	USA	Automobiles & Parts
Johnson Controls	USA	Automobiles & Parts
Disney (Walt) Company	USA	Media
Rogers Communications	CAN	Telecommunications
TransAlta Corporation	CAN	Utilities
Baxter Intl	USA	Health Care
Citigroup	USA	Banks
Humana	USA	Health Care
NYSE Euronext	USA	Financial Services
Yahoo	USA	Technology

Source: FTSE. *Factsheet.* "ESG Ratings – Global & Regional Leaders." March 2012, http://www.ftse.com/Indices/FTSE4Good_ESG_Ratings/Downloads/Regional_Leaders.pdf, (accessed June 8, 2012).

Global

Company	Country	FTSE's Industry Classification Benchmark (ICB) Supersector
Vivendi	FRA	Media
Westpac Banking Corp	AU	Banks
Nokia	FIN	Technology
Bank Hapoalim	ISR	Banks
Norsk Hydro	NOR	Basic Resources
UBS	SWIT	Banks
Aviva	UK	Insurance
BT Group	UK	Telecommunications
Diageo	UK	Food & Beverage
Go-Ahead Group	UK	Travel & Leisure
WPP	UK	Media

---

4. FTSE Group, originally formed by the Financial Times and the London Stock Exchange, is a registered company whose name, FTSE, is licensed by the London Stock Exchange to the FTSE Group.

Dow Jones Sustainability World Index

The objectives of this index – one of several Dow Jones Sustainability Indexes – are to include "global sustainability leaders" based on a corporate sustainability assessment by SAM Group, http://www.sam-group.com, an investment company whose focus is "sustainability investing." "The index represents the top 10% of the largest 2,500 companies in the Dow Jones Global Total Stock Market Index^{SM} based on long-term economic, environmental and social criteria."[5]

Top 10 Companies in the Dow Jones Sustainability World Index 31 May 2012

Company	Country	Industry
International Business Machines	United States (US)	Technology
General Electric Co.	US	Industrials
Nestle S.A.	Switzerland	Consumer Goods
Johnson & Johnson	US	Health Care
HSBC Holdings PLC (UK Reg)	United Kingdom (UK)	Financials
Novartis AG	Switzerland	Health Care
Intel Corp.	US	Technology
Vodafone Group PLC	UK	Telecommunications
GlaxoSmithKline PLC	UK	Health Care
Samsung Electronics Co. Ltd.	South Korea	Technology

Source: CME Group Index Services LLC. *Fact Sheet*. "Dow Jones Sustainability World Index^{SM}," May 31, 2012, http://www.sustainability-index.com/djsi_pdf/publications/Factsheets/SAM_IndexesMonthly_DJSIWorld.pdf, (accessed June 7, 2012).

---

5. CME Group Index Services LLC. (2012, May 31). *Fact Sheet*. "Dow Jones Sustainability World Index^{SM}," May 31, 2012, http://www.sustainability-index.com/djsi_pdf/publications/Factsheets/SAM_IndexesMonthly_DJSIWorld.pdf, (accessed June 7, 2012).

Examples of Corporate Social Responsibility Reporting

Company (Alphabetical)	
Coca-Cola Enterprises Inc	Corporate Social Responsibility and & Sustainability Report 2010/2011: http://www.cokecce.com/assets/uploaded_files/CCE_CRS_Report_2010-2011_1.pdf
Intel Corp	http://www.intel.com/content/www/us/en/corporate-responsibility/corporate-responsibility-report-overview.html
Mountain Equipment Co-operative (MEC)	[Accountability Report]: 2011 Summary Report: http://www.mec.ca/media/Images/pdf/accountability/accountability-2011-summaryreport_v1_m56577569831149663.pdf complete online report: mec.ca/accountability
Nike Inc.	Website: http://nikeinc.com/pages/responsibility ; 2010–2011 Sustainable Business Performance Summary: http://www.nikeresponsibility.com/report/
Starbucks	Website: http://www.starbucks.com/responsibility
TD Bank Financial Group	Corporate Responsibility Report 2011: http://www.td.com/corporate-responsibility/Report2011.jsp
TELUS Corporation	TELUS 2011 Corporate Social Responsibility Report: http://csr.telus.com/en/
Vodafone Group plc	Website: http://www.vodafone.com/content/index/about/sustainability.html; Sustainability Report 2011/2012: http://www.vodafone.com/content/index/about/sustainability/sustainability_report.html
Volkswagen	Website: http://www.volkswagenag.com/content/vwcorp/content/en/sustainability_and_responsibility.html; Sustainability Report 2011: http://www.volkswagenag.com/content/vwcorp/info_center/en/publications/2012/04/SR_2011.bin.html/binarystorageitem/file/VWAG_NHB_2011_e_web_neu.pdf

Sources: The Works Design. (2011, August) *CSR Reporting: Best Practices from 2010.*
http://www.worksdesign.com/doc/csr-best-practices.pdf, (accessed June 7, 2012).
Ceres. *Ceres-ACCA Reporting Awards*, http://www.ceres.org/awards/reporting-awards.
Chartered Accountants of Canada. *2011 Corporate Reporting Awards Winners.*
http://www.cica.ca/about-cica/corporate-reporting-awards/item54465.aspx (accessed June 7, 2012).
Corporate Knights: The Company for Clean Capitalism, http://www.corporateknights.com.
CSR Wire: The Corporate Social Responsibility Newswire, http://www.csrwire.com.

Appendix B:
Governance Framework Requirements

Governance Framework

The objective of a governance framework is to ensure that an organization's activities, through the actions of its employees and agents, are in the best interests of its stakeholders. According to past practice, boards of directors have overseen the corporation on behalf of the owners to make sure activities were in the best interest of the company, of the shareholders, really, and the board was expected to institute such governance mechanisms as they needed to ensure that the company optimally achieved its strategic objectives. Without appropriate governance mechanisms – suitable strategies, guidance through an ethical culture, encouragement, monitoring, reporting, rewards, and penalties – employees and agents could engage in suboptimal activities such as putting their interests ahead of the organization's, or placing the organization's reputation at significant risk.

Relatively recently, during the 1990s, corporate accountability expanded to include a broader set of stakeholders. In 1994 and 1995, pronouncements from the Toronto Stock Exchange (now the TSX) and the CICA introduced the thinking that boards of directors were required to foster an ethical corporate culture. Recognizing this, at around the same time some major public accounting firms incorporated stakeholder risk analysis into their audit methodologies, as a means of identifying their clients' business risks, and therefore their own audit risks.

The role of the board and its relationships with other actors in the governance framework is portrayed in Figure 1.

In general terms, the board of directors is expected to further the prospects of the company through:

Figure 1 Appendix B
Corporate Governance Framework

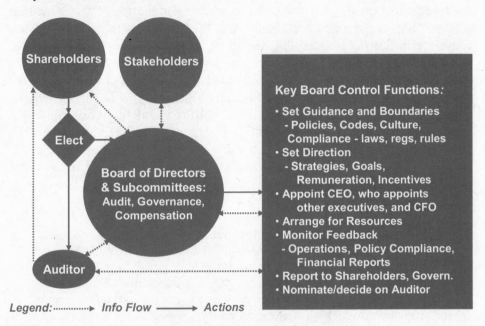

- Oversight – setting or approving strategies and processes, monitoring actions, and improving on actions or correcting errors when necessary
- Ensuring appropriate strategies & objectives reflect values, ethics, competitive advantage, and risk assessment; meeting challenges and stakeholder expectations; and incorporating both long– and short–term time horizons
- Ensuring appropriate actions by:
  - Appointing & monitoring performance for the CEO and CFO
  - Promoting ethical leadership – values and tone at the top
  - Creating and approving ethical guidance – culture, code and rules, learning, encouragement, decision making, internal controls, monitoring mechanisms, enforcement, feedback
  - Providing adequate resources
  - Monitoring compliance with laws, rules and regulations
- Reporting to stakeholders for support incorporating
  - Transparency, integrity, comprehensiveness
- Nominating the auditor

The board's responsibility can best be achieved by developing and maintaining an ethical corporate culture. In fact, directors and senior officers are legally responsible for the creation and maintenance of a system that ensures that employees act ethically, and the quality of that effort has become a criterion for the establishment of a "due diligence" defence that would relieve a corporate director from legal liability for the misdeeds of employees. In its 1994 *Report of the Toronto Stock Exchange Committee on Corporate Governance in Canada*, the TSE (now TSX) stated that directors have a responsibility to ensure that an ethical culture exists in an organization.[1] The Canadian Institute of Chartered Accountants (CICA) followed in 1995, by setting out the appropriate criteria for control of a corporation. Specifically, they identified an organization's ethical culture as a fundamental element of its internal control.[2] For example, *Guidance on Control*, issued by The CICA, states:

> Shared ethical values influence all behaviour in an organization. Together with an understanding of mission and vision, they constitute the basic identity that will shape the way an individual, group, organization or board will operate, and they provide stability over time. Shared values contribute to control because they provide a guide for individual, group or team decision-making, action and policy.[3]

Similar developments in the U.S. have focused on how the directors have put systems into place to ensure that ethical and operational problems do not occur. The U.S. *Sarbanes-Oxley Act of 2002* for example, was enacted to reform corporate governance and disclosure in an effort to restore credibility eroded by Enron and other corporate scandals, and to facilitate capital markets that rely on trust in the fact that shareholders, and the public interest, will not be misled and subverted. In response, governance regulations have been revised to some extent around the world.

Consequences can be severe under the *1991 U.S. Sentencing Guidelines*, unless the "due diligence" protection is available. Legal cases like *Caremark National Inc.* (1996)[4] have reinforced the need for directors to maintain information systems that monitor ethical performance, and proactively seek out and rectify causes of ethical problems.

---

1. *Report of the Toronto Stock Exchange Committee on Corporate Governance in Canada*, December 1994, paragraphs 4.3 and 4.4.
2. *Guidance for Directors – Governance Processes for Control* (Toronto: Canadian Institute of Chartered Accountants, December 1995), page 2, paragraph 8. See also pages 8 & 9 of that document for a discussion of approving and monitoring the organization's ethical values.
3. *Guidance on Control* (Canadian Institute of Chartered Accountants, November 1995), paragraph 59.
4. See Law Case Summary at the end of this appendix.

The Report of the Toronto Stock Exchange Committee on Corporate Governance in Canada made this point very well:

> Having said that directors have no corporate law duty to act in the best interest of any particular stakeholder group [*other than shareholders*], it is obvious that a board cannot make decisions without understanding the implications of its decision for this broader group of stakeholders. In making decisions to enhance shareholder value the board must take into account the interests of other stakeholders. In today's environment it is difficult for a corporation to prosper if it is not "on side" with all its stakeholders.[5]
>
> (Italics added)

Decisions integrating shareholder and stakeholder interests are not as difficult as previously thought. They can be made using stakeholder impact analysis and philosophical techniques that are discussed in Chapter 8.

Directors wishing to be up-to-date would be well advised to join an organization such as the Institute for Corporate Directors (ICD), which has developed an education and certification process (ICD.D), and provides information through its website at http://www.icd.ca; or the NACD (National Association of Corporate Directors), which can be found online at http://www.nacdonline.org/nacd/governance.asp.

Regulation of ethical conduct

Of course, many things that are unethical are illegal, and corporations, whether private or public, have to follow the law. However, as emphasized by Lynn Sharp Paine, merely following the law is not sufficient to satisfy stakeholders, or to maintain the integrity and reputation of a business. Corporations are subject to many kinds of rules and regulations concerning such matters as employee health and safety, product safety, environmental performance, and various forms of licensing. Public companies in most of the world are also subject to a vast array of detailed regulations concerning governance, insider trading, and financial reporting rules that in a large entity require an army of people to administer. The scope of these regulations expanded as a result of corporate financial scandals that came to light in the 1980s, and continues to do so. More and more regulatory pieces have come into play.

---

5. "Where Were The Directors? Guidelines for Improved Corporate Governance in Canada," *Report of the Toronto Stock Exchange Committee on Corporate Governance in Canada* (Toronto: December 1994): Section 4.17, p. 21.

Financial Regulation

Financial regulatory initiatives that apply to public companies in North America aimed at shareholder protection include the following:

- Regulations of stock exchanges and securities commissions that require companies to publicly disclose compliance with corporate governance criteria, and in Canada, the audit committee charter.
- *Sarbanes-Oxley Act* (SOX) in the U.S., and equivalent securities polices in Canada that are in the process of being implemented.
- The establishment of bodies to oversee the performance of auditors in Canada, the U.S. and many other countries worldwide.

All these rules and regulations have an ethical base, although they may not usually be considered in that light. Dealing with a bureaucrat about an arcane regulation relating to the applicability of an insider trading rule is not usually considered to be an exercise in applied ethics, and understandably so. But in recent years, in response to highly publicized ethical and legal lapses by large corporations, the United States Congress has reacted with legislation, and other countries, including Canada, have followed. This legislation has primarily focussed on the particular interests of investors and shareholders, who were cheated out of millions of dollars. As an aside, it is interesting to note that legislators and regulators do not seem to be nearly as concerned about protecting the interests of other stakeholders who lost millions, such as employees. However, after the 2008 housing market collapse, the political pressure became immense, and some concern was expressed on the plight of those who could not meet their mortgage payments and had their homes foreclosed. In response to the 2008 financial crisis (see Chapter 10), the *Dodd-Frank Wall Street Reform and Consumer Protection Act* was signed by U.S. President Barack Obama on July 21, 2010, in an effort to control the behaviour of U.S. financial institutions.[6]

Details of regulatory requirements outlined in this appendix may be found on the websites of the relevant regulatory body. In North America these would include:

---

6. A *Brief Summary of the Dodd-Frank Wall Street Reform and Consumer Protection Act* may be found at http://banking.senate.gov/public/_files/070110_Dodd_Frank_Wall_Street_Reform_comprehensive_summary_Final.pdf.

- U.S.A.
  - SEC http://www.sec.gov
  - PCAOB http://www.pcaobus.org/
  - NYSE http://www.nyse.com
- Canada
  - CSA http://www.csa-acvm.ca/
  - CPAB http://www.cpab-ccrc.ca
  - Ontario Securities Commission (OSC) http://www.osc.gov.on.ca/
  - TSX http://www.tsx.com/

Guidance on the application of these regulations may also be found in publications of law and accounting firms. These are usually more user friendly for non-experts.

A useful example of modern governance can be found in the Rogers Governance Report which is available online at http://www.shoprogers.com/corporategovernance/corporategovernance_overview.asp.

Toronto Stock Exchange governance disclosure requirements

Larger Canadian public companies are required to file an Annual Information Form (AIF) that, among other things, requires companies to append their audit committee's charter and to state whether they have complied with certain recommended (and voluntary) corporate governance criteria.

Sarbanes-Oxley Act (SOX) and Canadian equivalents

In 2002 the U.S. Congress passed the *Sarbanes-Oxley Act*. The important thing about this legislation is that it focussed directly on ethical conduct by senior management, and others such as boards of directors and audit committees, who have management oversight responsibilities. While this legislation is primarily related to honesty in financial reporting, and the U.S. Securities and Exchange Commission (SEC) was given responsibility for applying the act, its effect is much broader. For example, the audit committee is held responsible for monitoring complaints from employees about the honesty of management in relation to financial reporting.

The primary aspects of the SOX legislation and resulting regulation are:

- A requirement that public companies evaluate and disclose the effectiveness of their internal controls as they relate to financial reporting, and that independent auditors for such companies "attest" (i.e., agree, or not) to such disclosure and express an opinion on the adequacy of internal controls as they relate to financial reporting. Subsequent to its initial enactment, this requirement was softened, especially for small registrants.

- Certification of financial reports by chief executive officers and chief financial officers. Criminal liability can attach for knowingly certifying inaccurate reports.
- Auditor independence, including outright bans on certain types of work for audit clients, and pre-approval by the company's audit committee of all audit and non-audit work.
- A requirement that companies listed on stock exchanges have fully independent audit committees that oversee the relationship between the company and its auditor.
- A ban on most personal loans to any executive officer or director.
- Employee protections allowing those corporate fraud whistleblowers who file complaints within ninety days of termination or other disciplinary action to win reinstatement, back pay and benefits, compensatory damages, and costs.

Similar requirements are now part of Canadian securities regulation, except that the Canadian Securities Administrators (CSA) do not require auditor attestation of management's report on its internal controls. The independence requirements for auditors were established by the Canadian accounting profession, rather than securities regulators, and are in some respects more rigorous than those of the SEC.

For reasons of lack of space, and because they are constantly changing, it is not the purpose of this publication to provide guidance on compliance with securities regulation in North America. Guidance on these matters is readily available from the regulators themselves, with much needed interpretive guidance from accounting firms and law firms. Rather, our purpose is to emphasize how legislators and regulators are moving into ethical behavioural issues.

For example, the SOX and Canadian regulations requirements to report on the adequacy of their internal controls over financial reporting, use the so-called COSO[7] criteria. One of the most important of these criteria is "tone

---

7. The Committee of Sponsoring Organizations of the Treadway Commission (COSO), http://www.sox-online.com/coso_cobit_coso.html, is a voluntary private sector organization dedicated to improving the quality of financial reporting through business ethics, effective internal controls, and corporate governance. It arose in response to serious financial reporting frauds that had occurred in the 1980s. In 1992 COSO developed a framework and criteria for reporting on internal controls that had become widely accepted in the U.S. prior to the SOX legislation. Although a somewhat different framework was developed in Canada, the COSO framework now appears to have become universal.

at the top," which emphasizes the importance of demonstrably ethical behaviour by CEOs and other senior officers. COSO's criteria also specifically emphasize that business ethics represents an important element of the risk management process.

Both the U.S. and Canada have many other regulatory bodies that influence financial reporting and auditing in specific industries, especially those relating to the provision of financial services.

Oversight of the public accounting profession

Failure of auditors to catch some of the accounting frauds of the eighties and nineties had ethical dimensions, and led to tougher auditing and independence standards in North America, and internationally.

The Public Company Accounting Oversight Board (PCAOB) was created by the SOX legislation in the United States, and reports to the SEC. One of its mandates is to oversee and inspect the performance of audits of public companies. All firms that perform such audits are required to register with PCAOB; large firms are inspected annually and smaller ones less frequently. The inspections are rigorous and failure to comply with recommendations and requirements of PCAOB can result in drastic penalties.

PCAOB's equivalent in Canada is the Canadian Public Accountability Board (CPAB), which conducts similar inspections of audit firms that audit public companies. Its power stems from a requirement of the Canadian Securities Administrators (CSA) that requires all reports on registrant companies to be from auditors in good standing with CPAB.

Both PCAOB and CPAB are independent of the public accounting profession. Both bodies focus on more than just technical compliance with auditing, accounting, and independence rules. They consider a firm's quality controls, particularly those relating to the need for emphasis on audit quality and independence, including "tone at the top."

Non-financial Regulation

Most companies are affected by laws and regulations related to their particular business. The focus of many of these requirements is fundamentally ethical, whether it be public or employee safety, or environmental in nature. In almost all cases, if a company runs afoul of such requirements, it incurs not only legal penalties, but also reputational damage, occasionally of a catastrophic nature. In fact, even if not penalized under law, the revelations involved may still damage reputations.

Summary

The fact that legislators and regulators are moving further into the business ethics field should not lead to complacency or a belief following the rules is enough to stay out of trouble. Far from it. Regulations tend to focus on form, sometimes at the expense of substance. Governance processes and internal control structures will work well only if those responsible for implementing them act in an ethical manner. When it comes to audit committees, for example, it appears that Enron had all the right structures in place. Indeed, some have said the audit committee's mandate was exemplary. However, the process failed because the people who were involved were not as diligent as they should have been. Diligence in matters ethical is a business imperative, whether or not there are rules requiring it.

Readings

Len Brooks, "Sniff Tests," *Corporate Ethics Monitor*, 7:5 (1995): 65.

Reprinted with permission of The Publisher of The Corporate Ethics Monitor, EthicScan Canada Ltd., Toronto. Not to be reproduced without permission in writing.

Sniff Tests

How many times have you wished there were a few key questions you or your employees could ask about an activity to assess quickly whether it is ethical, or whether further ethical study is needed? How many executives wish their employees had asked such quick but fundamental questions before taking an action that ultimately turned out to be very embarrassing for them and damaging for their organization? Why not head off such problems by developing tests for your organization to use to clarify whether an action is ethical or unethical, to sniff out unethical activities before they become troublesome, and to identify when and how an activity should be changed to make it ethical.

Sniff tests can focus the attention of decision makers on the impact of the activity or option on the organization's stakeholders, including the decision maker. For instance, to test whether the activity is fair, the decision maker could ask: *Would I regard this as fair if this were done to me?* A follow-up question that addresses remedial concerns could be: *How would I want the activity changed if I were the focus of it?*

Ethical decision making does not always make everyone happy. But to test whether the activity is right, a sniff test might be: *Is it legal?* But this is not a strong enough test on its own because there are many activities that are legal but not ethical. Some sniff-test questions that may be useful here are: *What would the public think of this activity if the reasons behind the decision were on TV or the front page of tomorrow's newspaper?* or *What would my children think of this?* or the acid test, *What would my mother think of this?*

There are often trade-offs to be made between various stakeholders because few activities are good for everyone. Trade-offs can be raised and assessed by the following chain of questions: *Does every stakeholder benefit from this activity? Is the harm caused to one or more of the parties offset by the benefits created for others? Is there any harm being created that is permanent or contrary to organizational guidelines? After looking at all potential benefits and harm caused in the next 10 years, is the net benefit marginal? Should I consult my superiors about the risk inherent in this activity?*

Ethical problems tend to become much worse over time than most decision makers expect. Consequently, sniff tests that probe the future are useful, such as: *What's the worst-case ethical scenario that could result from this decision? Have I considered that a whistleblower usually emerges and that secrets rarely stay secret? Is there any problem that could arise beyond the ten-year time horizon that I should take into account?*

Unethical activities often spring from arrangements that fail to protect the ethical position of the organization, so it is wise to pose some sniff tests about the organizational framework that spawns decisions, such as: *Do personnel in this area understand the organization's ethical expectations? Are personnel in a position where the gain from unethical activity can outweigh the chance of being found out or the penalty involved? Is there a timely ethics audit or review of activities and organizational arrangements in this area?*

Sniff tests can be helpful, even essential. David Nitkin, whose work at EthicScan created the concept, believes that sniff tests represent a means for top executives to have confidence that all their personnel can and will apply a consistent set of tests and, as a result, reach similar conclusions to ethical dilemmas. Wouldn't you rather head off an ethical dilemma that smells before it is too late?

LAW CASE SUMMARY: CAREMARK NATIONAL INC.

Reprinted with permission of the author, Prof. L.J. Brooks. All rights reserved.

Late in 1996, the Chancery Court of the State of Delaware, a very influential court in corporate matters, handed down a decision that changed the expectations of directors for monitoring the affairs of the organizations they direct. The change held in the *Caremark National Inc. Case* was to require directors to monitor organizational activities even when there is no cause for suspicion of wrongdoing.

Until the *Caremark* decision, the guiding case was the Delaware Supreme Court's 1963 decision in *Graham v. Allis-Chalmers Manufacturing Co.* In *Allis-Chalmers*, a case involving director's liability for violations of U.S. antitrust laws, the Court had found that, "absent cause for suspicion," a board of directors had no legal duty to create a system for monitoring or compliance of organizational activities. This allowed directors to argue an ostrich defence in the event of wrongdoing to the effect that they had, "seen no evil nor heard no evil," and had made their decisions in good faith and to the best of their ability. As a result, the fiduciary duties of directors, and the duty of care were somewhat circumscribed from the level of responsibility that some stakeholders felt reasonable.

The Chancery Court took the view in the *Caremark Case*, a derivative lawsuit involving kickbacks to health care providers in violation of the federal Anti-Referral Payments Law, that the directors could be liable for recovery of some of the company's $250 million in fines from its directors for breach of their duty of care by failing to take good faith measures to prevent or remedy the violations. The Court noted, since employee actions could prevent a corporation from achieving its strategic goals, "that a director's obligation includes a duty to assure in good faith that [an] information reporting system, which the Board concludes is adequate, exists and that failure to do so under some circumstances may, in theory at least, render a director liable for losses caused by non-compliance with applicable legal standards." Moreover, due to the issuance of the U.S. Federal Sentencing Guidelines on November 1, 1991, and their subsequent integration into expectations, directors must now consider the due diligence defence criteria that those guidelines have spawned when advancing their good faith defence. This means that the Chancery Court no longer considers a corporate compliance and monitoring program to be optional.

For further information, the reader is referred to an article by Frank M. Placenti in *The National Law Journal*, on Monday June 23, 1997 (pages B5, B6). Further insights are possible if higher courts modify the Chancery Court's *Caremark* decision. But until then, directors are well advised to be ethically proactive in the development of strategic plans, operating policies and in the monitoring of performance.

Jim Goodfellow and Allan Willis, "CEO Challenge," *CAmagazine* 40:1 (2007): 35–42.

Reproduced with permission from CAmagazine, published by the Canadian Institute of Chartered Accountants, Toronto.

In three short years, chief executive and chief financial officers have been required to certify financial info in the name of bolstering integrity

"Since 2004, three waves of CEO and CFO certification have washed over corporate Canada, and there are more to come. All are aimed at restoring investor confidence in financial reporting and related controls by improving accountability and transparency – terms seldom heard during the '90s, a time of heady growth, but which, since 2001, have resurfaced as key business, governance and disclosure principles.

Certification was introduced to Canada in 2004 when the Canadian Securities Administrators (CSA) required the CEO and CFO of a reporting issuer to certify the financial information in quarterly and annual filings. In 2005, that was expanded to include certification about disclosure controls and procedures. Last year, the third wave arrived. It requires certifying officers of TSX and TSX-V issuers to file the full annual certificate for financial years ending on or after June 30, 2006 – which, for many reporting issuers, means the calendar year ended December 31, 2006.

The full annual certificate in CSA Multilateral Instrument 52-109 expands the certification to require CEOs and CFOs to state they have "designed such internal control over financial reporting, or caused it to be designed under our supervision, to provide reasonable assurance regarding the reliability of financial reporting and the preparation of financial statements for external purposes in accordance with the issuer's GAAP."

In addition, they are required to certify that the annual Management's Discussion and Analysis (MD&A) discloses any changes in internal control over financial reporting (ICFR) that occurred in the latest interim reporting period that have materially affected, or could materially affect, the ICFR.

This third wave of certification applies only to the design of ICFR, not its operating effectiveness. That will be introduced in a fourth wave of certification, yet to come.

In March 2006, CSA Notice 52-313 announced that the CEO and CFO certificates of TSX and TSX-V issuers will be expanded to include certification of the effectiveness of the issuer's ICFR as of the end of the financial year and certification that the certifiers have "caused the issuer to disclose in the annual MD&A [their] conclusions about the effectiveness of internal control over financial reporting." The CSA's proposed rules for this fourth wave of certification were to be released by the end of 2006. (At press time they had yet to be published.)

As the certifications for Canadian reporting issuers continue to unfold, they will take a direction different from certification rules in the US. Unlike Securities Exchange Commission registrants, issuers in Canada will not, according to CSA Notice 52-313, be required to provide a separate management report on ICFR, nor will they have to obtain their auditor's opinion from an internal control audit or an opinion on man-agement's assessment of the effectiveness of ICFR.

Readers may wish to review the CSA's proposals in addition to the discussion here, which focuses on helping CEOs and CFOs, their management teams and their audit committees finalize the assessment of ICFR design and the disclosures needed in their annual MD&A to meet the certification requirements from June 2006 onward.

The top-down, risk-based approach

The current requirement to assess the design of ICFR creates a challenge. In effect, it requires certifying that ICFR exists on paper, without requiring testing as to whether it actually works in practice, especially during any particular reporting period. Therefore CEOs and CFOs need an organized, disciplined and documented process for assessing and documenting their conclusions concerning the design of ICFR in order to support their certification and MD&A disclosures.

The September 2006 CICA publication Internal Control 2006: The Next Wave of Certification provides a straightforward, business-focused, top-down and risk-based approach for CEOs and CFOs to follow in assessing and certifying the design of ICFR. This approach will also help companies prepare for the future evaluation of the effectiveness of ICFR.

To be effective and efficient, a top-down, risk-based approach requires at least two things. First, there must be a focus on the tone at the top, that is, the interaction between the board of directors and the CEO in establishing the control environment and the culture of integrity. Second, there must be a sound process for identifying principal business risks, including financial reporting and disclosure risks. The effectiveness of a top-down, risk-based approach to assessing ICFR design is consistent with findings reported in the August 2006 paper Internal Controls – A Review of Recent Developments issued by the International Federation of Accountants. This notes a convergence of thinking over the past two years in various countries' and bodies' pronouncements about internal control, emphasizing the importance of the tone at the top and a focus on risk as the essential features of internal control.

Further, companies should view their assessment of ICFR as a business improvement opportunity, not just a regulatory com-pliance task. The assessment of ICFR presents management, boards of directors and audit committees with the opportunity to reassess what ICFR is intended to achieve: control over financial reporting and disclosure risks. Companies should design and implement ICFR to achieve their business objectives as well as satisfying their external reporting obligations. After all, without effective ICFR, how can senior management and boards of directors be certain that decisions taken on the basis of internal financial information are being made on a sound basis?

The International Federation of Accountants paper stated an interesting finding from a recent UK review of its internal control code: "It was felt that those companies that viewed internal control as sound business practice were more likely to have embedded it into their normal business processes, and more likely to feel that they had benefited as a result, than those that viewed it primarily as a compliance exercise."

In summary, the tone at the top and the control environment, a focus on risk, the extent of active CEO involvement and appropriate board oversight are critical elements of ICFR. A top-down, risk-based approach is also likely to be more practical than the approach taken to date in the US for satisfying Section 404 of the Sarbanes-Oxley Act.

Accountability and transparency

The CSA's certification regulations are basedon two fundamental principles: accountability and transparency. The accountability principle is achieved through separate and personal certifications from the CEO and the CFO.

The transparency principle is applied at four levels. The first, the content level, refers to the degree to which the information in the filings enables readers to reliably assess and interpret the financial condition, results of operations and cash flows of the issuer. The second level, a process level, refers to the reliability of disclosure controls and procedures (DC&P), and disclosures of any material weakness in them. Now, the third level – also of process – has been added to address the design of ICFR and include disclosures about changes in ICFR. In future, as a fourth level, there will have to be disclosures arising from management's conclusions from their evaluation of the effectiveness of ICFR.

Unfortunately, many issuers seem to have missed the messages about transparency and accountability, which are embedded in the CSA disclosure requirements. The certification requirements about DC&P call for CEOs and CFOs to state that they have caused the issuer to disclose in the annual MD&A their conclusions about the effectiveness of the DC&P as of the end of the period covered by the annual filings.

However, based on a sample of 286 issuers selected from across the country, the CSA found, according to CSA Staff Notice 52-315 in September 2006, that: "Approximately 28% of issuers in our sample, however, failed to include this disclosure in their annual MD&A. This widespread noncompliance with such a clear and basic requirement shows that many issuers are not paying adequate attention to their disclosure obligations. We are particularly concerned by the failure to include the disclosure regarding disclosure controls and procedures in the annual MD&A given that, in most cases, the certifying officers specifically represented in their certificates that they had caused the issuer to include this disclosure in the annual MD&A."

Clearly, this disclosure requirement has hit the CSA's radar screen, and it will undoubtedly continue monitoring compliance with it.

What is less clear is whether the CSA will expand its focus to assess the level of effort CEOs and CFOs are putting into their assessment of DC&P, or to assess whether any material weaknesses exist in it. Perhaps it will take challenges and decisions in the courts under civil liability to ultimately clarify the expectations and consequences concerning the judgments made in the process of the evaluations and related personal certifications.

Materiality

Materiality in relation to a design weakness should be based on the extent to which it would increase the risk that errors that could mislead investors would be made or not be detected in the issuer's published financial statements prepared in accordance with the issuer's GAAP.

The accounting literature contains guidance in making materiality determinations from both qualitative and quantitative perspectives. Unfortunately, little Canadian guidance is available to help management evaluate the likelihood of errors occurring, or what would constitute a low versus high likelihood. Current US guidance – Rule 2 of the US Public Company Accounting Oversight Board – defines a material weakness as "a significant control deficiency, or combination of deficiencies, that results in a more than remote likelihood that a material misstatement of the annual or interim financial statements will not be prevented or detected." The bottom line is CEOs and CFOs must use their professional judgment in assessing their findings with respect to the design of ICFR and determining the appropriate disclosure in the MD&A.

Three levels of disclosure may be considered in evaluating a weakness in the design of ICFR:

- Type A – weaknesses considered material, which should be disclosed in the MD&A as well as to the audit committee and external auditors
- Type B – weaknesses not considered material but significant enough to be communicated to the audit committee and external auditors, and
- Type C – weaknesses that are not significant from an external reporting perspective but should be communicated to the appropriate member of management for remediation.

CEOs and CFOs should develop, in consultation with internal auditors, external auditors and the audit committee, their own criteria for applying these categories in practice.

Disclosure in the MD&A

The CSA Staff Notice 52-316 in September 2006 has made it clear that the CEO's and CFO's individual conclusions about the effectiveness of the DC&P should include the disclosure of identified weaknesses in ICFR:

> "Given the substantial overlap between the definitions of DC&P and ICFR, it is our view that the certifying officers therefore should cause the issuer to disclose in the annual MD&A the nature of any weakness [this is taken to mean any weakness that would cause the certifying officers to doubt whether the design of ICFR provides reasonable assurance regarding the reliability of the financial statements and whether they are in accordance with the issuer's GAAP] in the design of the issuer's ICFR, the risks associated with the weakness and the issuer's plan, if any, to remediate the weakness. If no such plan exists, theissuer should consider disclosing its reasons for not planning to remediate the weakness."

As a matter of prudence, management should also investigate and correct any financial statement errors that may have occurred as a result of the ICFR design weakness in the current reporting period and in future reporting periods until the weakness is remediated.

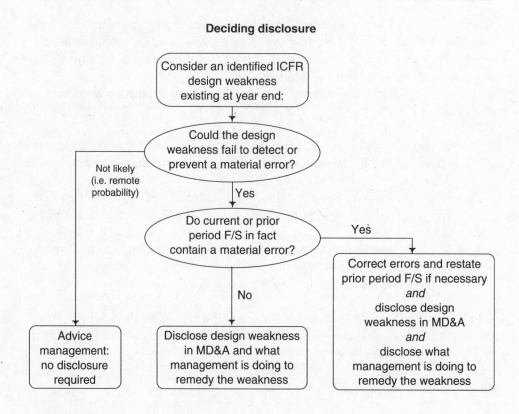

Deciding disclosure

Consider an identified ICFR design weakness existing at year end:

Could the design weakness fail to detect or prevent a material error?

Not likely (i.e. remote probability)

Yes

Do current or prior period F/S in fact contain a material error?

Yes

No

Advice management: no disclosure required

Disclose design weakness in MD&A and what management is doing to remedy the weakness

Correct errors and restate prior period F/S if necessary *and* disclose design weakness in MD&A *and* disclose what management is doing to remedy the weakness

For example, suppose a material weakness in the design of ICFR is detected and disclosed in the 2006 annual MD&A. Management should conduct an investigation to ensure this weakness did not result in material errors in the 2006 financial statements before these statements are finalized and released. Then they should conduct a similar investigation in the first quarter of 2007, and in subsequent quarters, until the ICFR design weakness is corrected. To do otherwise could leave the CEO, CFO and the company's directors exposed to legal and/or regulatory actions if there were a material error in the financial statements and they had done nothing to ensure the financial statements were fairly presented when they were aware that a material design weakness existed in ICFR.

The chart "Deciding disclosure," may be helpful to CEOs and CFOs in deciding about MD&A disclosures of weaknesses in ICFR design.

The CEO/CFO certificate for 2006 also requires CEOs and CFOs to disclose in the MD&A any material changes in their ICFR that were made in the most recent interim reporting period (e.g., fourth quarter for annual MD&As). This applies to changesthat have materially affected ICFR and those that are reasonably likely to do so in the future.

Q4 change disclosure

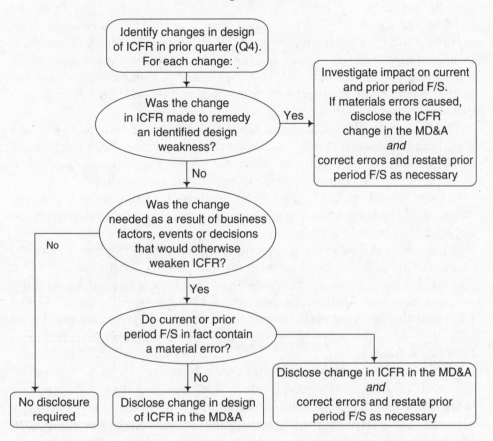

The chart "Q4 change disclosure," page 38, may be helpful in deciding about disclosures of fourth-quarter changes in ICFR design.

Signing certificates when material ICFR weaknesses exist

CEOs and CFOs will face a dilemma when they come to sign their certificates in situations where:

- an uncorrected material weakness in the design of ICFR has been identified as of the end of the reporting period,
- appropriate MD&A disclosure has been made about the weakness, and
- appropriate steps have been taken to ensure the weakness has had no material effect on the financial statements.

The wording of the required certification cannot be altered or amended and the certificate explicitly states that the CEO and CFO "have designed ICFR to provide reasonable assurance regarding the reliability of financial reporting and the preparation of financial statements for external purposes in accordance with the issuer's GAAP." However, the disclosure of an ICFR design weakness in the MD&A suggests that reasonable assurance as to the reliability of financial reporting does not exist. Faced with such a dilemma, what are CEOs and CFOs to do?

The September 2006 CSA Staff Notice 52-316 stated, "In our view, the certifying officers can certify the design of the issuer's ICFR if the issuer's disclosure about the identified weakness presents an accurate and complete picture of the condition of the design of the issuer's ICFR."

In such a situation, CEOs and CFOs are advised to bring the matter to the attention of the audit committee and consult legal counsel to determine an appropriate course of action.

If the issuer is disclosing a remediation plan for an identified material weakness in ICFR, it would be wise for that plan to clearly indicate what actions will be taken and when, as well as the commitment and capability to carry them out. Further, the plan should be approved by the CFO, the CEO and the audit committee and the disclosures should be continued until the audit committee is satisfied that the remediation plan has been fully implemented.

Management and audit committees are advised not to try to rationalize why an ICFR design weakness is not material and therefore does not need to be disclosed, in order to avoid the contradiction that might otherwise appear to arise between the disclosures in the MD&A and the wording in the required certificates.

Implications for smaller issuers

Small companies with limited resources may have certain ICFR design weaknesses (e.g., segregation of duties) that are difficult or wholly unreasonable to rectify. Because of this, many small companies may need to conclude that their ICFR is ineffective. They will, therefore, have to disclose the material weaknesses in ICFR in the MD&A and also, by consequence, have to report in the MD&A that their disclosure controls are ineffective.

As noted above, the CSA's Staff Notice 52-316 indicated in September 2006 that issuers should "disclose in the annual MD&A the nature of any weakness in the design of the issuer's ICFR, the risks associated with the weakness and the issuer's plan, if any, to remediate the weakness. If no such plan exists, the issuer should consider disclosing the reasons for not planning to remediate the weakness."

There are, however, actions that management and the audit committee may wish to consider that are less costly than re-mediating the ICFR design weakness, in order to provide investors with assurance that the ICFR design weaknesses have not resulted in material error in the financial statements. For example, the audit committee could engage the external auditor to perform quarterly reviews of interim financial statements. If the audit committee engages auditors to perform quarterly reviews, this fact should be disclosed in the MD&A.

Conclusion

The requirement to certify the design of ICFR cannot be avoided. Management can, however, carry out its ICFR design assessment process in a way that ensures ICFR supports both internal business decision-making and the reliability of external financial reporting. By taking such an approach, the time and effort spent in ICFR design and a top-down, risk-based assessment will be more likely to earn a return on the investment made. It may also help to support a due diligence defence by management and the board, should one ever be required. Finally, the actions taken and lessons learned now in assessing the design of ICFR will be of value in future when CEOs and CFOs face the fourth wave of certification – the annual evaluation of ICFR operating effectiveness.

Jim Goodfellow, FCA, is chair of the CICA's Canadian Performance Reporting Initiative-Board and partner at Deloitte & Touche LLP

Alan Willis, CA, is an independent consultant in corporate governance, performance measurement and performance reporting. He coauthored with Jim Goodfellow CICA's September 2006 guidance for management and directors, Internal Control 2006: The Next Wave of Certification

S. Prakash Sethi, "Codes of Conduct for Global Business: Prospects and Challenges of Implementation," *Principles of Stakeholder Management* **(Toronto: The Clarkson Centre for Business Ethics & Board Effectiveness, 1999), 9–20.**

Corporate Codes and Critics

In the United States and Western Europe, corporate codes of conduct have become *de rigueur* for most large corporations. According to recent studies, 60 to 70 percent of major US corporations have issued codes of conduct, and many of the largest foreign multinationals have done so as well. These codes usually attempt to state the company's mission, values, and goals, and to describe its relationship to various stakeholders, both internal and external. Unfortunately, most of these codes suffer from a number of flaws:

- They are presented as public statements of lofty intent and purpose, but lack specific content.
- While they mention the corporation's commitment to its customers, employees, etc., they ignore the rights of these key stakeholders in their dealings with the company.
- They make no provisions for internal implementation, and code compliance is not integrated into the organization's procedures and reward structure; hence, managers and employees are often uninformed about the codes and their content, and do not take them seriously.
- They provide no basis or framework for communication with external communities about the efforts and results (success or failure) of the corporation in achieving the codes' objectives.

The inevitable result of these defects is that corporate codes of conduct are often treated with disdain by knowledgeable and influential opinion leaders among various stakeholder groups, as well as by outside analysts and the public at large. To be sure, there are a handful of companies whose codes of conduct are taken more seriously by their constituencies. Notable examples are those of Motorola, Levi Strauss, Texas Instruments, Sara Lee, and Mattel. However, the very smallness of this group reinforces my point. And, with the exception of Mattel, none of these corporations has chosen to make public either the process by which it seeks compliance of its code within its own organization (particularly by its overseas subsidiaries and strategic partners), or the results of its compliance efforts. Nor have the corporations, with the exception of Mattel, subjected their codes or processes to independent outside verification.

The weakness of corporate commitment to code compliance is all too apparent. After thirty years of research and teaching in this field, I can point to only one major corporation that has asked external independent monitors to examine its code compliance and has made the results public. This example is Nestle, the Swiss-based multinational corporation and one of the world's largest manufacturers of food and related products. Nestle was confronted with worldwide public boycotts of its products, and demonstrations by advocates of the poor and developing countries for its alleged improper marketing and promotional activities in the sale of infant formula products in these countries. Although inherently safe, these products were too expensive and largely unnecessary in these settings. Poor and uninformed mothers in developing countries were pressured into buying these products through intense promotion. Eventually, the World Health Organization enacted an International Code of Marketing of Breast-Milk Substitutes (Infant Formula Code) which banned most advertising and promotion of such products. Nestle was strongly opposed to the development of this Code. Nevertheless, after the Code was enacted, Nestle announced its willingness to abide by the Code and arranged for independent verification and compliance monitoring. The outcome was highly salutory. Within a period of less than four years, Nestle's reputation was largely restored, and the boycott against the company's products was called off.

Since that time, only one US multinational corporation has voluntarily promulgated a global code of conduct that committed itself to independent monitoring by an external group of credible and experienced persons charged to make a public report of their findings. That company is Mattel, one of the world's largest producers of children's *toys* including Barbie, Hot Wheels and Fisher Price products. This experience, and my personal involvement in it, will be further discussed below.

Corporate Response to Criticism

There have, of course, been a few other notable positive responses by major corporations, both individually and collectively, to public criticism. The promulgation of the Sullivan Principles by US firms operating in South Africa is a significant example. For the most part, however, multinational corporations have responded to public pressures in two lesseffective ways:

- They claim to abide by all local laws and standards. They also declare that their practices are driven by competitive market forces, low worker productivity, and the extra cost of doing business in different countries. Furthermore, they claim, often with some justification, that wages and working conditions in their own plants are superior to other plants in these areas.
- They promulgate voluntary codes of conduct that appear to address the concerns of their critics. Unfortunately, these weak and haphazard efforts often reveal the *absence* of long-term strategies to deal with underlying issues, as well as inadequate programs of public communication. Very few companies have created codes of conduct or "best practice" by which they can actually guide and evaluate their overseas operations, or the conduct of their local partners and suppliers.

Companies are often seen as being dragged into action only when public pressure becomes too intense to ignore. Alternatively, companies have resisted change by spending incredible amounts of time and effort in discussions about code formulation. This can be seen in the case of the apparel industry's code of conduct. President Clinton announced this initiative with great fanfare in June, 1997, but only after many years of intense public pressure. It then took almost eighteen months for the various parties to come to a specific agreement about what would be audited, who would do the auditing, and what type of report would be published. As a result of these delays and disagreements, the entire process is viewed by the public with great skepticism. As a matter of fact, two of the leading public interest group participants in the negotiations have refused to sign the new accord and have denounced it as too weak. Moreover, if experience to date is any indication, the implementation process is also likely to be subject to intense discussions among the participants, with resultant delays. Thus, it will be quite some time before anyone will have an opportunity to evaluate the importance and effectiveness of this code. The consequence of these failings has been further public antagonism and pressure on the corporations. Thus, rather than gaining public support and recognition for their efforts, the companies involved are being denounced for bad faith. There are also efforts to pursue legislative and regulatory approaches at national and international levels that would compel companies to undertake desired actions.

The Imperative of Global Codes of Conduct

Let me state categorically and unequivocally my belief that corporate codes of conduct are here to stay. Further, they are both necessary and desirable. When properly developed and implemented, codes of conduct can provide the corporation with a voluntary and flexible approach to addressing some of society's concerns, both in general and in the market-place. Codes can serve both corporate interests and public purposes and can strengthen free market institutions, as well. Effective use of codes can restore public faith in the market economy as the best avenue for enhancing human welfare, advancing regional economic development, and strengthening democratic institutions.

Public sentiment and perspective play a very important role in defining the parameters of discretion that a society will allow the leaders of its various social, political, and economic institutions. In the present instance, as well as in many previous instances involving social issues, the fight for the hearts and minds of the public have invariably been led by corporate critics. Companies, fearing lack of public trust, have refrained from a proactive stance and have instead limited themselves to disputing their critics' charges. This is a losing battle and will always remain so. By yielding the initiative to their critics, companies have allowed their critics to shape the agenda in ways that put business in a perpetually defensive mode, talking about "what they may have done wrong" instead of "what they are doing right."

Codes of conduct offer an invaluable opportunity for responsible corporations to create an individual and highly positive public identity for themselves; that is, a reputation effect that can have a direct result on their bottom line in terms of increased revenues, customer loyalty, expanded markets, a productive work force, and a supportive political and regulatory environment. Furthermore, an increased level of public confidence and trust among important constituencies and stakeholders would lead to greater freedom for management in the running of their business operations, and insulate them from the actions of other, less scrupulous firms in the market-place.

Voluntary codes serve to achieve a larger public purpose in a manner, that is flexible and pragmatic and take into account the unique set of problems faced by an industry or by different companies. *They* also allow the moderate elements among the affected groups to seek reasonable solutions to the issues involved, even before these issues are captured by more radical elements whose primary interest may be in escalating the level of social conflict, rather than fashioning mutually acceptable and feasible solutions.

And they avoid the need for further governmental regulation that is invariably more expensive and less efficient (because of political considerations and the need to create regulations that cover all possible situations and contingencies).

Creating a Code of Conduct

The remainder of this paper is devoted to a discussion of the development and implementation of a meaningful code of conduct for globally active corporations. This discussion will draw on my own experience as chair of the Mattel Independent Monitoring Council for Global Manufacturing Principles (MIMCO).

Characteristics of a Viable Code

A corporate code of conduct is in the nature of "private law" or a "promise voluntarily made," whereby an institution makes a public commitment to certain standards of conduct. The fact that issuance of a code is "voluntary" reflects the flexibility of action afforded to a corporation. Commitment to a code affirms that corporations and their critics share a common interest in improving the conditions of their interaction, and in mutually satisfactory resolution of underlying issues.

For a code of conduct to have any reasonable chance of meeting the expectations of all parties involved, the following conditions must be met.

- The code commitments must be economically viable for the corporation, given the dynamics of its technology and competition, and the economic and sociopolitical realities of the environments within which it operates.
- The code must address substantive issues that are of importance to the corporation's various constituencies, particularly employees, communities, and governments.
- The code must be specific about performance standards that can be objectively measured.
- Important constituencies of the corporation must be engaged in the code formulation and implementation process.

Development and Implementation

Development and implementation of a multinational code of conduct is a challenging task because of the differing orientations and concerns of the diverse parties involved; their disparate assumptions about the feasibility of particular goals and benchmarks; and disagreements about the means that are appropriate and feasible to achieve agreed-upon goals. Another major hurdle arises from the organizational ethos and decisionmaking processes of corporations and other participative and public interest groups. A corporation's primary focus is on the efficiency of processes and the optimization of outcomes. Participative and deliberative processes, e.g., open consultations and procedural norms, are adopted only as means to achieve desired ends and are not seen as values themselves. By contrast, many stakeholder groups place tremendous importance on consultation and information sharing, not only as steps in effective decision-making, but as values themselves. Thus, from their perspective, efficient use of time and resources may take second place to consultation and involvement; and corporate actions that appear to jeopardize participative processes are viewed with distrust.

Assuming that there is adequate commitment to widespread participation and involvement in code development, the next step is to determine the scope of the proposed code. This includes:

- Definition: What aspects of corporate activity and impact are to be included in the code?
- Measurement and Verification: How should corporate performance in these areas be measured, and how should the accuracy of this information be verified?
- Accountability and Reporting: To whom should the corporation be accountable for its performance, and how should this information be made public?

Specificity in all of these matters is critical because an ambiguous code tends either to become meaningless, or to expand into varied meanings as different groups stretch its terms to suit their particular interests. Code requirements must be translated into quantifiable and standardized measurements so that objective and consistent observations can be made by different people, over time. Code compliance must become an element of management routine that is integral, rather than peripheral, to the firm's normal operations. And, most importantly, indicators of code compliance must reflect results rather than intentions: goals met or unmet, not merely actions taken in pursuit of goals.

Two final points on implementation are these:

- The company's top management must be strongly and unequivocally committed to the code, and code compliance must be an

element of performance evaluation at all levels of management.
- The company must be willing to expose its record of code compliance to external verification. This last step is particularly important if the firm expects to achieve "reputation effects" and the benefits of stakeholder trust and collaboration, as well as public approval.

Independent Monitoring Systems

One of the most critical aspects of code implementation is the creation of an independent monitoring system. Independent monitoring is necessary for the public to see that companies are indeed doing what they proclaim to be doing. Unfortunately, most companies with codes are extremely reluctant to subject themselves to independent outside monitoring and public dissemination of monitoring results.

This is an area of great disagreement between corporations and their critics, and a major source of public distrust about corporate motives and performance. Reluctance to share information is sometimes justifiably based on the fear that the company will be subjected to inappropriate pressure and harassment, rather than be applauded for the progress it has made. However, inadequate disclosure inevitably suggests that there is something to hide, and suggests a lack of faith in the ability of stakeholders to appreciate and encourage good corporate conduct. It is ironic that corporations expect their financial performance to be publicly reported and audited by independent outsiders for the benefit of investors, but are unwilling to provide other information-often much less sensitive of comparable concern to other vital constituencies.

Companies have often argued that many indicators of code compliance are internal measures, not conventionally subject to outside review, and that confidentiality makes it easier to take corrective actions through a system of "carrot and stick." This line of argument, however, has not been successful in previous situations involving crises of public confidence and is doomed to failure in the current global socio-political environment. Neither advanced nor developing countries will allow companies to operate any longer under a "veil of secrecy" where issues of human rights and ethical/moral conduct are concerned.

There are currently two approaches to creating and implementing codes of conduct with appropriate performance verification and public reporting processes. One involves industry-wide effort; the other suggests that individual companies should develop their own approaches, based on their unique circumstances. We briefly consider the advantages and disadvantages of each.

Industry-Wide Effort

The case for an industry-wide effort is based on the premise that companies in an industry face similar sets of problems, competitive conditions, and external pressures. Therefore, a combined approach should be feasible, cost effective, and place all companies on the same competitive footing with respect to these issues. An industry-wide approach also gives participating companies a united position with which to respond to their critics and public at large.

There are, however, serious flaws to this logic:

- An industry-wide approach requires consensus before any action can be taken. It therefore plays into the hands of those companies who are least inclined to undertake substantive action, and thus can postpone implementation through endless discussion, procrastination and obfuscation, thereby defeating the purpose of the exercise and inviting public ridicule and distrust.
- It forces industry performance standards to the lowest common denominator; i.e., the company with the weakest record sets the pace for the entire industry.
- It reduces incentives for individual companies to improve their own performance based on their own particular circumstances.
- Since these industry-wide efforts invariably depend on "voluntary compliance" and rarely incorporate monitoring or enforcement measures, poorly performing companies remain undisciplined and taint the record of the entire industry.

I do not believe that, at the present time, an industry-wide approach is either feasible or desirable in most cases. Since very few industries have even a modicum of "commonly accepted" standards or performance criteria in *any* area of public concern, an effort to develop common performance criteria might appear to be-and might actually become-a form of anti-competitive collusion. Moreover, at the current stage of code development and public acceptance, an industry-wide approach is likely to be very disadvantageous to the companies that are seeking to develop creative, innovative responses to human and social concerns.

Independent Approach

I believe that for a company that is strongly committed to a substantive and effective code of conduct, a "go-it-alone" strategy is preferable at the present time. The direct economic benefits emanating from increased stakeholder trust, cooperation, and loyalty should provide ample incentive; and enhanced public reputation should translate into a more hospitable external socio-political environment over the long term. A go-italone company has the flexibility to fashion a code of conduct that takes advantage of its unique capabilities and to develop new systems and procedures of permanent value (and perhaps of market value to other firms as well). Successful individual firm experience may well permit the gradual development of multi-firm approaches.

Monitoring Council

Whatever the specific substantive content of a code of conduct, and whatever its level of sponsorship (division, corporate, or industry), its ultimate success depends upon the verification of its results by independent reviewers. I refer to these individuals as a "Monitoring Council." Such a Council should consist of three to five members with impeccable credentials for independence, knowledge, and, if possible, code formulation and implementation. The Council must have credibility with all constituent groups, including corporate directors and managers, governments, and other stakeholders. I do not believe that it is appropriate to include specific stakeholder representatives as Council members, since the Council's purpose is to determine the extent to which the company is meeting its public commitments, as expressed in its code. (Stakeholder representatives may well be included in consultations concerned with the drafting and revision of a code, which is a different matter.)

The principal task of a Monitoring Council should be oversight, with responsibility for verifying not only the results of field audits but, even more importantly, the company's responses to deficiencies when they are uncovered. Field monitoring of code compliance should be separated from verification and reporting, which should be the sole purview of the Council. The Council should develop a mechanism for receiving information and complaints about corporate performance from both within and outside the company. It should make regular public reports about the company's compliance with its code, and the content of these reports and the manner of their presentation should be the sole responsibility of the Council. The Council should, of course, make every effort to ensure that all facts in its reports are accurate, and that all conclusions are fully justified. Under the best of circumstances, the monitoring function should be viewed as a cooperative effort in which both the monitors and the corporation's field managers strive to ensure compliance. Under the worst of circumstances, where monitors and managers view each other as adversaries, the entire code implementation process will be a failure.

Mattel Experience

Mattel, the world's largest toy manufacturing company, announced the creation of its Global Manufacturing Principles (GMP) in November, 1997. The Code created a set of standards that would apply to all of the company-owned plants as well as those of its more than 300 primary contractor manufacturing facilities around the world. As part of its code formulation and implementation process, the company also committed itself to the establishment of an independent council to monitor its operations to ensure compliance with GMP. It is called the Mattel Independent Monitoring Council for Global Manufacturing Principles (MIMCO). To the best of my knowledge, it was the first time that a major multinational corporation voluntarily committed itself to independent monitoring by outside observers who had complete authority to make their findings available to the public.

In establishing the Council, Mattel was trying to identify itself as a socially responsible company and good corporate citizen. Mattel believed that it was important that its policies, operational procedures, and performance measures under the GMP should receive broad public recognition and acceptance. Mattel also considered it extremely important that the relevance and adequacy of the GMP, as applied to the company's overseas operations, particularly in developing countries, be recognized and accepted by its employees and managers worldwide.

The Council currently consists of three members: Dr. S. Prakash Sethi, Distinguished University Professor of Management, Zicklin School of Business, City University of New York; Dr. Murray Weidenbaum, Distinguished University Professor of Economics, Washington University in St. Louis, and a former chairman of the Council of Economic Advisors; and Dr. Paul McCleary, President and CEO of ForChildren, Inc., and former President and CEO of the Save the Children Foundation.

In accepting their assignment, Council members received a number of important assurances from the company's top management:

- Mattel will ensure that the code meets or exceeds all pertinent host country laws and best industry practices in the areas of its operations.
- The company is committed to the code and will devote the necessary resources to ensure compliance to it by field managers in the company's owned and controlled plants, and will cooperate and assist the company's major vendors to comply with the code.

- The company will create a highly objective, quantifiable, and out-come-oriented set of standards that will add substance and comprehensiveness to the code and ensure the code's implementation in a meaningful manner.
- The company will make every effort to work toward the enhancement of these standards in an evolutionary manner that will enhance the financial and social well-being of its workers, and also contribute to the economic growth of the countries involved.

During its first phase, MIMCO will focus its efforts on auditing those twenty or more plants that are owned or controlled by Mattel. These account for close to 70 percent of Mattel's world-wide production. A very large part of Mattel's production operations are based in the Asia-Pacific Region: Peoples' Republic of China, Indonesia, and Malaysia. This audit will therefore cover the topics that have been of major public concern in those areas: workers' health and safety, wages, and living conditions. We expect this phase of the audit process to be completed by April 1999, and our findings will be made public soon thereafter.

An audit is only as good as the questions it asks and the activities and issues it covers. We have spent the last six months developing a highly objective, quantifiable, precise, and statistically rigorous set of instruments that will be used in conducting field audits. These will cover, among other things:

- Workers' environment, health and safety, and working conditions.
- Wages and working hours.
- Living conditions.
- Communications with the management concerning their living and working conditions, new employee orientation methods, and regular training programs.

Mattel has already completed extensive in-house audits to ensure that its own plants, and those of its major suppliers, are in compliance with GMP. Where necessary, it has also worked closely with the company's suppliers to help them improve their operations to meet Mattel's standards – frequently at Mattel's expense. And, in a number of cases, where suppliers have been unable or unwilling to make such an effort, Mattel has discontinued its business relationship with them. Mattel has established a single global task force with members located in its Asian Region headquarters in Hong Kong and in its corporate headquarters in El Segundo, California. This task *force* has been responsible for generating the necessary databases for Council use in creating audit protocols; these, in turn, will be used by the independent auditors appointed by, and reporting to, the Council.

Concluding Thoughts

The emerging global economic order of the 1990s has once again brought capitalism and its principal actor, the multinational corporation, to new levels of prominence and power. Unlike the 1960s, when multinational corporations were seen as a threat to national sovereignty and political freedom, the dominant contemporary view seems to be that the multinational corporation is – or certainly can be – an agent of positive change. However, beneath this veneer of hope and expectation, lies distrust in the unaccountability of the corporate behemoth and the fear of its potential for doing harm whether through misjudgment or abuse of power.

The contemporary tensions between business and society – which will certainly extend into the next millennium – do not arise from obvious conflicts between right and wrong, guilt or innocence. Their more subtle sources are, for example, alternative concepts and combinations of equity and inequity, the distribution of potential social and economic benefits, the virtue of frugality and the sin of undue accumulation, and the morality of principles versus the morality of situations. We realize that we live in an increasingly interdependent, global society where the welfare of the individual human being is deeply, and often unpredictably, embedded in the operation of the entire system. In this complex environment, we cannot pretend to separate moral principles from institutional practices, political power from economic influence, or human and environmental values from material wealth.

The large corporation must become an active agent for social change if it is to make the world safe for itself. Rules of law, democratic institutions, and the ethics of competition and the marketplace are requirements for the continued success of multinational corporations and, indeed, contemporary capitalism. The corporation can no longer pretend to be a reactive participant within the social system, responding (positively or negatively) to pressures and goals arising from other groups. As a dominant institution in society, it must accept responsibility for independent initiative, both with respect to its own goals and the formation of the public agenda. Effective participation requires that the corporation be able to articulate who and what it is from a social perspective, and what role its processes and products play in society. This articulation is, in fact, the ultimate purpose and result of a corporate code of conduct.

David Selley, "Bribing foreign government officials now illegal," *management ethics* (February 1999): 1–3. Also available online at: http://www.ethicscentre.ca/EN/resources/February%201999%20methics .pdf

In December the federal government passed the *"Corruption of Foreign Public Officials Act"* (the Act) which, effective in mid February, makes it a criminal offence punishable by up to five years in jail to pay a bribe to a foreign public official to gain a business advantage. The media either didn't notice or chose to remain silent. By most estimates Canadian companies are not aware of this Act and the effect it may have on the way they do business. In late 1997, the 28 OECD member countries had approved a Convention that would outlaw major bribery of government officials and, according to Milos Barutciski, a lawyer with Toronto law firm Davies Ward & Beck, the Canadian legislation has done a good job in implementing the requirements of that convention. Barutciski chaired a Canadian Bar Association Task Force on International Corruption that provided input to, and support for, the Canadian implementation of the Convention. So what previously has been a business and an ethical issue, now also becomes a legal issue for Canadian companies and their officers and directors. In fact, it has always been a legal issue in the countries in which a bribe has been paid. There is no country in the world where bribery of public officials is legal, or publicly acceptable. One has only to look at the current travails of the International Olympic Committee (IOC), and the developing revelations in Indonesia. What is new with this Act is that bribing a foreign government official is now illegal in Canada broadly in the same way it would be illegal to pay a bribe to a Canadian government official.

The Act covers loans, awards and advantages of any other kind made directly or indirectly to a government official to obtain a business advantage by inducing that official to act or refrain from acting in some way. Government officials include elected officials and others. Governments include political subdivisions of countries, government agencies and also international organizations formed by governments.

A typical case might be paying an agent to assist in obtaining a government contract to, say, build a dam, and instructing the agent to use some of the funds to bribe a government official to award the contract to their principal, rather than to another bidder. Of course, if the other bidders bribe too, this will become a mug's game for all bidders. The Act also makes it an offence to deal in the proceeds of bribery and clarifies that any payment that falls within the ambit of this Act is not deductible for income tax purposes. Finally, the Act exempts "facilitating payments" to junior public

The Centre at Ten Years Old

"The whole objective of the Centre has been to shake our society of its complacency, to question a status quo that too often accepts as inevitable those activities which are bad not only for our moral character, but for the bottom line as well."

The Centre held its 10th anniversary celebration on December 2, 1998 at the Royal Bank of Canada where special recognition was given to the Centre's founding directors. David Olive, a founding director himself and senior writer with *The National Post*, gave a tribute to the achievements of the past ten years to about 70 of the Centre's past and present corporate and individual supporters, as well as many former and current directors. He lauded the progress that the Centre has made over the past decade in bringing issues to light. "We've made the forceful point that ethics isn't an arcane set of rules. It is merely an appreciation of the consequences of behaviour that may bring regret and injury to ourselves and others." He described the Centre as "part of the vanguard" that has raised the level of moral tolerance and sounded a call to action. David also reminded us that much needs to be done. He challenged the Centre "to be more aggressive in identifying soul-destroying ethical lapses, and the chronic ethical abuses that still characterise too many aspects of business life." He concluded by saying he was excited by the prospect of the Centre's growing role as a forum for ideas and solutions in a world far more attuned to ethical values than ten years ago. Sincere thanks are due to The Royal Rank for use of their outstanding premises for our celebration.

officials that are demanded in order to perform tasks of a routine nature, such as issuing vehicle or business licences, or import and export documentation which are common in many countries. While such practices are generally harmful to the countries concerned, they are not easy to eliminate in the short term. From the point of view of the OECD Convention and the Act they can be argued to not confer a business advantage because all businesses pay these amounts as a matter of course. Like all legislation, there will be opportunities for differing interpretations and room for loopholing, but the wording is strong and unequivocal in its primary thrust – elimination of major bribery and corruption by Canadians of foreign officials for business advantage.

The OECD Convention, and the Canadian Act, resulted from the strenuous efforts of many multi-national businesses, governments and NGOs, particularly Transparency International (TI), a non-profit international organization based in Berlin whose mission is to get rid of major bribery in international business transactions. TI has fought for this legislation for many years in many countries. Professor Wes Cragg of the Schulich School of Business at York University is president of the Canadian Chapter of TI. He is proud of TI's pivotal role internationally, and in Canada in persuading the government to push the legislation through before the December 31 deadline. This was critical to the success of the entire OECD initiative because the Convention was required to be ratified by five major countries in order to become effective, and Canada was the last of the five to sign on. The Bill was passed quickly by the Senate and then zipped through all three readings in the House of Commons in one day.

Cragg and other proponents of the Act recognize that legislation, even in the 28 OECD countries and the handful of others that have signed on voluntarily, cannot stop the practice, but because these signatories account for approximately 80% of world trade a significant reduction in bribery is anticipated. Previously, some Canadian businesspersons and their advisors have been somewhat cynical about this issue; they have taken the approach that they would of course rather not pay a bribe, but that's the only way business can be done in some countries. In most cases they will now think twice (at least) before doing something that could send them to jail for five years. For many, hopefully most, the mere fact that it is illegal will dissuade them from participating. Most companies' codes of ethics start with the requirement that they will comply with the law!

Michael Davies, vice-president and general counsel for GE Canada, a strong proponent of the OECD Convention and heavily involved in its development, believes that many large Canadian companies have in recent years developed codes of conduct that include prohibitions against paying major bribes. Many companies, he said, including GE, walk away from deals because they are unwilling to pay bribes. Such companies may simply need to reinforce their current codes by stressing the illegality of what before had merely been contrary to their code. However, Davies believes an educational effort may be necessary for other companies that operate in this environment so that they are aware of the Act and are helped to understand the issues involved. The lack of media coverage to date has not helped. The Financial Post finally published an editorial on the Act on January 20th. It was not entirely favourably inclined to the legislation. On the other hand, The Economist (January 16th) devoted a strongly supportive editorial and a three page article to the coming into force of the Convention. This is consistent with the Economist's editorial stance in favour, except in exceptional circumstances, of unfettered free markets and trade. Paying bribes to obtain or retain business has been a major impediment to the smooth operation of markets and flow of trade and can seriously distort outcomes, to the detriment of everyone except the recipients of the bribes and their Swiss or other off-shore bankers.

Why would big business be so much in favour of this initiative? After all, large companies are not associated in the public's mind with asking for more rules. In addition to ethical considerations, though, big business is looking for a level playing field. The United States has had legislation banning foreign bribery for many years. US companies said they were put at a competitive disadvantage when bidding on major contracts against competitors from Germany, France, Britain and other home bases for multi-national business, including Canada. Now the playing field will be level for most of the world that exports capital investment and business.

Or will it? Legislation is one thing; enforcement is another. The OECD Convention requires signatories to establish a monitoring and reporting process on enforcement. The Canadian Act requires the Ministers of Foreign Affairs, International Trade and Justice to report annually to Parliament on implementation of the convention – an unusual provision that should be interesting to watch. Cragg points out that TI is strongly urging the OECD to develop its own effective monitoring mechanisms to ensure member countries enforce the Act. If some major countries do not live up to their commitment the overall effect of the Convention will be drastically reduced, not only because companies from those countries may continue to pay bribes but because then companies from other countries will lose competitiveness if they do not follow suit – the level playing field will have been ploughed up.

Compliance within companies is not guaranteed either. For example, nobody pretends that the US Foreign Corrupt Practices Act has stopped all bribery by US companies nor that codes of conduct that prohibit bribes are always effective. There are, however, other mechanisms that may discourage the kinds of bribes covered by this Act. Senior management and boards of directors will likely become more conscious of situations in which they, or their subsidiaries in other countries, may be asked for a bribe. They may become more sensitive about unusually large agency fees. Companies that do business in high risk areas will consider the potential for illegal bribes in their risk management processes, if they did not before. For public companies, their auditors have to change the way they look at evidence that bribes covered by this Act may have been paid. Now that they are illegal, they are covered by the requirements of generally accepted auditing standards that relate to illegal acts. Auditors must understand their client's business sufficiently to be able to assess the risk of breaches of laws and regulations that might materially affect the financial statements. According to Diana Hillier, Director of Assurance Standards for the Canadian Institute of Chartered Accountants (CICA), this would require an auditor of a company with major business transactions in high risk countries to be alert for evidence that illegal bribes may have been paid. Auditors are not required to design procedures to investigate whether any have been paid, however, unless they find evidence that makes them suspicious, such as an unusually large agency fee. If auditors find evidence that an illegal bribe has been, or might have been paid, they must first assess whether the consequences may be material to the financial statements. Often they would not be, but even in this case CICA standards require the auditors to report the matter to senior management and the board, and if they are not satisfied that appropriate action has been taken the standards suggest seeking legal advice on their options. Large public accounting firms will no doubt be informing their audit personnel about the Act, and building awareness into their audit processes.

In short, the OECD Convention, and the Canadian Act are an important first step that can have only positive effects. With strict enforcement by the OECD countries, large scale bribery of foreign public officials will significantly diminish and provide a strong incentive for companies to resist pressure to pay bribes. It must be recognized, however, that there are a few major players that have not signed on (Hong Kong and Singapore, for example) and if individual companies, or entire industries, continue to believe they must pay bribes to get the business they need to stay alive, they will probably be able to find ways of hiding the bribes and loopholing the law. Only time will tell whether this seriously detracts from the effectiveness of the Convention and Act. For now, though, we can rejoice that a major step has been taken that might eventually rid the world of this scourge on international business and on domestic economies.

> Companies that do business in high risk areas will consider the potential for illegal bribes in their risk management processes...

If you are involved in any way in international business, it is relatively easy to arm yourself with two key pieces of information about this issue. The first is the Act itself (also known as Bill S-21), which consists of only six short paragraphs, the related amendment to the Income Tax Act, and a few other amendments that only lawyers need to worry about. The second vital piece of information is TI's so-called "Corruption Perception Index", based on the perception by business executives of which countries are the most susceptible to bribery. This index is widely publicized, and is available

from TI Canada's web site, www.bus.yorku.ca/program/TranIntl/index
.htm, or from TI's main site at www.transparency.de. If you are doing business with government officials or their agents in countries at or near the
bottom of TI's list, you ought to take special steps to ensure that your company is not breaking Canadian law.

Beneficiaries of the OECD convention, if it works, will include: companies in Canada and other OECD nations whose codes of ethics and values
have prevented them from paying bribes and who have walked away from
deals that other less scrupulous companies have won; companies and their
owners, who will no longer have to bear the cost of paying the bribes, or
inflated agency fees; the ordinary people in countries low on the TI index
whose economies have been distorted and rendered less efficient because
of misallocation of resources; employees on the front line of international
business transactions who will be under less pressure, or will have added
support to resist; and international organizations such as the World Bank
and IMF whose efforts to deal with financial problems of the developing
world will be less distorted by diversion into off-shore bank accounts of
moneys that should have gone to development. A few, though, will lose a
great deal. We should not shed any tears for them.

*David Selley, FCA is past-chair and a director of the Canadian Centre for Ethics & Corpo-
rate Policy and a consultant in auditing standards, methodologies and technologies.*

Graham Tucker, "Ethical analysis for environmental problem solving,"
Agenda for Action Conference Proceedings, the Canadian Centre for
Ethics & Corporate Policy, 1990, 53–57.

Introduction

Today, no company can claim to be "ethical" unless it is demonstrating a
concern for the environment. The focus of this conference is on the tools of
ethical analysis and problem solving that can provide a practical framework for action.

Before finalizing a business decision, an executive should ask a series of
questions designed to ensure the best possible choice is made both for the
shareholders as well as other stakeholders. These questions ought to be
asked in the following order to canvass the values shown:

1. Is it profitable? (market values)
2. Is it legal? (legal values)
3. Is it fair? (social values)
4. Is it right? (personal values)
5. Is it sustainable development (environmental values)

These questions have been built into the "five-box" framework for ethical analysis which is shown in Figure 1.

Figure 1 Questions

The focus on values is critical to the proper analysis of business decisions
because morality, which is becoming more and more critical to the health of
corporations and society, cannot be legislated. It depends on the value
system of corporate leaders and employees. Moreover, the tough choices
required among alternatives often defy quantification and must be based
on the values of the decision-maker.

Nowadays, it is not safe to judge a propsective action just on its
contribution to profits, because the action may not be legal. Even if it is
profitable and legal, society will penalize the company if the action is not
also perceived to be fair and right. Recently, as the fragility of our global
environment has become clear, society has begun to demand that corporate
actions fit into the sustainable development of our economy.

The application of the "five-box" framework for analysis will be
developed below in the analysis of the Kardell Paper Co. case, after a

discussion of some terms used in ethical analysis and the outlining of a framework for ethical problem solving.

Some Important Distinctions

It's important that we make important distinctions (a) between management and leadership and (b) between being legal and being ethical. Lack of clear distinction in these areas causes a lot of confused thinking in business ethics.

When managers are successful, usually it is because they are high-energy, hard-driving individuals who know how to play by the rules of the game. They efficiently and single-mindedly strive to achieve the goals of the organization. But they may or may not be leaders.

Robert Greenleaf, author of the book *Servant Leadership*, defines leaders as "those who better see the path ahead and are prepared to take the risks and show the way." The characteristic which sets leaders apart from managers is their intuitive insight and the foresight which enables them to go out ahead and show the way. Why would anyone accept the leadership of another, except that the other sees more clearly where it's best to go? The manager, by contrast, tends to be part of the bureaucracy that wants to preserve the status quo. The managerial role determines the values. Managers do what's expected of them. That role often overrides the managers' personal values.

Role responsibility can be very powerful. The management of Johns-Manville knew for years that its product asbestos was linked by scientists to lung cancer in its employees. Similar situations existed with the Ford Pinto and the Dalkon Shield.

Managers often feel powerless to act outside of their prescribed role; they feel that they don't have the authority to buck the system. The corporate authority may be sanctioning the unethical behavior. It takes the moral authority of a leader to change the system, and this is often notably lacking in both politics and business.

Robert Greenleaf points out that the failure of businesspeople to use foresight and take creative action before a crisis arises is tantamount to *ethical failure,* because managers in these cases lack courage to act when there is still some freedom to change course. Many managers opt for short-term profit at the expense of long-term viability. On that basis there are probably a lot of people walking around with an air of innocence which they would not have if society were able to pin the label "unethical" on them for their failure to foresee crises and to act constructively when there was freedom to act.

Figure 1
A Framework for Ethical Analysis – Changing Ground Rules and a Sustainable Future

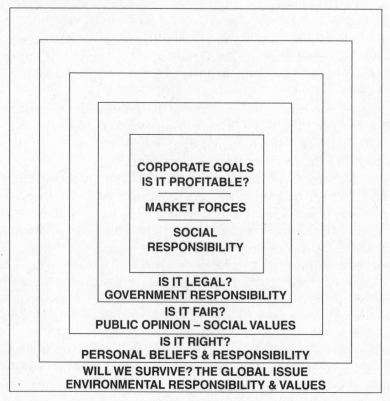

CORPORATE GOALS
IS IT PROFITABLE?

MARKET FORCES

SOCIAL
RESPONSIBILITY

IS IT LEGAL?
GOVERNMENT RESPONSIBILITY
IS IT FAIR?
PUBLIC OPINION – SOCIAL VALUES
IS IT RIGHT?
PERSONAL BELIEFS & RESPONSIBILITY
WILL WE SURVIVE? THE GLOBAL ISSUE
ENVIRONMENTAL RESPONSIBILITY & VALUES

Similarly, it is important that we distinguish between being legal and being ethical. The law is frequently quite distinct from morality. It is mainly concerned with the minimum regulation required for public order, whereas ethics attempts to achieve what is "best" for both the individual and society. Thus it's possible to be operating within the law and yet be unethical. The legal limits for a certain pollutant may have been established before it was discovered to be unsafe at that level. The company may be operating legally. Yet by knowingly endangering the health of workers or the community, the company is acting in an unethical manner.

Many corporate codes of ethics express a commitment to keeping the letter of the law, but that may not protect them from censure when the new data becomes public knowledge. Obviously we have to have laws and regulations to avoid the chaos of a lawless society. However, the ethical crunch that is being experienced by the business world today is that the communications revolution is putting more information in the hands of the public. It used to be possible to exercise power and control by withholding or concealing information. If you don't know that asbestos dust is giving you lung cancer you can't do anything about it. The public now finds out very quickly what is going on, and it is demanding ethical conduct because this affects its well-being.

We have recently witnessed dramatic changes in Eastern Europe, as shared information has empowered previously powerless people to rise up and take control of their own destiny in seeking a better life. Precisely the same power is at work in our society, changing the rules of the game for business. Five years ago, the concern for the environment ranked sixth in the value system of the Canadian public. Today it ranks number one. This in turn is empowering government to enact much tougher regulations. Those companies that are either too entrenched in the old rules or lack the foresight to see the long-term consequences of what is now perceived by the public to be unethical behavior will fail. Whereas those companies which use a combination of ethical foresight and good business and have the courage to make the changes required, will survive and prosper.

Legislation may provide a level playing field, but legislation alone cannot solve the problem. Similarly, strong corporate statements about environmental values also are useless if business does not have the ethical will to comply with them. The health of our environment depends more than anything else upon corporate moral leadership, which reflects the personal values of executives and employees. And this is where we move from theory to the realm of applied ethics, which is concerned with the practical outcome of business decisions.

Value Judgments

The name of the game is making value judgments in the light of our personal values. I want to say a few words about values so that we can have a common language in this conference.

Values are the criteria by which we make our judgments or choices, and establish our goals and priorities. For most of us, there is a bit of a gap between our ideal personal values and our actual or operative values, and we need to be honest about what our values really are.

The situation is complicated for us today as social values are changing, and this is redefining ethical standards. The ground rules are changing.

Studies have shown the following characteristics resulting from people having clear or unclear values:

A FRAMEWORK FOR ETHICAL PROBLEM SOLVING

Consider the following issues while employing the eight steps listed below:

1. Establish objectivity.

Who is doing the analysis and what interests do they represent?

What are the ground rules of the company and of the decision-making group?

2. Scan the situation; identify the problem.

Separate out the "core problem" from the subproblems. Whose problem is it? Why is it a problem?

3. Analyse the problem.

Use the "five-box," or "five-question" framework (the chart on the following page) to analyze the situation. What are the operative ground rules or values from the perspective of corporation's existing rules, as well as the legal, public, personal and environmental implications. Who makes the decision? Who are the stakeholders? What are their ground rules? Is it fair to all concerned?

4. Determine the cause of the problem.

Why and how are the rules being broken? Are the rules being broken Prima facie or Categorical? Is there any justification? Specify the cause.

5. Establish the objective.

Describe the desirable outcome, or end-point. Is it achievable? How would you measure it? What is the time frame?

6. Explore the options.

Brainstorm possible solutions. Create alternative courses of action.

7. Decide on the best solution.

Who will be affected by each option? Evaluate the impacts from each option on each group of stakeholders. Which option maximizes the benefits and minimizes the burden? Will it pass the five-box ethics test?

8. Plan and implement the solution.

Unclear values	*Clear values*
Apathetic	Know who they are
Flighty	Know what they want
Inconsistent	Positive
Drifter	Purposeful
Role player	Enthusiastic
Indecisive	Decisive

Both individually and corporately, it is to our advantage to develop a clear set of values, because confused values will result in confused ethical decisions.

Ethical analysis usually uncovers value conflicts which occur below the surface of our thinking. They can't be settled by rational argument. Only as we listen respectfully to each other's value perspective is it possible to find a reasonable accommodation of the difference. This is why stakeholder analysis is so important.

Rule Ethics

This brings us to the two basic ethical concepts we will apply in our case study today. The first is rule ethics.

Rule ethics states that you make your decisions about right or wrong on the basis of valid ethical principles, norms or ground rules. In other words, we ask, "Will this proposed action be violating civil law, or company policy in the code of ethics?" This is a good place to start, but as mentioned before, it may not produce ethical decisions. The decisions that result may be legal – but if the ground rules have changed, they may not be ethical.

The next level of Rule Ethics consists of the the rules or principles that come out of our moral traditions, which in our society are mainly the Judeo Christian moral norms such as "Thou shalt not kill, steal, lie, cheat or oppress."

The underlying question in Rule Ethics is, Whose rules are you following? It used to be that the corporation had its own rules, which related only to market forces, and it was not felt to be necessary to consider the values of society. That is, "What's good for General Motors is good for the rest of us." Cynically, the Golden Rule has become, "He who has the gold makes the rules."

Utilitarianism, Or End-point Ethics

John Stuart Mill said that, "To determine whether an action is right or wrong, one must concentrate on its likely consequences – the end point or end result. What is the greatest benefit for the greatest number?"

This led to cost-benefit analysis: does the benefit justify the cost? And to risk-benefit analysis: does the benefit justify the business risk?

In other words, you begin with Rule Ethics, in which the stakeholders test a decision by asking:

Is it legal?
Is it fair?
Is it right?
Is it environmentally sound?

Then you move to the end-point ethics, which seeks the greatest benefit for the greatest number – and this, finally, forces us to make some trade-offs to achieve the greatest good.

So far, we have been considering the process of ethical analysis. However, there is a tendency to think that having analyzed the problem we have solved it. Unless we take it to the next step of rational problem solving, nothing much is – going to happen.

The process I am going to introduce is ethically neutral. The thing that makes it ethical is the particular values and ground rules you apply in the process. If the ethical analysis has been done thoroughly, you will have already sorted out the values that you will apply at the various decision points in the problem-solving process.

Creative problem solving involves lateral thinking, or second-order thinking.

First-order thinking is the obvious course of action that first occurs to the mind of the manager or executive.

Second-order thinking involves "refraining" the problem and considering it from a different perspective.

For example, if you look at a business problem from the perspective of each of the five boxes on the chart, you might generate some creative alternatives which might not come to mind if only the corporate box is considered. It will take courage for every business enterprise to make the ethical shift for a sustainable future, but some can and *are* leading the way.

Graham H. Tucker was founder and Director of the King-Bay Chaplaincy in Toronto, and acting executive director of the Canadian Centre for Ethics and Corporate Policy. Mr. Tucker was author of The *Faith-Work Connection*.